# The Making of the Christian Mind

**Other Books of Interest from St. Augustine's Press**

Giulio Maspero, *The Mystery of Communion: Encountering the Trinity*

Kevin Hart, *Contemplation and Kingdom: Aquinas Reads Richard of St. Victor*

Wayne J. Hankey, *Aquinas Neoplatonism in the Summa Theologiae on God: A Short Introduction*

Étienne Gilson, *Theology and the Cartesian Doctrine of Freedom*

Karl Rahner, S.J., *Ignatius of Loyola Speaks*

St. Anselm of Canterbury, *Proslogion*

John of St. Thomas, *Introduction to the Summa Theologiae of Thomas Aquinas*

James V. Schall, *On the Principles of Taxing Beer: And Other Brief Philosophical Essays*

James V. Schall, *The Regensburg Lecture*

Promise Hsu, *China's Quest for Liberty: A Personal History of Freedom*

Rémi Brague, *Moderately Modern*

Allen Mendenhall, *Shouting Softly: Lines on Law, Literature, and Culture*

Josef Pieper, *A Journey to Point Omega: Autobiography from 1964*

Peter Kreeft, *Socrates' Children: The 100 Greatest Philosophers*

Peter Kreeft, *Ethics for Beginners: 52 "Big Ideas" from 32 Great Minds*

John von Heyking, *Comprehensive Judgment and Absolute Selflessness: Winston Churchill on Politics as Friendship*

Joseph Bottum, *The Decline of the Novel*

Barry Cooper, *Consciousness and Politics: From Analysis to Meditation in the Late Work of Eric Voegelin*

D. Q. McInerny, *Being Ethical*

Roger Scruton, *The Politics of Culture and Other Essays*

Roger Scruton, *The Meaning of Conservatism*

Roger Scruton, *An Intelligent Person's Guide to Modern Culture*

Leon J. Podles, *Losing the Good Portion: Why Men Are Alienated from Christianity*

# The Making of the Christian Mind: The Adventure of the Paraclete

## Volume 1: The Waiting World

James Patrick

St. Augustine's Press
South Bend, Indiana

And He who sat upon the throne said,
Behold, I make all things new.
Revelation 21:5

Manufactured in the United States of America.

1 2 3 4 5 6 26 25 24 23 22 21

**Library of Congress Control Number: 2020947004**

∞ The paper used in this publication meets the minimum requirements of the American National Standard for Information Sciences – Permanence of Paper for Printed Materials, ANSI Z39.48-1984.

St. Augustine's Press
www.staugustine.net

Father Merrill Stevens
The Reverend Canon Howard Buchner
Sister Henry Suso Fletcher, O.P.

*Grato animo*

# *Table of Contents*

# *Foreword*

These chapters tell a story. They are not an argument but are written with the intent of making the thought of Christians as it developed over the first six centuries accessible, above all to a readership that even if not scholarly is well-read and historically engaged. In imitation of Saint Augustine this book might begin, "The glorious city of God is my theme in this work," with the qualification that the story told in these pages is not political or historical but intellectual. It is the story of the intellectual foundation on which the city of God must always rest, of the ideas that made a new world and of the men through whose books those ideas lived, making a new empire of thought and of moral possibility, giving humanity new horizons of hope, inspiring new literature, a new politics, and a new art. Their letters and books bore witness to the renovation of the human heart, a work to which the law and philosophy of the ancient world had aspired, but in which task these noble enterprises had not been successful. Thus the title *All Things New,* for the birth of Christ, his death on the cross in Jerusalem when Pontius Pilate was procurator, his resurrection and ascension, and the renewal of the human heart at Pentecost were decisive in human history in a way in which the defeat of the Persians at Marathon in BC 490, Octavian's victory over Mark Antony and Cleopatra at Actium in 31, the achievements of Gutenberg, Galileo, and Einstein, can never be. The events centered around the death and resurrection of Jesus gave new meaning to every life, to history, and to nature itself. "Behold I make all things new" says the voice from the throne of the Lamb (Rev 21:5).

This renovation required the creation of what on one hand looks like an institution in time, the Church, but which transcends time as the mystical body of Christ. The story of the earth-bound institution is told by Church historians. The story of the mystical body, its creation and its destiny, is God's story, which we know at best in part, darkly as in an imperfect mirror, its citizens enrolled in a book that only the Lamb of God can open. If these chapters were a history of Christian literature, it would be a pale imitation of Johannes Quasten's *Patrology*. If it were a systematic account, it would be a modern history of dogma, as in Jean Tixeront's three-volume *Histoire des dogmes* or Reinhold Seeberg's *Text-Book of the History of Doctrines.*

These essays are in large measure commentary on texts belonging to the first six centuries: from the *Didache,* written perhaps within fifty years of Pentecost, to such sixth-century benchmarks of Christian thought as the *Rule of Saint Benedict* and Boethius' *Consolation of Philosophy*. The early chapters are commentary on the role of living tradition, Scripture, Hebrew and Christian, and then upon texts belonging to the Apostolic Fathers, a title first employed by the French scholar Jean-Baptiste Cotelier in 1672 to describe a family of texts that includes ecclesiastical writers of the first and second centuries such as the anonymous authors of the *Didache,* the second-century *Epistle of Diognetus,* and the *Shepherd of Hermas,* a work much loved but finally excluded from the canon, as well as the letters of Clement, Ignatius, and Polycarp.

Succeeding the Apostolic Fathers and partly contemporaneous with them were the Apologists, such as Justin Martyr, the great Irenaeus, and Melito of Sardis, who made the case that Christianity ought not be punished but should be encouraged as superior to paganism and a blessing to the empire. Beginning in the late second century there was an engagement with heresy by Christian writers that produced a controversial literature replete with history and theology. Further afield are the documents that illuminate the context in which Christianity was born such as the Jewish apocalyptic literature, as well as texts that by their nature as theological outliers illuminate the faith of the Church such as the writings of the great Gnostics.

Attempts to catalog the literature that documents this process began with Eusebius, who in his *Church History,* written between 312 and 325, described the extant writings of Christians down to his own day. Eusebius was then a principal source for Jerome's *De viris illustribus,* short accounts of Christian authors and their works, written in 392 "to answer those who were accustomed to jeer at the intellectual mediocrity of the Christians."[1]

1 Quasten,1:1

Pope Gelasius enumerated books received and not received by the Church in his *Decretum Gelasianum* in the 540s. Cassiodorus of Vivarium writing in the 550s provided a catalog that included both Christian writers and classical sources of the liberal arts in his *Institutes of Divine and Sacred Learning*. A modern work such as Johannes Quasten's four-volume *Patrology*, which reviews the literature from its beginnings to Augustine, is much more than a catalog, offering as well short selections, commentary, and bibliography.

Whatever else the movement that proclaimed Christ the Savior of mankind may have been, it was a story told by men who wrote at a certain time in a certain place, who by their words gave form to the Christian mind. Their thought was influenced by ideas rooted in the past, secondarily from the Greek world, essentially from Judaism, and vivified by their incorporation into a new whole inspired by the advent of Jesus, his teaching, his sacrifice, and his double promise: that the fire of the Holy Spirit would come to establish the kingdom of the new heart in time and that he would return to renew creation and to welcome the company of the elect into his presence at the end of the age.

This is a story written from the viewpoint of the West, in part because for the first three centuries there was no great Eastern capital to provide a Greek center of scholarship and authority contrapuntal to that of Rome, and because until the sixth century, the age of Boethius and Gregory (after which a shadow fell across the West), the Church saw itself as formed intellectually chiefly by Rome and Alexandria. The East, through the efforts of such brilliant thinkers as Basil (330–79), Gregory of Nyssa (335–95), and Gregory Nazianzus (329–90) contributed opposition to the long series of virulent Christological heresies that were only put down by the great councils, ending with the Second Council of Constantinople in 553. It is often regretted that St. Augustine as a boy disliked Greek and never reached fluency in it, and dies on the eve of the Council of Ephesus in 430. Justinian (527–65), the last emperor to assert authority effectively in the western provinces, was the last emperor with facility in Latin and Greek, and while it is true that knowledge of Greek was never completely lost in the West, there was from the late second century a tension between traditions that were associated respectively with these two languages and with their geographical reach. As early as the late-second-century pontificate of Victor (189–98) there were difficulties about Easter and about prophecy; there was controversy over the Johannine apocalypse, the Acacian schism between East and West (482–519), then Iconoclasm, which raged from 725 to 843, and finally the schism of 1054. The account herein goes no further than the sixth century, when the division between East and West still lay in the future, and when the body of thought preached by the apostolic mission, established by the Gospels and empowered by Pentecost, was in principle complete. The makers of the Christian mind were unaware that before Gregory the Great died in 602 there would be born in Medina a prophet whose aggressive political theology would reshape the Mediterranean world, and that the invasions by the armies of Muhammad in conjunction with the persistent pressures of the Germanic tribes, the intransigence of conflicting Christological opinions, and the inability of the late Empire to defend its eastern frontier would together cause the cultural caesura called the Dark Ages that make the first six centuries unique and discrete in the intellectual history of Christendom.

These essays are not scholarly in the meaning associated with monographs and learned journals; the book does not survey the literature comprehensively or relate its arguments to contemporary academic discourse in more than an opportunistic way. With the exception of the suggestion that the non-Irenaean accounts of the origin of John deserve a second look, the insights and arguments presented do not move beyond the bounds of contemporary scholarship. The argument implied is incomplete, points along a line; there are gaps in the narrative that the text implies. The Hellenistic period is usually taken to end with Octavian's victory at Actium in 31 BC, but herein it includes the movements in religion and philosophy to Marcus Aurelius' *Meditations* of the 170s. Texts such as Melito of Sardis, Diognetus, Minucius Felix, Cyril of Jerusalem, and Arnobius are omitted reluctantly. These essays are also limited chronologically. The prefatory section sketches the influence of Greek philosophy, Hellenistic religion, and the faith of Israel, locating these as we find them in the reign of Augustus. The Christian story proper begins at Pentecost, inaugurating an epic in which the Holy Spirit is the divine hero, illuminating at every turn the makers of the Christian mind. It encompasses the intellectually creative period that was simultaneously the twilight of the empire and the matrix of the ideas that prophesied the vitality of the Christian world that would emerge in the ninth century.

These chapters are intended to be coherent in themselves, although each is related to what has gone before and what follows. They do not presuppose first-hand knowledge in the reader, but it may be hoped that the insights offered will drive this same reader to the sources. Taken together these essays undergird the proposition that the intellectual architecture of Christian thought is the crowning achievement of mankind in matters that touch our knowledge of God and of human nature and destiny. This first volume tells the story of the formation of the Christian mind from the first preaching of the Gospel through Irenaeus' *The Refutation and Overthrow of the Knowledge Falsely So-Called*, written near the end of the second Christian century. Subsequent volumes bring the story to the threshold of the Middle Ages with Boethius, Cassiodorus, and Saint Benedict.

Christianity is a survivor, not because it possessed the instruments of power but because, as Jesus of Nazareth said before Pilate, the foundation of the Kingdom is truth, its instruments of conquest are its renewing gifts; its consequences are the substitution of truth for error and ignorance, of faith for skepticism, of humility for pride, and of charity and friendship for emulation, all this realized never perfectly but always as possibilities having the power to make all things new.

The Feast of Saint John the Baptist, 24 June 2020

# *Acknowledgements*

The ability to write about the Christian literature of the first six centuries depends upon the successful efforts of manuscript hunters, collectors, editors, and translators who made accessible the literature lying outside the canonical scriptures that attests to the Christian mind at its origins. These texts would be inaccessible to twenty-first-century readers were it not for the labors of men like Jacque-Paul Migne (1800–1875), who collected from monastery and cathedral libraries the scattered texts that constitute the Christian intellectual patrimony, publishing them in 221volumes of the *Patrologia Latina* and 162 volumes of the *Patrologia Graeca.* These are still standard sources. In English-language scholarship the effort to make the Fathers accessible for an age in which facility in Greek and Latin was fading would include the *Library of the Fathers* begun by John Henry Newman in 1838 and continued by Pusey and Keble until 1888. This was followed by the *Ante-Nicene Christian Library* (1866–1872) and the American reprint, *The Ante-Nicene Fathers* (1884–1886). Two series of the *Nicene and Post-Nicene Fathers* brought the series to the seventh century. Immediately following the Second World War *Ancient Christian Writers* (1946) and *The Fathers of the Church* (1947) appeared. The Renaissance had seen some interest in the Apostolic Fathers, but popular translations of individual works into English began with the publication in 1891 of Lightfoot's *Apostolic Fathers*, a project followed by the SPCK translations of individual works, and finally by anthologies such as Cyril Richardson's *Early Fathers*, the first volume of *The Library of Christian Classics.*

The stories of many of the texts of the early Fathers are romances in themselves. The *Didache* or *Teaching of the Twelve Apostles*, known to Eusebius, was lost to modern scholarship until its chance rediscovery in 1872 in a monastery in Jerusalem. The larger part of Hippolytus' *Refutation of All Heresies* was found at Mount Athos in 1840. Irenaeus' important

*Demonstration of the Apostolic Preaching* was no more than a title until the discovery of an Armenian version in 1904. The apocryphal *Assumption of Moses,* which illuminates the context in which canonical Revelation was written, was not discovered until 1881. In the twentieth century knowledge of Gnosticism has been enriched by the discovery in 1946 at Nag Hammadi in upper Egypt of a well-preserved gnostic library that included, among other important texts, Valentinus' *Gospel of Truth* and the epistle to Rheginos, *On the Resurrection.* My debt, and the debt of every student of the thought that made the early Church, to these manuscript-hunters and translators is gratefully acknowledged. Their work made possible a renewed interest in the early Fathers, and encouraged scholarship. I also express my thanks to the generations of scholars whose erudition has since mid-nineteenth-century made possible the ever more fruitful study of early Christianity, the contexts in which it was born, and its opponents.

Finally, I thank the James L. and Mary D. MacFarlane Trust, and Mary Davis MacFarlane, whose generosity made this book possible.

# *Abbreviations*

ACW — *Ancient Christian Writers*
*Against Heresies* — Irenaeus, *The Refutation and Overthrow of the Knowledge Falsely So-Called*
Agapetus — *Advice to the Emperor Justinian*
*ANF* — *Ante-Nicene Fathers*
Bettenson — Henry Bettenson, *Documents of the Christian Church*, 3rd edition
*Church History* — Eusebius of Caesarea, *Church History*
*City of God* — *Augustine, City of God*
Clement — of Rome, *Letter to the Corinthians*
*Confessions* — Augustine, *Confessions*
*Consolation* — Boethius, *The Consolation of Philosophy*
*Constantine* — Eusebius, *Life of Constantine*
*Demonstration* — Irenaeus, *Demonstration of the Apostolic Preaching*
*Dialogue* — Justin Martyr, *Dialogue with Trypho the Jew*
*Didache* — *Teaching of the Twelve Apostles,*
Ignatius of Antioch
- *Eph.* — *To the Ephesians*
- *Magn.* — *To the Magnesians*
- *Phld.* — *To the Philadelphians*
- *Pol.* — *To Polycarp*
- *Rom.* — *To the Romans*
- *Smyrn.* — *To the Smyrnaeans*
- *Trall.* — *To the Trallians*

*JTS* — *Journal of Theological Studies*
Jowett — Benjamin Jowett, ed., *Dialogues of Plato*
Justin — *First Apology*
LCL — Loeb Classical Library

| | |
|---|---|
| *Martyrdom* | *Martyrdom of Polycarp* |
| *McKeon* | Richard McKeon, ed., *Basic Works of Aristotle* |
| *NHL* | *The Nag Hammadi Library in English.* Edited by James M. Robinson |
| *NPNF* | *A Select Library of the Nicene and Post-Nicene Fathers of the Christian Church*, First Series |
| *NPNF*[2] | *A Select Library of the Nicene and Post-Nicene Fathers of The Christian Church, Second Series* |
| Quasten | Johann Quasten, *Patrology* |
| *Richardson* | Cyril Richardson, *Early Christian Fathers,* volume 1 |
| *Rule* | *Rule of Saint Benedict* |
| *Shepherd* | *Shepherd of Hermas* |

# Part I
## *A Waiting World*

> And he hath made from one every nation of men to dwell on the face of the earth and determining beforehand their times appointed and the limits of their habitation, so that if they should reach out toward God they might find him, for he is not far from every one of us.
>
> Paul to the Athenians, Acts 17:26

> When the fullness of time had come, God sent forth his son, born of a woman.
>
> Galatians 4:4

Viewed from our present, the intellectual constitution of Christianity can be understood as an inspired incorporation of Greek thought, Jewish literature, and Roman civilization into one imperial whole shaped and perfected by revelation from God. As a system of thought Christianity was from the beginning syncretistic, not in the sense that it borrowed its principles from other philosophies or religions but through its ability, within the limits of the truth it guarded, to gather up the fragments, to create an organic tradition that took up the best of what had been thought and incorporate it into the larger vision of Christian wisdom. Justin Martyr's observation of the 150s, that whatever is true belongs to us Christians, meant that the religion of Christ would never be a cult, cut off from past human experience, but would rather welcome the best the human story had to offer so long as it was patient of the supernatural touch that lifted it above itself and above "the world."

When the making of the Christian mind began, this successful effort to incorporate the best of the Roman and Jewish worlds into the religion of Christ lay in the future. The faith and history of Israel had come to frustration when, after a century of disputes between the Egyptian Ptolemais and the Syrian Seleucids over control of Palestine, Antioch III (although defeated by Ptolemy IV at Raphia in Gaza in 217) allied himself with Jewish malcontents. Here began the aggressive program of Hellenization pursued by Antiochus IV (175—164), culminating in the introduction of worship of the Olympian Zeus in the Temple at Jerusalem in 167 (2 Macc. 6:2).

Events of great consequence are often set in motion in unexpected ways, as happened when the aged Mattathias, priest of Modein, a village seventeen miles northwest of Jerusalem, refused the order to offer unclean sacrifice by worshipping Antiochus' Zeus. Seeing a Hellenized Jew step forward to comply with Antiochus' order, Mattathias slew him at the altar, killed the attendant soldier, and destroyed the altar itself (1 Macc. 2:1–26). This inaugurated a guerilla war in which the irregular forces of Mattathias and his five sons, encouraged and assisted for a time by the Hasidim, the pious ones who are later to be associated with Qumran and the Essenes, created a successful nationalist movement. Judas Maccabaeus, who in BC 163 stormed Jerusalem, imprisoned the Syrian troops, and purified the Temple, was the hero of the movement (1 Macc. 4:34–46). In 142 his successor Simon (BC 142–34) obtained from Rome a decree granting Jews throughout the empire freedom to worship the God of their fathers. Simon was appointed "leader and High Priest forever, that is with hereditary rights, until a trustworthy prophet should arise." This decision was posted on a bronze tablet "in the precincts of the sanctuary" (1 Macc. 14:48). The period BC 142 to 63 AD, when Pompey brought Palestine under Roman rule, takes the name of Simon's family, the Hasmonaeans after Hasmoneus, the great-grandfather of the rebel Mattathias. With Pompey's invasion of Judea in 63 the Roman ascendency was consolidated, the reign of the Hasmoneans came to an end, and Judea, Galilee, and Samaria became parts of the vassal state of Palestine, with Judea governed by Roman surrogates. The most memorable of these would be Pontius Pilate, famous to the author of First Timothy (6:13), his name still recited wherever the Creed of Nicaea is said. When Caesar Augustus was succeeded by Tiberius in 14 AD, the Jews were two generations away from the destruction of their holy city and their temple in 69–70 by the Roman general Titus and their subsequent dispersion across the Mediterranean and Mesopotamia. The stubborn allegiance to God displayed by Mattathias and his sons would not fade as Israel was subsumed into the Roman world. The Roman Consul Agrippa, Augustus' auxiliary, scolded, "You are the only people who think it a disgrace to be servants of those to whom the whole world has submitted."[1]

The world in which the Church would successfully co-opt Plato and Plotinus, claim the Hebrew Scriptures as its own, and partly adopt *Romanitas*, including the piety and natural inspiration of Hellenistic religion, belonged to the future while the great age of philosophy and Greek poetry lay in the distant past. The traditional religion of the Roman republic was being invaded by cults bred up in the East—Mithras, Dionysius, and Isis—which went beyond conventional piety toward the gods to offer salvation to expectant souls. At the periphery of the philosophic world lay the ironic moralism of the Cynics, urging the abandonment of convention in favor of the radical pursuit of virtue, and the popular atheism of Lucretius.[2]

Christ came to a waiting world. Edward Gibbon, writing in the Age of Enlightenment, fretted that the monastic ideal had destroyed the noble Roman tradition of politics and piety. Christianity with its note of restraint and its sponsorship of the monastic life did not destroy a noble empire of ideas; it brought to perfection a rich culture which, left to its own resources, might well, given its trajectory, have dwindled into intellectual insignificance of Parthia. Rome looked prosperous and victorious. Its territorial expansion continued into the third century and seemed when Christ was born to know no limits. Victory in the Third Punic War (BC 146) against Carthage and her allies had given Rome hegemony in Spain and the western African coastlands. Greece and the Asiatic principalities were annexed between BC 150 and BC 100, little Judea and the surrounding territory in BC 63, Egypt in 30, and Britain in a series of wars begun in 40 AD. There were still men of genius like Plutarch and Cicero, philosophers who taught virtue and purity of life such as Seneca (BC 4–65AD) and Epictetus (50–135AD), and effective

1 Josephus, *Jewish Wars*, 2.16.4, ed. William Whiston, *The Works of Flavius Josephus* (Halifax, Nova Scotia: Milner and Sowerby, 1852), 507.

2 A. A. Long, *Hellenistic Philosophy* (New York: Charles Scribner's Sons, 1974), 110.

emperors like Augustus and Trajan, but despite continual efforts to restore and shore up the foundations, civil polity was at best brittle, religion was in decay, and philosophy a scene of contending sects, characterized by the skepticism of the late Academy in which nothing was quite true and the case might always be otherwise. When Augustus secured the empire, the civilization displayed all the cultural weaknesses that accompany decay. Literature was preoccupied with form, "resulting in the rule-ridden traditionalism and tiresome 'echoing' of Cicero and Vergil, its emphasis on aesthetic effect. . . , exhibiting every form of dexterity possible to authors who aspired to virtuosity without any regard for truth."[3] Architecture was on its way to Hadrian's villa at Tivoli (120 AD), where every trick of variety, surprise, and effect was employed using a classical vocabulary, by way of Augustus' own Altar of Peace (BC 13) and Nero's Golden House (50 AD), both arguably examples of the appeal to monumentality and complexity when imagination has failed.

By admiring the body for its natural beauty and nothing more while simultaneously denying that the flesh had any finality beyond the grave, the culture laid itself open to the sorrows of an egregious carnality, the grisly consequences of which Justin describes: state sponsorship of prostitution, the abuse of abandoned children, temple prostitution, and mutilation for sexual purposes.[4] This unchecked sensuality was located in the highest level of society. Nero made free to enact a public marriage to the boy Sporus, and Hadrian (98–117) erected across the empire statues of his departed favorite Antinous whom, says Justin, "everybody, through fear hastened to worship as a god."[5] Rumor exaggerates, but the claim that at the end of the second century the Emperor Commodus (180–92) maintained a stable of 300 concubines and 300 boys for his pleasure elaborated the public perception of the imperial behavior.

Octavian's impressive accomplishments as the emperor Augustus overlaid the decline of a civilization that had exhausted its vitality in civil wars

3 Charles Norris Cochrane, *Christianity and Classical Culture* (New York: Oxford University Press, 1957), 146.

4 Justin 29 (Richardson, 260).

5 Hans Urs von Balthasar suggested in his *Theology of Glory* (San Francisco, Calif.: Ignatius Press, 1989) that the "entranced gaze of the spectator" as the naked youth steps into the stadium, their bodies displaying a kind of radiance, "is the origin of Greek pederasty" (95).

and political ineptitude. His reign inaugurated an era of restoration in which piety was encouraged, temples restored, and peace maintained in Italy. On 4 July BC 13 Augustus was present at the dedication in the Campus Martius of the *Ara Pacis*, the great altar celebrating the Augustan peace, whose recollected fragments now stand again by the Tiber.[6] Despite intermittent bad government, irresolvable political tensions, bad emperors, invasions, and almost perpetual wars of defense and conquest, the Augustan order and its Christian successors would persist in the West for six centuries, establishing the stability within which Christianity grew. Paul's gratitude for the emperor and the administration of law that punished wickedness and praised the good was typical, and with him began the custom of prayer for the emperor (1 Tim. 2:1–3). The world had peace thanks to the Romans, and even Christians could walk without fear on the roads and travel wherever they pleased. Superficially, the empire was the apotheosis of secular success, embellished with the formalities of the republic but at heart a popular despotism that had successfully enforced peace after a century of civil war.

Yet the world Augustus won twenty-seven years before Christ was born in Bethlehem, understood in terms of its then-present moral accomplishments and possibilities when Tiberius succeeded in 14 AD, was a dying world, waiting to be vivified by the religion of Jesus the Galilean. The Roman historian Tacitus, writing at about the time of Ignatius' letters, about 110 AD, reflecting on the preceding half-century, wrote: "Things holy were desecrated. There was adultery in high places. The Mediterranean swarmed with exiles and its rocky inlets ran with blood. The reign of terror was particularly ruthless at Rome. Rank, wealth, and office, whether surrendered or retained, provided grounds for accusation, and the reward for virtue was inevitable death."[7] Christianity with its optimism, its notes of restraint and its sponsorship of the family and the monastic life as sacred

6 In 1568 fragments were discovered beneath a palace behind S. Lorenzo in Lucina and were purchased by the Grand Duke of Florence, the Louvre, and other museums. In 1891 the fragments were identified as fragments of Augustus' altar and the complicated process of excavating the remaining parts was undertaken in 1903. Finally in 1927 the *Ara Pacis* began to be reassembled on a site on the left bank of the Tiber east of the Ponte Umberto I.

7 Tacitus, *Histories* 1.2 (trans. Kenneth Wellesley [Penguin Books: Baltimore, Md.: 1964], 22).

institutions, did not destroy a noble empire of ideas; it saved an intellectual and moral culture which, left to its own resources, would have met the fate of Nineveh and Tyre. This inspired effort to take the achievements of the Roman and Jewish worlds and make the religion of Christ lay in the future when Octavian defeated Antony at Actium in BC 31.

There was not much of the peace described by Paul as "passing all understanding" (Phil. 4:7). There was in the midst of new-found Augustan order an expectant longing that neither Dionysius nor Mithra could fulfill. In the age of the Maccabeans, in Alexandria the revenant voice prophesied in the name of the ancient Sibyl:

> But when Rome shall o'er Egypt also rule,
> Governing always, then there shall there appear
> The greatest kingdom of the immortal King
> Over men. And a holy Lord shall come
> To hold the scepter over every land
> Unto all ages of fast-hastening time.[8]

A century later Virgil in the fourth Eclogue foresaw the birth of a child:

> Justice returns, returns old Saturn's reign,
> With a new breed of men sent down from heaven.
> Only do thou, at the boy's birth in whom
> The iron shall cease, the golden race arise. . . .
> He shall receive the life of gods, and see
> Heroes with gods commingling, and himself be seen of them,
> And with his father's worth
> Reign o'er a world at peace. . . .[9]

Jerusalem looked forward to the advent of the "trustworthy prophet" foreseen by the bronze tablet posed in the temple precincts. Now the city

8 *Sibylline Oracles*, 3.724–1003, Milton S. Terry, *Sibylline Oracles Translated into Blank Verse* (New York: Eaton and Mains, 1899).

9 Constantine cites this "messianic" Eclogue at the opening of the First Nicean Council in 325, Eusebius, *Oration of Constantine*, 19–20 (*NPNF*[2] 1:575–76).

was alert for the appearing of "that prophet" (John 6:14), whom eight centuries earlier Isaiah had prophesied (9:6–7):

> For to us a child is born, to us a son is given,
> And the government will be upon his shoulder,
> And his name will be called
> Wonderful, Counselor, Mighty God,
> Everlasting Father, The Prince of Peace.
> And of the increase of his government
> And of peace there will be no end.

Into this waiting world, this much-welcomed, fragile Augustan peace, Christ was born.

# One
## *Reason Seeking Faith*

> As it happened those who first handled [philosophy], and who were therefore deemed illustrious men, were succeeded by those who made no investigations of the truth, but only admired the perseverance and self-discipline of the former as well as the novelties of the doctrines; and each thought that to be true which he learned from his teacher.
>
> Justin Martyr, *Dialogue with Trypho* 2

> They were able, indeed, to get some notions of reality but not to find it, since they did not deign to learn about God from God.
>
> Athenagoras, *Plea Regarding Christians* 7

Philosophy often seems remote from life. Yet in an uncanny way the thought of philosophers, necessarily preserved in books, drifts down from the heights of formal reflection where the great teachers preside down to the schoolroom and lives of the literate and semi-literate. It settles at last in the half-conscious assumptions through which every man engages the world. The studied reflections of Plato's Academy, Zeno's Stoa, and Aristotle's Lyceum influenced thought in the age of Augustus and still influence and form thought after two thousand years. Philosophy, and the principles and habits of thought it encourages, goes with us into the ordinary paths of life and undergirds and conditions our encounters with the other disciplines. This certainly is true of the relation between philosophy and theology, for there is no account of God's supernatural acts and revelation that does not presuppose the natural wisdom of philosophy as a foundation relating it to the world of thought and nature.

It was the providential good luck of the Christian enterprise that near the beginning it won the allegiance of the philosopher and apologist Justin (100–165), who, writing in the age of Antoninus Pius (138–61), gave a catalog of the philosophical schools available to him in his search for truth, naming as living witnesses to the philosophic tradition Platonists, Stoics, Peripatetics or Aristotelians, Theoretics, and Pythagoreans.[1] With the exception of the Theoretics, about whom nothing beyond Justin's use of the name is known, these same schools would have been represented a century earlier when the apostolic mission was born in Pilate's Jerusalem. Justin does not name the contemporary representatives of the schools he encountered, but each had its teachers in the age of the Antonines, 138–92.

Philosophy had begun with an attempt to understand nature. The Milesians, so named from their city of Miletus in Asia, established the Greek poetic tradition. They wrote perhaps around BC 600, a half-century after Homer's *Iliad*, the heroic story of the Mycerean Greek's expedition against Troy, and Hesiod's roughly contemporaneous *Works and Days*, the poetry of agricultural life. The Milesians began to find intelligibility in the natural world by attempting to identify its basic element, that from which everything is composed. Thales concluded that all bodies consist of and return to water, that water in which the earth floats, while Anaximander (610–546) conceived the more complicated idea that the four elements—earth, air, fire and water—by their interaction produce a condition he called limitlessness, the great ocean of being from which all things were born. His colleague Anaximenes (585–528), another Milesian, considering this unsatisfactory, proposed air as the basic element. Heraclitus (535–475) believed that in an ever-changing world, formed by logos or reason, all beings were composed of fire, "an exchange for fire as goods for gold," a foundational insight that would later be represented by the scientific principle that matter and energy are the reciprocal stuff of the universe. At mid-fifth century BC Parmenides, in his criticism of Heraclitus' doctrine of opposites—light and dark, heat and cold—posited what would later be called the principle of non-contradiction or identity: a thing cannot be itself and some other thing at the same time in the same way, an

1 *Dialogue* 1–2 (*ANF* 1:195).

insight that would ever after be the anchor of rationality. Democritus (BC 460–370) proposed atoms, uniform in size but differentiated by matter, existing in the void, as the stuff from which the world is composed, beginning the search for ever-smaller and more "basic" particles which continues today. The Christian Middle Ages inherited the synthetic commonplace that all is composed of earth, air, fire, and water, which convention was in turn the remote ancestor of the periodic chart of two hundred-plus elements.[2]

Having begun with an attempt to understand the natural world, philosophy turned with Socrates (BC 469–399) to explore the world of the soul, of goodness in its relation to virtue and self-knowledge, and of the mystery of truth. But the founder of metaphysics as we know it was his disciple Plato (BC 429–347), whose insight that all of nature and all thought is formed by and exemplifies transcendent ideas, anticipated by Pythagoras' interest in number and geometry, would, in one way or another, serve as the first principle of intelligibility for two thousand years.[3] A world in flux was in principle unknowable, but if everything represented a type of form or substance, knowledge of a more than probable kind was possible. Christian writers presupposed this great Platonic insight, undergirded as it was by Israel's knowledge of the transcendent, name-giving, hence form-giving, God. The Platonic Academy in Athens, founded by Socrates' disciple Plato, took its character from its defense of this principle. Although other interpretations of the dialogues would be developed, this insight was ably represented through the early fifth century and the age of Theodosius II. This gift of philosophic intelligibility, reinforced and spread in the West by Augustine (354–430), was so firmly ensconced as a premise of Christian thought that the pagan Academy was let to disappear with the proclamation of an imperial decree in 529.

Plato's sometime disciple Aristotle always maintained that he differed

2 See John Burnett, "The Milesian School," in *Early Greek Philosophy* (London: Adam and Charles Black,1892; repr., 1971), 39–79.

3 Plato noted in the *Phaedo* his disappointment that having been led by Anaxagoras to the belief that "mind is the disposer and cause of all," I then "found my philosopher altogether forsaking mind or any other principle of order, but having recourse to air, ether, and water," 98b (Jowett 1:482); G. M. A. Grube, *Plato's Thought* (London: Methuen, 1935), 18–19, 48–49.

from his friends the Platonists in only one thing: that the forms or ideas, whose existence he did not question, were not separable, not known by pure insight apart from experience of the things themselves, but were discovered by a process of engagement with nature that resulted in knowledge of intellectual realities not very different from Plato's forms. A. E. Taylor wrote of Aristotle, "He seems to say that these simplest truths are apprehended intuitively, or on inspection, as self-evident by Intelligence or Mind. On the other hand, he says that they are known to us as a result of induction from sense-experience. Thus he seems either to be a Platonist or an empiricist, according as you chose to remember one set of his utterances or another . . . . His final conclusions on all points of importance are hardly distinguishable from those of Plato."[4] Both Plato and Aristotle were what historians would later call realists, although in different ways, who between them created a vast corpus of philosophical insight on which the mind of the Mediterranean world and its dependencies has been nourished for twenty-five centuries.

Aristotle's following, the Peripatetic school, so-called after the covered walkway of the Lyceum, was represented in the first century BC by Andronicus of Rhodes, who recalled it to its roots by publishing a new edition of Aristotle's texts. When Justin wrote at mid-second century there would be echoes of Aristotle everywhere, but the Peripatetic school as such had ceased to be influential after Strabo in the late second century, and as Justin found them the Peripatetics were engaged in the un-philosophic task of teaching for fees.[5] The school persisted in Alexander of Aphrodesias, who began lecturing at Athens in 198 AD.

The philosophy of Plato's Academy descended from the age of the great founder and his contemporary Theophrastus to his successor Arcesilaus (BC 213–129), who chose to develop the skeptical side of the dialogues, which often ended with a *sic et non*, rather than the systematic, metaphysical Platonism that later would appeal to Augustine. At mid-first century BC Platonism would be perpetuated by Cicero (BC 106–43) and secondary figures such as Albinus, author about 151 AD of a textbook on Plato's philosophy; Apuleius (123–90 AD), best known as author of the *Golden Ass*

4 A. E. Taylor, *Aristotle* (New York: Dover Press, 1955), 30, 37.

5 A. A. Long, *Hellenistic Philosophy*, 226.

but also of a much criticized exposition of Platonism (*On the Doctrine of Plato*); and Plutarch (46–120 AD), who was touched by the academic tradition. Numenius of Apamea (150–200 AD),[6] who had developed the thought of the Academy in a mystical way, anticipated the Neo-Platonism of Plotinus (205–70 AD).

The unnamed Platonist whom Justin would meet as he began his search for truth, offering the prospect that through Plato's philosophy Justin might see God, was an exception to the pattern of skepticism that marked the later Academy. The promise philosophy offered but could not fulfill would persist in the beautiful text of Plotinus' *Enneads*, which about 260 described the journey of the soul through the Platonic realm of ascending intelligibilities to something beyond: "The self thus lifted, we are in the likeness of the Supreme, if from that heightened self we pass still higher—image to archetype—we have won the end of all our journeying."[7] Outside the embrace of Christianity the inheritance of Plato would continue its drift either into the theosophical fantasies of Iamblichus (250–325 AD) or into the skepticism that earned the rebuke of Augustine's *Against the Academics* in 386.

The Stoics whom Justin mentions in his account of his search were a school of moral and philosophic thought founded upon the principle that virtue is knowledge, specifically knowledge of the world as it is with its pleasures and pains, a knowledge which gives the wise man the ability to bear nobly what must be borne and to enjoy such pleasures as may be justly attainable. The name is derived from the Greek word for porch, referring to the Painted Porch, the public hall in Athens that flanked one side of the great piazza in which the Stoic founder Zeno of Citium (335–263) and his successors taught in a line that endured unbroken until at least 260 AD. It was the Stoics who popularized the idea that the world is shot through with the reason that inhabits both the world of nature and the mind of man. At the end of the Republic Stoicism had been ably represented by Lucius Annaeus Seneca (BC 4–65 AD). His intellectual successor Epictetus (55–135

6 Kenneth Sylvan Guthrie, *Numenius of Apamea, the Father of Neo-Platonism* (London: George Bell and Sons, 1917), 30–31.

7 Plotinus, *Enneads*, 6.9.11. Stephen McKenna and B. S. Page, trans., (Chicago: William Benton, 1952), 360.

AD) gave the school his *Discourses* and *Enchiridion* or *Handbook*, which followed Socrates in presenting philosophy as a way of life, a way that began by accepting death with courage: "Let death and exile and all other things that appear terrible, especially death, be daily before your eyes, and you will never entertain any abject thought, nor too eagerly covet anything."[8] Fear thus overcome, it remained to build the virtuous soul; "of the art of living, the subject matter is each person's own life."[9] There would typically be a tinge of Stoicism in the thought of every philosophic Roman, and indeed in Christianity itself. In his *Dialogue with Trypho* Justin mentioned Stoicism just a few years before the Emperor Marcus Aurelius wrote his famous *Meditations*, the great classic of the philosophic insights of the thoughtful among the pagans, in 154.

The common-sense philosophical insights of those that John, Paul, Ignatius, and Justin would assume, were to be found among these ideas of the philosophers; but when Christian writers first engaged Plato, philosophy, once a fruitful and noble tradition, was in danger of becoming eclectic and febrile.[10] Writing a little more than a century after Pentecost, Justin as he recounts in his *Dialogue with Trypho*, found all of the schools wanting. The Pythagoreans had nothing for beginners, those who had not mastered the mathematical arts of the quadrivium: astronomy, music, arithmetic, geometry. Peripatetics, the disciples of Aristotle, wanted the fee settled before instruction began, a sure sign of an anti-philosophic temper. The Stoics, caught up in reflection on the ambiguities and pain of the human situation, had nothing to say.[11] Justin admired the teaching of the Platonists, but their belief in the uncreated nature of the ideas and the natural immortality of the soul would prove incompatible with his Christian profession.[12] Perhaps it is not remarkable that Justin does not mention in his search for truth what was certainly a popular philosophy among his contemporaries—the school called the "garden" on an analogy to Zeno's

8 Epictetus, *Handbook* (Hard, trans., 292).

9 *Discourses*, 1.15.1 (Hard, trans., 36).

10 "A number of the commonplaces had been absorbed by Jewish Greek writers" (Arthur Darby Nock, *Early Gentile Christianity* [New York: Harper and Row1964]), 96, note 1.

11 Justin 2 (Richardson, 242).

12 *Dialogue* 4–5 (*ANF* 1, 196–97).

painted porch—that followed the doctrine of the fourth-century teacher Epicurus, who taught that the soul is not immortal but material, and that pleasure is the guide to life, with pleasure understood as encompassing not only freedom from pain and the enjoyment of pleasures of the body but those pleasures afforded by living virtuously. The philosophy of Epicurus was popularized in the first century BC by Lucretius' long poem *On the Nature of Things.*[13]

With the epistemological skepticism of the late Academy, their doctrine that, as many of the dialogues suggested, any question might be answered in more than one way, and the virulent materialism of Lucretius as background, Justin suggested that the reason for the weakness of the philosophical witness to this apparent barrenness of philosophy as he found it, was the tendency of each school to admire and perpetuate the thought of their distinguished founders while ignoring the philosopher's first task, which is not to defend what has been thought but to think truly. "Reason requires that those who are truly pious and philosophers should honor and cherish the truth alone, scorning to follow the opinions of the ancients, if they are worthless."[14]

In contrast with Roman religion, which was tolerant and eclectic, philosophy was often a realm of emulation and contention. As it happened, it was the co-opting by Christians of Plato and Aristotle that gave fresh life to the ancient philosophies. Hilaire Belloc wrote: "It was not the spread of the faith which undermined the high civilization of pagan antiquity; on the contrary, the faith saved all that could be saved. . . ."[15] When in 529 the Emperor Justinian closed the schools of philosophy that did not teach

13 Lucretius, *On the Nature of Things*, trans. A. E. Stallings (New York: Penguin, 2007).

14 *Dialogue* 2 [Richardson, 242].

15 Hilaire Belloc, *The Crisis of Civilization* (New York: Fordham University Press, 1937), 46. And see David Bentley Hart, "To return to my principal point, the Christianity of the early centuries did not invade a world of noonday joy, vitality, mirth and cheerful earthiness, and darken it with malicious slanders of the senses. . . . Rather, it entered into a twilit world of pervasive spiritual despondency and religious yearning, . . . as a religion of glad tidings, new life, and that in all abundance" *Atheist Delusions: The Christian Revolution and Its Fashionable Enemies* (New York: Yale University Press, 2009), 143.

the orthodox faith,[16] the useable elements of Plato's metaphysical vision and of Epictetus' ethics had been so thoroughly incorporated into the body of Christian learning and apologetics that the pagan schools were otiose. But five centuries earlier, as the republic became the empire, Plato's Academy, Aristotle's Lyceum, and the Stoa, splinters of a larger vision though they were, represented a noble achievement of the classical world the importance of which has never diminished.

Inevitably Plato, mediated to the West by Augustine, would become the principal guide for Christian philosophers and theologians for the first millennium of Christian intellectual life.[17] Platonism's transcendent vision made Justin believe, mistakenly he concluded, that by following this philosophy he would soon see God, "for this is the end of Plato's philosophy."[18] Platonism's defense of the intelligibility of nature was a bridge to the doctrine of the Word that enlightens every man, through whom all things were created, that the Gospel of John would render fundamental to Christian thought. Platonists were not materialists; at their best they believed in the possibility of certain knowledge based upon eternal, transcendent ideas.

Considered as truth, the ideas are objective realities that general terms connote. It is from this aspect that Plato thought of them as mathematical formulae which governed the physical world and brought order out of chaos, laws that governed every human action as well as the movements of the stars and planets, the one right way of doing things in the moral sphere.[19]

16 Justinian did not propose to suppress pagan philosophy but to deny teachers not of the faith support from the public purse. That the action was aimed specifically at the Athenian Academy is unclear. See James Hannam, "*The Emperor Justinian's Closing of the School of Athens*," 2016 (http://jameshannam.com/Justinian, htm).

17 Augustine had wrestled with the skeptical academic Platonism of Cicero until he came finally to accept a "realist" interpretation of Platonism, which, modified by Plotinus and John 1:1–14, became the Platonism of the Christian Fathers. See Augustine, *Eighty-Three Questions*, Number 46, written about 391, which Thomas Aquinas used almost nine centuries later as his authority for the article "On Ideas," question 15 of part 1 of the *Summa Theologica.*

18 *Dialogue* 2 (*ANF* 1:195).

19 Grube, *Plato's Thought,* 50.

But there were dangers. There is surely something to Tertullian's charge that philosophy, by which he would have meant Plato, encouraged the dualism represented by that virulent gloss on the Christian Gospel called Gnosticism, and the case can be made that the Fathers, having more or less adopted Plato, were required to expend much effort keeping its native anti-incarnational bias, barely contained in the theology of Clement of Alexandria and intrinsic to the thought of Arius, in check. The idealist theme inherent in Platonism and Pythagoreanism, which fell so easily into a theology of emanations, would offer a target of opportunity to heresy until the fifth century. The brilliant theologian Origen (185–254) would be its victim and this emanation philosophy would in turn subtly undergird Arianism, the doctrine that Jesus was not God of God but the highest creature—nothing in history could share the being or substance of the One—at the turn of the third century.

The involvement of philosophy in theological reflection was to be expected: thinkers like John the Evangelist and Paul, without once making formal reference to any philosophy, perhaps lacking knowledge of any Platonic text, wrote within certain presuppositions that are closely related to the thought of the Academy on its systematic side. Although anticipated to some degree by the Wisdom literature (Wis. 7–8) and by the Stoic conception of a world shot through with reason, the ideas of a world made in the image of the Eternal Word who is also a divine-human person in John 1:1–18, the Pauline ideas of the cosmic Christ in whom all things exist (Col.1:15–20), like the participation of Christians in Christ, are given intelligibility by a vernacular appreciation of Plato's doctrine of ideas, apart from which every thing and every person is an isolated, formally unique, theoretically unknowable something.

Finally, there existed in the intellectual environment of the first and second centuries a kind of half-philosophic, half-religious presupposition that would influence Christian thought just as it had shaped the Hellenistic world. In the background of Greek, and hence all Roman, philosophy there was always the shadow of Orphism, an archaic dualism that proclaimed the soul to be eternal, kin to the Gods, and the body to be a prison for the soul from which it would be released only by death. The tag *sēma, sōma,* the body is a tomb, was a commonplace in Hellenistic culture. This dualism would resonate with the philosophies of Plato and Pythagoras, and for the unphilosophic, possessed nonetheless of a mind that seemed to preside with transcendent constancy over the ever-changing world of coming to be and passing away while its creature the body decayed, the first principles of vernacular Orphism, held uncritically, seemed self-evident. This dualism, taken with other influences such as the Hermetic literature of Egypt, would be a staple of Gnosticism, that anti-incarnational shadow Christianity that Paul and John and Ignatius considered the bitter enemy of the religion of the resurrection of the body (1 Cor. 15:12–34, 1 John 2:22, 2 John 7).

As the quest for philosophic truth described by Justin Martyr in the opening chapters of his *Dialogue with Trypho* shows, there was no shortage of teaching and learning in schools that laid claim to truth. Justin was proudly a philosopher, but the philosophic enterprise as he found it was a cacophony of contending voices, disciples representing the interests of the great masters of the past. True, the philosophers Justin interviewed were engaged in an impossible task; the attempt to answer the questions that occur always and everywhere about virtue, the meaning of life, and the nature of God, relying solely on reason. Some were more successful than others and their heritage is an intellectual treasure which ever nourishes the mind of the West. Not to know Plato's *Laws*, the *Republic*, the *Theaetetus,* and the *Phaedo*; not to know something of Aristotle's *Metaphysics* and *Ethics*, Cicero, Marcus Aurelius, to mention only the most obvious, is to miss the gifts that reason brought to the Mediterranean world.

These gifts were fragile, always claiming more than could be realized, until the Word became flesh. It is of the very nature of the philosophic quest at its best to raise questions to which it can give only suggestive but incomplete answers. Philosophy can argue with some success that belief in one Creator is reasonable, but it cannot convince the human heart to believe without the providential witness of the Holy Spirit and the authority of divine revelation. What Paul said of the limits of human knowledge applies *mutatis mutandis* to the philosopher's task: reason sees as in a glass, an imperfect mirror, darkly (1 Cor. 13:12), but it does indeed see. To find fruition philosophy must fall silent so as to listen to the voice of divine wisdom; reason without revelation will always finally be blind.

Christian revelation gave the enterprise of the philosophers—of Plato, Aristotle, the Stoics, the Pythagoreans—a future by rescuing the thought of the Hellenistic world of the first century AD from the futility that belongs to a search for truth that frames great questions to which it has but partial answers and imagined systems, sometimes as with Plotinus of great beauty, that do not lead beyond themselves. For Christians in the age of Justin truth as the classical world had known it was scattered everywhere, waiting to be perfected and incorporated into the majestic whole of Christian doctrine. Until the advent of the Arabian commentators on Aristotle and the flowering of the universities in the twelfth century, philosophy would be found not in the systematic treatises of philosophers such as Justin had been before his conversion, but embedded in the theological tradition that began with the Johannine prologue and Justin Martyr, and would find its medieval flourishing in Augustine, Bonaventure, and Aquinas. Christian theologians and apologists were always philosophers, but philosophers were also theologians, as was Cicero when he wrote *The Nature of the Gods* and Epictetus when he wrote his *Discourses*, and as the founders Plato and Aristotle had also been.

# Two
## *Everything Is Full of Gods*

> In the question now before us, the greater part of mankind have united to acknowledge that which is most probable, and that which by nature we are led to suppose, namely, that there are Gods.
>
> Cicero, *The Nature of the Gods* 1

"Everything is full of gods." These words of the distinguished philosopher Quintus Aurelius Symmachus (340–402 AD), writing when the neo-paganism encouraged briefly by the Emperor Julian was being dismantled by the Emperors Gratian (367–83) and Valentinian II (383–92), were a commonplace representing a fundamental theological insight of the Hellenistic world. Nature was not in the post-Cartesian sense of the word natural at all, for it was alive with divine presences. There was about it all a comforting but sometimes unsettlingly character. One might meet a god around any corner or a stranger might indeed be a god in disguise. Omnipotent though Jupiter (Zeus) was, both he and lesser members of the divine company had favorites and were capable of pursuing grudges, of jealousy and grief, as at the death of Marcellus, Augustus' favorite nephew, in BC 23.[1]

Atheists the Romans for the most part were not; the inhabitants of the Hellenistic world were a religious people in the sense that they believed everything to be full of gods, the gods and man to be of one race, and human events to be governed by the divine influence of the stars. Unlike the Jews for whom God's utter transcendence was the ground of his every perfection, pious Romans saw the world as alive with superior beings, gods who communicated with them by signs, by dreams, by natural events and

1 *Aeneid*, 6.870–71 (LCL 63:595–98).

prodigies, by lightning, and prodigies of nature, all of which the college of *augures,* observers of signs, especially the behavior of birds, and *haruspices,* diviners who read the entrails of sheep, could interpret.[2] Cicero was an augur, an official diviner, the author of a work *On Divination* calculated to show the limits of the practice and to discountenance fortune-telling and necromancy.[3] The other important means of discerning the will of the gods was the Sibylline books, Greek verse-oracles, always consulted by the Senate in times of crisis, that while they did not prophesy the future as did Isaiah or the prophet John, did indicate the divine favor or disapprobation toward human enterprises. This collection was believed to have originated with the purchase of three books of oracles from the Cumaean sibyl by the last Tarquin king in the late sixth century BC. Having made their way into Roman provenance, the Sibylline Oracles were kept in a chamber beneath the Temple of Jupiter on the Capitoline, guarded when Augustus gained the principate in BC 27 by the *quindecimviri,* fifteen distinguished Romans, who were assisted by two Greek-speaking translators.[4]

Gods in a sense lived in temples but also in groves and inhabited springs. Nature itself was a theophany, full of gods, crowned by the stars, themselves "divine and eternal animals . . . circling as in a dance."[5] There were gods for everything and every activity. The door was the separation between the world and the household. Janus was the god of the door, Janus Patulcius opened the door, Janus Clusivius closed it. Arnobius of Sicca,

2 J. H. W. G. Liebeschuetz, *Conformity and Change in Roman Religion* (Oxford: At the Clarendon Press, 1970), 7– 29.

3 R. M. Ogilvie, *The Romans and Their Gods in the Age of Augustus* (New York: W. W. Norton. 1969), 6.

4 In BC 82, they were severely burned, necessitating the collection of oracles from Erythrae, the island of Samos, Sicily, and Africa. They were removed in BC 12 to the Temple of Apollo on the Palatine, associated architecturally with the house of Augustus, where they remained until they were destroyed in 405 by the Roman general Stilicho (Ogilvie, *Romans and Their Gods*, 62–63; H. W. Parke, *Sibyls and Sibylline Prophecy in Classical Antiquity* (London: Routledge, 1988); "Octavian and the Thunderbolt: the Temple of Apollo Palatinus and Roman Traditions of Temple Building," *Classical Quarterly* 56 (2006): 149–68.

5 Plato, *Timaeus* 40d (Jowett, 1.21–22); Aristotle *Metaphysics* VI.1, 1026a (McKeon, 779).

who flourished in the reign of Diocletian (284–305), in his work *Against the Pagans*, still wrote as though Limintinus presided over the threshold, and Cardea over the hinges.[6]

At the center of Roman worship, as with almost every Mediterranean people except the Jews, who worshipped a jealous God, was no particular body of doctrine but the fact of sacrifice, the necessity for establishing a right relationship with those who controlled life and nature. About BC 50 Varro in his *Res divinae* cataloged Roman sacrificial practice, describing the sacrifice appropriate to each festival, a work analogous to Leviticus in the Hebrew Scriptures. Roman life was ordered by an elaborate calendar, one purpose of which was to mark out the days on which sacrifice was to be made to the appropriate god.[7] As with the Jews, for whom the center of the land and people was Jerusalem and the temple, and within the temple the ark containing the law, the center of the thing called simply Rome was the city on the Tiber, and at the heart of the city the temple of Jupiter with the Twelve Tables of the law affixed. But there was this difference. The laws enshrined in the ark were intended to establish a living relationship with the unnamable deity and to define the moral goodness he found pleasing. The laws of the Twelve Tables were partly that, but were mostly customary, rules to ease the day-to-day life of Romans, written originally for an agricultural people, punishing slander, describing the rights of the heads of families, prohibiting marriage between patricians and plebeians, and establishing rights-of-way.[8]

Romans understood purity as a matter of ritual observance and did not pay much attention to the elevating effects of worship beyond conventional expressions of piety or honoring what had been and ought to be honored. Although the mystery religions, Mithra and Dionysius, would have differed significantly on this point, relations with the gods of Rome were typically not about salvation but about success, about making one's way through life with one's share of blessings while avoiding disasters. One did not love the gods; one tried to maintain a good relation with them by offering sacrifice.

6 Ogilvie, *Romans and Their Gods*, 11.

7 Ibid, 70–80.

8 Stephen Steinberg, "The Twelve Tables and Their Origins: An Eighteenth-Century Debate," *Journal of the History of Ideas*, 43 (1982): 379–96.

Sallustius, writing in the fourth century, composed his defense of paganism too late to be considered typical of the age of Justin Martyr but he is nevertheless an important witness to the nature of sacrifice. "Prayers divorced from sacrifices are only words; prayers offered with sacrifices are animated words, the word giving power to the life and the life animation to the word." Sacrificial practice reflected a near-universal conviction, "the intermediary between life and life should be life, and for this reason living animals are sacrificed by the blessed among men."[9] But when Sallustius, who is after all the contemporary of Julian the Apostate, goes on to say that we sacrifice to gain union with the god, he is displaying not so much the influence of traditional Roman piety but of Neo-Platonism and the mystery religions.

The great events that formed imagination were accomplished through sacrifice. Human sacrifice, always rare, was outlawed in BC 97, but there had been noteworthy exceptions.[10] The sacrifice of Iphigenia was notorious and Athens had been founded, the great temple consecrated, by the sacrifice of the daughters of Erectheus, whose story decorated the interior frieze of the great temple to Athena.[11] Sacrifices were to be accomplished with care and solemnity. The universal intuition summed up in the word *sacer* reflected the understanding that something could be made holy by handing it over to the immortal gods who lived beyond the veil of present experience, a meaning held in an analogous way by the Hebrews. The state maintained an elaborate schedule of sacrifices and establishing the day and type of sacrifice, whether the day was a working day or a festival day, on which business could not be pursued, seems to have been a principal purpose of the calendar, although sacrifices generally seem to have been routine, not occasions for any great public celebration. Privately, sacrifice would be made either to gain a favor or to fulfill a vow. The god having fulfilled the request,

9 Sallustius, *Concerning the Nature of the Gods and the Universe,* 16, ed. and trans. Arthur Darby Nock (Cambridge: University Press, 1926; paperback edition, 2013), 29, 31.

10 Human sacrifice had been prohibited at Rome in BC 97. See Leibeschuetz, *Continuity and Change in Roman Religion*, 138, n. 4.; Ogilvie, *Romans and their Gods*, 87–88.

11 Joan Breton Connelly, *The Parthenon Enigma* (New York: Alfred A. Knopf, 2014), 126–48.

which the suppliant had made by tying the wax tablet on which his petition was written to the god's statue, sacrifice was in order. An analogous practice continued in Christianity, with petitions scratched on the tombs of martyrs, or with the petitions attached to the statue of Our Lady of Good Birth in Sant' Augustino in Rome, itself a place of sacrifice. "It is easy to underestimate the emotional impact of the sacrificial rite. It was an impressive spectacle which had associations with all the most solemn moments of a Roman life. Above all there was the emotion aroused by the act of killing."[12]

Family sacrifice was often made by offering a small cake, but solemn sacrifice required the offering of life. The one sacrificing would first purchase an animal that must be perfect; the animal and the one sacrificing must be clean. He would also employ a flute player and make arrangements with a priest.[13] Then he would begin by entering the temple and offering fervent prayer, standing, kneeling, or sometimes prostrate. One must know the god's name. Prayer must be perfect. The animal must be decorated and must be willing, or at least not unwilling, as the panels fronting the seats of the senators in the still-extant Curia, the senate house built in the reign of Diocletian (AD 284–305), illustrate, depicting beribboned, obviously well-satisfied oxen and swine.

Then the solemn ritual would begin, not in the temple, but at an altar before the temple door. Fire would be lit on the altar. An attendant would command silence. The priest would draw the knife from the animal's head to its tail. The one offering sacrifice, facing the temple door, would address a carefully written prayer to the god within. The *popa,* the temple servant, standing on the right of the animal, would ask, "Do I strike?" The animal would be struck with a well-aimed blow that would stun and bring it to its knees. The knife man would then slit the animal's throat, holding the head down if the sacrifice was to a god of the underworld or up if to a heavenly god. The sacrifice not only repaid a debt, but the vitality of the god was sustained by sacrifices. Thus the prayer to the god might include the phrase "be you increased."[14]

12 Liebeschuetz, *Continuity and Change in Roman Religion,* 80.

13 Probably not one belonging to one of the four colleges of priests, whose membership consisted of politically important citizens, but one of the *flamines* attached to the temples of certain gods. See Ogilvie, *Roman Religion*, 108–09.

14 Ogilvie, *Romans and Their Gods*, 42

The priest, the man offering the sacrifice, and his friends would then eat the offering, as at the Exodus (12:5–10), as at Sinai (Exod. 24:5–8), as at every Passover, and in the unbloody sacrifice that would form Christian life and liturgy.[15]

Rome was famous for its piety even after the late republican decline; in the second century BC the Greek historian Polybius could write: "The respect in which, in my opinion, the Roman constitution is most markedly superior is in its view of the gods. It seems to me that superstition, which we criticize in other people, is precisely what gives the Roman state its cohesion."[16] There were exceptions, among whom Lucretius (94–55) is notable, his *De Rerum Natura, On the Nature of Things,* being an attempt to drive religion and all its superstitions from the life of the literate Roman on behalf of a 'scientific' understanding of nature, arguing in a voice such as Voltaire might have used in the eighteenth century or Herbert Spencer in the 1880s The telling example offered by the rationalists in their polemic against traditional Roman religion, whose exponents would in extremity offer human sacrifice, was Iphigenia:

> To be impurely slaughtered, at an age when she should wed,
> Sorrowful sacrifice slain at her father's hand instead.
> All this for fair and favorable winds to sail the fleet along!
> So potent was religion in persuading to do wrong.[17]

Lucretius and rational religion did not carry the day. The Romans were a pious people and their life is unintelligible apart from the omnipresence of the gods. Reinforcing, while often criticizing, religion there was always a piety of the philosophers, rooted in texts like Plato's *Republic* and his *Laws,*

15 Ogilvie, *Romans and Their Gods*, 50. That an entire animal sacrifice could not have been consumed by those sacrificing occasioned Paul's warning that Christians should not eat meat sacrificed to idols, the left-overs being a major source of urban supply (1 Cor. 8:1). Pliny would not have understood the harmless food Christians shared as a sacrifice, there being no animal offering (Bettenson, 4).

16 Polybius, *Histories,* 6.56 (trans., Robin Waterfield [Oxford: University Press, 2010]), 411.

17 Lucretius, *On the Nature of Things*, lines 98–101, trans. A. E. Stallings (London: Penguin Books, 2007), 6.

works in which Plato argued the existence, justice, and benevolence of the gods against the vernacular willingness to accept their capriciousness and amorality.[18] This philosophic tradition would develop in different ways into the philosophers' religion of the Stoics, represented best perhaps by the *Discourses* of Epictetus and the *Meditations* of the Emperor Marcus Aurelius, and later into the quasi-religion of the Neo-Platonists like Plotinus (205–269 AD) and Iamblichus (250–325 AD). Stoicism, at least as represented by Epictetus, assumed the existence of God as the ground of virtue and cosmic order.

Despite these rationalizing attempts, negative in Lucretius' *De Rerum Natura*, and in various ways constructive in the works of Plato, Marcus Aurelius, and Epictetus, like almost all people throughout time, Romans were interested in, if not haunted by, the ideas of an afterlife; that is, while most Romans would find the resurrection of the body impossible and even distasteful, and the Christian notion of the renewal of creation risible, they did not believe that death ended personal existence. The ancestors were somewhere. Every Roman family worshipped the *Lares*, "the deified spirits of the ancestors who still took an interest in the family," to whom prayer and some small sacrifice of wine or incense might be offered daily.[19] There was the belief that the spirits of the departed, their *Manes*, lingered at the places of their burial.[20] For the average Roman there was the realm of Hades where, according to the most fully developed account, the departed were judged by Minos and assigned, after being dipped in Lethe, the pool of

18 Plato, *Laws* 10, 898–904 (Jowett, 2:640–49) and Cicero, *On the Nature of the Gods* 3.36: "Supposing, which is incontestable, that there are gods, they must be animated, and not only animated but endowed with reason, united, as we may say, in civil agreement and society, and governing together one universe, as a republic or city." C. D. Yonge trans., *The Nature of the Gods and on Divination* (Amherst, N. Y. : Prometheus Books, 1997), 73.

19 Ogilvie, *Romans and Their Gods*, 101.

20 In many Roman tombs one finds a small tube directed downward toward to the remains. This was used to offer ritual nourishment to the departed, especially at the celebration of the Parentalia, 13 to 24 February, to include departed ancestors in a commemorative family meal. Famously, Saint Monica, who had practiced the custom of visiting the tombs of ancestors in Africa, abandoned this usage because in the fourth century it was no longer the practice among Christians in Italy.

forgetfulness, to Elysium, while the unjust are delivered to the Furies and assigned to the tortures of Tartarus.[21] For great generals and the founders of cities there was life in the milky way, among the stars, as befell Scipio Africanus in Cicero's *Dream of Scipio*.[22] For brave soldiers there were the Isles of the Blessed, or the Elysian Fields.

The sacrifices of Roman religion had always been offered to propitiate the gods, although the degree to which they offered relief from personal guilt (as distinct from misfortune, civic danger, or folly) is unclear. While there was always exhortation to virtue (Aristotle, Cato, Cicero, Epictetus, and a host of others), no proposal regarding a specific way of personal holiness gained currency during the Roman republic. Cicero asked, "Who ever thanked the gods that he was a good man? We thank them indeed for riches, health and honor. For these we invoke the all-good and all-powerful Jupiter; but not for wisdom, temperance, and justice."[23] Those virtues were to be worked out in the Roman soul, where character fixed by the stars met that power to form the soul that was the mark of a free man.

As the republic wore down, there developed what might be called a market for a set of salvation religions. In the beginning there had been Orphism, the religion of Orpheus, which made the idea that the body is the tomb of the spirit a commonplace, and which influenced Plato and his successors. The state cult of the Egyptian Isis gradually became a popular religion of personal devotion to the goddess. Dionysius took up a place as guardian of the soul on its journey into the underworld. The cult of

21 Elysium, the Elysian fields, and the Isles of the Blessed might be seen as geographical, located at the western edge of the earth.

22 Cicero, *Republic,* VI.16 (Niall Rudd, trans., *The Republic and the Laws* [Oxford: University Press, 1998]), 89.

23 Cicero, *On the Nature of the Gods*, 3.36 (trans. C. D. Yonge, 137). The attempt to understand the typical Roman's relation to the gods is challenging. Cicero's point holds, but contrasting with his rather detached view was the opinion of the Greek Dio Chrysostom, a cynic philosopher contemporary with Ignatius, who described Greek affection for the gods as analogous to the longing of a child for an absent parent, "rightly loving them for their beneficence and kinship, and being eager in every possible way to be with them and hold converse with them" (Dio Chrysostom II, (LCL) *Twelfth, or Olympic Discourse,* trans. J. W. Cohoon (London: Heineman, 1939). 53.

Mithras, an eastern import that became famous about the time of the Flavians (69–92 AD), featured sacramental meals and a ritual like baptism, through which members were initiated by being cleansed by the blood of the bull. The initiate, having been crowned with a garland, took it off saying, "Mithras is my garland." These were salvation religions that with regard to type shared some imaginal ground with Christianity.

There was always the picture of the religion of the noble Romans, the state cult with the *pontifex maximus* and the vestal virgins and the peasant religion of the *Lares,* the deified spirits of dead ancestors, and the *Penates* who watched over the larder. The premise, which would endure into the Constantinian century, held that piety towards the gods was always rewarded by divine protection for the state and victory for the legions. But the religion of the Romans throughout the decades that separated the dictator Sulla (BC 137–78) from Augustus, had endured an ever more intense crisis, in which traditional pieties gave way at the periphery to oriental cults, to magic, to divination, and to astral determinism; Romans never, until Christianity broke the spell, lost their belief in the necessity that was ordained by the stars.

In the end Augustus' attempt to revive Roman religion from the decay into which it had fallen during the civil wars was a very modest success. About 110, Pliny, the governor of Bithynia, wrote the Emperor Trajan a letter in which he held out the hope that Christianity, which both he and the Emperor considered an irrational superstition, was losing adherents while temples were being rebuilt.[24] This optimism, pleasing to Trajan's ears, would not be justified by events. Nevertheless, Roman religion had a kind of future, for just as Christianity would fulfill and perfect Judaism, it would gather up and perfect the motives and practices of the Romans in a popular system which, if not evocative of a life-ordering faith, provided an emotional and conceptual framework within which meaning and intelligibility could be discovered.

Those citizens of the Roman world who became Christians joined a revolution. Yet the habits of the Roman religious world were not left behind but were woven into the texture of Christian experience. The Thessalonians understood what sacrifice was for they had offered sacrifice to the gods they

24 Pliny to Trajan, Bettenson, 3–5.

knew. They had, as Paul wrote in the early forties, in response to his preaching "turned to God from idols, to serve a living and true God" (I Thess. 1:9–10). He reminded the Corinthians (10:18) that they knew well one law of sacrifice: "Are not those who eat of the sacrifices partakers of the altar?" Romans of the age of Clement and Victor were familiar with the herald's cry on the occasion of some public sacrifice "*Favete linguis*," check your tongues, creating the silence which presaged the moment when life was offered to the gods.

The Roman round of ceaseless animal sacrifices is alien to modern sensibilities, which view the death of any living thing with (an often just) horror, reflecting a nicety that obscures the meaning of the sacrifice of the Christian sacrament and renders the Epistle to the Hebrews, as well as the Pauline references to the sacrificial death of the Lord, obscure. The Roman sensibility that the right relation with the god was established by the offering of life to life, which the Jerusalem priesthood would have shared, did, however, find a deep echo in the one sacrifice that survived the decline and disappearance of Roman religion. Jesus had said, "This is my body which is given for you; you do this," and Paul in his First Letter to the Corinthians, reminded his readers that whenever they celebrated the supper they displayed or set forth the death of the Lord (11:26).

Just as the regime of sacrifice in both Israel and Rome cannot have failed to be influential on the understanding of the Eucharistic sacrifice, just so, in an analogous way, the Christian calendar is rooted in Jewish practice and in the Roman calendar, while reflecting as well the natural cycle of the seasons. Over time the Roman week of eight days was replaced by the seven-day Christian week borrowed from Judaism and Genesis. Easter, the first and still greatest Christian festival, set the Passover, as it were, in a new key, and after a period when it was celebrated (at least in Asia) on the fourteenth day of the Jewish month Nissan, its date was determined by astronomical calculation. In Rome the new year traditionally began in March, the season of nature's regeneration. Hippolytus wrote about 204 in his *Commentary on Daniel* that Christians esteemed December 25 the birthdate of Jesus and March 25 the date of the great sacrifice.[25] In the Middle Ages,

25 Quasten considers the date in Hippolytus "an interpolation, although added very early" (2:173).

March 25 was New Year's Day as well as the Feast of the Annunciation to the Blessed Virgin Mary by the Angel Gabriel, or Lady Day. Nine months after March 25 is Christmas, the celebration of the birth of the Lord, which falls near the December feast of Saturnalia, a time of feasting and gift-giving, reflecting Saturn's benign, generous, and liberating character.[26] Saturn's name is preserved in Saturday, still a day of liberation.

That something of the Roman festival survived in the Christian celebration attests not the derivative nature of the Christian calendar but the assimilative power of a living religion, able to pick up the fruitful fragments of the classical past. Sometimes the process was one of substitution. The feast of Lupercalia, celebrated in early February, involved the (unusual) sacrifice of a goat and a dog, whose blood would be smeared on the Luperci, who then would run a race. The Lupercalia was still celebrated in 494 when Pope Gelasius I banned it and substituted the Feast of the Purification of the Blessed Virgin. Just as Christian theology perfected philosophy, just as the New Testament perfected the Hebrew Scriptures, in an analogous way the religion of the Christians corrected and perfected the Greek and Roman experience of God. Christian thought and practice would be a palimpsest which even as it overlaid what had gone before with something of a world-refreshing newness, offered a recollection of the classical anticipations that could still be glimpsed beneath its successor. Edward Gibbon's mistaken judgement of Christianity was rooted in his cynicism regarding the religion of the Romans. He wrote, "The various modes of worship, which prevailed in the Roman world, were all considered by the people, as equally true; by the philosopher, as equally false; and by the magistrate, as equally useful." But beneath this ill-concealed relativism there was the spark that enabled the idol worshipper of Corinth or Ephesus or Rome to see in Jesus the original of those aspirations that had made Roman piety famous.

Luke remembered that standing on the Areopagus, in the very shadow

26 The calendar/almanac made by the illustrator Filocalus for the wealthy Roman Valentinus in 354 dates the festival of the nativity as "eighth day before the calends of January [December 25] birth of Christ in Bethlehem Judea [VIII kal. Ian. Natus Christus in Bethleem Judae]." See R. W. Burgess, "The Chronograph of 354: its Manuscripts, Contents, and History," *Journal of Late Antiquity* 5 (2012):345–96.

of the great architect Ictinus' magnificent temple to the eponymous god of Athens; there, amidst the clutter of votive offerings that for caution's sake included the altar to the unknown god, the learned Pharisee Paul offered his apology for faith in Christ by reminding the great council that they shared something of a common piety based upon the participation of humankind in the life of God (Acts 17:28). One of their poets, Epimenides, who had flourished in the age of Thales, had written, God is not far from each one of us, for "In him we live and move and have our being," and another, the stoic poet Aratus (BC 315–240), wrote "For we are indeed his offspring." In his *Republic* Plato described work of true legislators as the making of a constitution worthy of men shaped by their kinship to the gods: "They will first look at absolute justice and beauty and temperance, and again at the human copy; and will mingle and temper the various elements of life into the image of a man; and thus they will conceive, according to that other image, which, when existing among men, Homer calls the form and likeness of God."[27] Justin's contemporary Epictetus wrote, "If a person could be persuaded of this principle as he ought, that we are all originally descended from God, and that he is the Father of gods and men, I conceive he would never think meanly or degenerately of himself."[28]

The Roman world was waiting for Jesus, son of God, son of Mary. "If through delight in the beauty of these things men assumed them to be gods, let them know how much better than these is their Lord, for the author of beauty created them" (Wis. 13:3).

27 501d (Jowett, 1:762).

28 Epictetus, *Discourses* 1.3.1 (Hard, trans., 10).

# Three
## *Israel's Promise*

> I could wish myself to be anathema from Christ for my brethren, who are my kinsmen according to the flesh, who are Israelites, to whom belong the adoption as of children . . .
>
> Romans 9:3

Saint Paul wrote these words in a mood of pensive regret, realizing that save for the few who had come to belief his own people were rejecting the Messiah, whom they had been taught to expect by both the ancient prophets and their near-contemporaries, the authors of such works as the *Assumption of Moses* and *IV Ezra,* the apocryphal appendix to canonical Ezra. Looking back from his place as an apostle of a messianic movement, rejected by his own people and despised as atheistic and uncivil by the Gentiles, Paul saw a glorious inheritance: "They are the Israelites, and to them belong the sonship, the glory, the covenants, this giving of the law, the worship of God and the promises; to them belong the patriarchs and of their race according to the flesh is the Christ" (Rom. 9:4–5). There had been the glory days of David, forever the great king (Matt. 5:35), and his son Solomon, when Israel had stretched from the eastern desert to the Mediterranean, and from Galilee to the Gulf of Aqaba (1 Kings 9:26), when the Queen of Sheba had come seeking wisdom (1 Kings 10:1). But when Paul wrote, the great period of national existence lay a millennium in the past.

As it had happened, the history of God's chosen people would from its beginnings contradict the modern myth of progress. The nation could not maintain its unity; at their father's death the sons of David, Rehoboam and Jeroboam, divided the kingdom, making Jerusalem the capital of Judah and Shechem the capital of Israel or Ephraim. Despite the advice of the great prophets, Isaiah, Jeremiah, and Ezekiel, the kings of both kingdoms,

Judah and Israel, routinely relied on their own judgment and prowess rather than on God. In 721 the northern kingdom would be destroyed by the Assyrians and in 589 Judah would go captive into Babylon, only to be set free by the Persian power fifty years later. The nation was then subject to Egypt, then to the Greek Seleucids, against whom in 168 BC the Maccabees foment a successful if short-lived rebellion, and finally after 63 to the Romans, which is where we find them as the events described in the New Testament unfold. Their history was a story of national pride maintained in the face of political oppression accompanied by spiritual decline; unfaithfulness, refusal to trust in God's promise, idolatry, and a hardness of heart that would stone the prophets sent by God to awaken Israel to its true destiny (Matt. 23:37).

Given the political failure and theological confusion of the Jews when Octavian gained the empire in BC 27, there was then no reason to believe that they would play an important part in the future of the Mediterranean world. Within the cosmopolitan Roman empire there were many peoples who would in their national character have little place in the new world Christ would bring. The Parthians who had defeated the Romans at Carafe in BC 53 would in turn be defeated by Mark Antony in the campaign of 40, an event that would inaugurate their dissolution. After the Roman onslaught of BC 146 Carthage was never again a great Mediterranean power. Petra, the rose-red city of Nabataeans, would be forgotten. There was little reason to believe that a tiny people that the Romans seem to have overlooked until they became involved in Rome's Egypt troubles of the first century BC—occupying an unpromising territory along the Jordan River, writing in a language that, except among the congregations of the dispersion, would have been incomprehensible more than fifty miles from the capital Jerusalem—that this people would carry with them the meaning of life and of creation. The angel of the Lord told the shepherds: "To you is born this day in the city of David a Savior who is Christ the Lord" (Luke 2:11). "Salvation is of the Jews" (John 4:22).

Their importance would be found not in political success but in the fact that God had made to Abraham and his heirs forever a promise he would not repent. Having elected them, God would cause Abraham's sons to be a light to the nations even when their own interests remained resolutely narrow and parochial. The Jews had become identifiable in the history of the near East by about 1500 BC, when God had called their father Abraham to go from Haran in Mesopotamia to Canaan with the promise that he would give Abraham descendants as numerous as the stars and Canaan as their own land (Gen. 12–15). What they had been before the call of Abraham was the representatives not of a particular people but of humankind in all its folly, its women involved with errant angels (Gen. 6:1–5), building towers to know God on their own terms (Gen. 11:1–9), never free of idolatry, so given to iniquity that God, regretting having made them, destroyed all things living except Noah and his family in the great flood. When the waters receded God gave the first promise and the first covenant, by which he gave the gift of stability to chaotic nature and promised that flood waters would never again destroy mankind (Gen. 8:22, 9:8–17). This covenant was made with all mankind; and as a sign of God's fidelity he gave the rainbow (Gen. 8:13–9:12).

It was then that God chose Abraham and his descendants, not because they were great but because he loved them (Deut. 7:8). This second covenant, God's promise to Abraham that he would have descendants as numberless as the stars who would inherit a good land, set them on the way to Canaan by a circuitous route that included slavery in Egypt, from which they were redeemed by the particular providence of God's Passover lamb, whose sprinkled blood caused the angel of death to pass over the houses of Israel's first-born (Ex. 12). Then, led by the signs of God's presence, smoke by day and fire by night, Israel came to Sinai, where Moses was given the law, publishing the eternal form of justice that would be pleasing to God (Exod. 20:1–17), and, as an effectual sign of the covenant, promising Israel his presence in the tabernacle (Exod. 25:22–23). Covenants are made with sacrifice, for in Israel, no less than in Rome and Greece, relationship with God was founded upon sacrifice. The sacrifice which sealed the first covenant was the sacrifice of all clean animals (Gen. 8:20–21). Thus the sacrifice of the Passover Lamb to purchase the lives of the first-born of Israel (Exod. 12:1–13). Thus the sacrifice of the oxen at Sinai, their blood thrown upon the altar and the people to unite Israel with God (Exod. 24:5–8). Leviticus is a book written to describe the purposes and ritual actions and offerings that constituted acceptable sacrifice. The Aaronic priesthood existed to offer sacrifice that made atonement for priest and people (Lev. 9:9–7). Any Roman priest would have understood the command of Leviticus that when an Israelite presents his offering, "whether in payment of a vow or as a freewill offering which is offered to the Lord as a burnt offering to be accepted, you shall offer a male without blemish. . . . You shall not offer anything that has a blemish" (Lev. 22:18–19). The author of Hebrews spoke of the old covenant as well as the new when he wrote, "Everything is purified with blood, and without the shedding of blood there is no atonement for sin" (Heb. 9:22).

The promise that God had given Abraham would be fulfilled along the path that led Abraham's sons into Canaan. There, against the warning of the prophet Samuel (1 Sam. 8:4–32), Israel chose to be governed by a king, which choice was later to illustrate the providential irony of their God as he transformed the rebellion of Israel and their chosen king Saul into the reign of David, who would be forever the great king, the father of the Messiah. For although God had warned against the monarchy, and although the first king, Saul, whose story is told in the First Book of Samuel, was a political and moral failure and perhaps a suicide, and although almost all Saul's successors, a few like Hezekiah excepted (2 Chron. 32: 26–30), were failures, kingship would somehow be redeemed in the chosen person of David, "the man after God's own heart" (1 Sam. 13:14). Christ would be called king of Israel (John 1:49, 19:21), king of kings (Rev. 19:16), and root or origin of David as well as David's son (Rev. 22:16).

The Jews had a promise, a history, and a book. They understood that they were but one people, chosen from among the vast progeny of the earth, but they also understood that they were the particular subjects of God's promise, a people, the smallest and least significant, chosen by God to fulfill his purpose in creating man. They, or some among them, also understood, at least intermittently, that their particularity, their closeness to God, gave them the responsibility to be a light to the nations. The wonderful, self-deprecatory character of their literature is represented by the book of Jonah, in which the prophet is enraged because the Ninevites have heeded his call, unwillingly given, to repentance. This character is also represented in their Books of Kings, in which king after king is distinguished as having done more evil than his predecessor. After their exile in Babylon, the universality of their mission would be forgotten in their all-too-human pride in their place in God's providence, a pride reinforced by the difficulties of maintaining their existence as a people and a nation.

Throughout their post-exilic history, from the return from Babylon in BC 539, there had been development in Jewish theology. According to the Pentateuch, especially Exodus and Deuteronomy, God had providentially brought his people into existence as the promised succession of Abraham. He had given them a law. Their duty was to love the Lord and to keep his commandments, and the fulfillment of the law would bring blessing and prosperity, disobedience would bring punishment and death. Their literature effloresced as a kind of philosophy in Wisdom and Baruch, and into sacred narratives that dealt with the great themes of life. The Book of Job posed the possibility that God might allow affliction to break human pride and to bring Job to himself. Ecclesiastes would offer a poetic reflection on the seeming meaninglessness of life without God. The prophets would condemn wickedness and counsel obedience, and would begin to teach that the kingdom was not of this world, but that it lay beyond the coming Day of God, when the Lord would appear to mete out justice and to establish a renewed creation marked by peace in his presence.

Finally, there was a literature that, developing the prophetic theme, despaired of history, represented by Daniel and by books that lay outside the Hebrew canon such as the *Book of Enoch* and the *Assumption of Moses.* The failure of the Maccabean experiment, begun with the rebellion against the Greek Seleucids in 163 and ending with Roman conquest and occupation just a century later, seemed to confirm the belief that the salvation of the nation would be achieved by a supernatural intervention of God, the coming of an anointed king, the Messiah, who would bring an age of justice and peace. Whether this Messiah would establish an earthly kingdom, bringing an entirely new order of reality, was controversial; at Jesus' ascension the disciples asked (Acts 1:6), "Lord, will you at this time restore the kingdom to Israel?"

Meanwhile the religious establishment, the temple priests, and the Pharisees continued to preach salvation through sacrifice and devoted adherence to the law; the Hasidim, the pious ones, continued to look for divine intervention; the Sadducees continued to counsel accommodation to the occupying Roman power; the Zealots prepared for revolution. As it happened, the most vibrant movement was the movement for repentance and purity as the last days dawned advocated by those like John the Baptist who saw themselves as inheritors of the prophetic tradition with its pronounced apocalyptic themes. The relation between John the Baptist, the Essenes, and the Qumran community is inferential but impressive.[1] These communities provide anecdotal evidence of a broad-based movement directed toward fulfilling the thirst for righteousness. It was from this prophetic movement that one of its prophets, John the Baptist, believed by Christians to have been called to his vocation at his birth by God, came to proclaim Jesus (Luke 1:39–44).

The days of Augustus and Tiberius found Judaism expectant. As Jesus of Nazareth taught and did signs, he gained disciples, so many that the Pharisees feared the whole world would follow him (John 12:19). It was surely not Jesus' teaching regarding inner righteousness and single-hearted love for God and his law that inspired the rejection of his mission by the Jews of Jerusalem. His moral teaching could be understood, at least superficially, as an extension of strands of thought in normative Judaism that included the Hasidim, the pious ones, and the Pharisees. What enraged the Jews was Jesus' claim to be the son of God; not a son of God, a not unfamiliar idea in the Hellenistic world,[2] but the Son of the majestic, omnipotent Creator whose very name was too holy to be written. Insofar as Judaism had been faithful, it had done so by resisting the temptation to worship the *baalim* of the Canaanites and the images of the Greek gods, indeed anything on the earth, above it or beneath it (Exod. 20:4–5). Was all this to be forgotten in the face of the claims of a prophet from Galilee who had been put forward by an enthusiastic mob? The crowd in Pilate's courtyard shouted that Jesus made himself the Son of God; "crucify him" (John 19:7).

1 A good account of the similarities between the community of the Dead Sea scrolls and early Christianity is Jean Danielou, *The Dead Sea Scrolls and Primitive Christianity*, trans. Salvator Attanasio (New York: New American Library, 1962).

2 Michael Peppard argues that "the social and political practices of adoption during the Roman Empire, especially those of the ruling imperial families, can indeed help us to re-imagine divine sonship and resurrect the 'son of God' metaphor" (*Son of God in the Roman World: Divine Sonship in its Social and Political Context* [Oxford: Oxford University Press, 2011]), 175. This granted, the authors of Mark 1:1 ("the gospel of Jesus Christ, the Son of God") and Matthew 26:65 ("tell us if you are the Christ, the Son of God") had in mind more prominently the image of God as unapproachably holy in Isaiah 6:1–5.

Fervent interest in the prophet who had been proclaimed king of the Jews at the Passover quickly became settled hostility. The martyrdom of Stephen was not a unique case of the zealous desire to purify the people of a dangerous heresy (Acts 7:8–60). After his conversion Paul, who had first known Jesus as a false messiah, blaspheming and misleading Israel, would begin by visiting the synagogues, for should Jews not welcome the Messiah? But soon he would visit them no more (Acts 13–14). Thus would begin the battle of official Judaism against the Incarnation, and from that time believers in Jesus' Messiahship would be persecuted as heretics. The enmity between Jews who believed in Jesus' Messiahship and those who did not would soon make the unbelieving Jews partners with the Roman authority in the persecution of Christians.[3]

Rejected by the synagogues, Christians would never in turn reject the very past in which the mission of the Lamb of God was rooted and which made their faith and their mission intelligible. They would read the Hebrew Scriptures as prophecies now fulfilled and, while always hoping for the salvation of the Jews, would see themselves as the new Israel. For Paul and his contemporaries in apostleship, the scriptures were the Hebrew Scriptures, either in Hebrew or in the Greek translation called the Septuagint. Israel was the root; the *ekklesia* of Jesus, those called out of the world by his Spirit, was the engrafted branch (Rom. 12:24).

When Augustus commanded the great census that brought Mary and Joseph to Bethlehem (Luke 2:1), no one would have foreseen that this obscure people would become the nation remembered more than Persia or Babylon or Egypt, because Christ would be born of the Jews and because the Jews possessed not a great architecture or poetry but a book. In the days of Augustus, the political greatness of Israel was a memory and the moral ideals that had shaped the nation in the beginning were obscured. Palestine was a province of the Roman Empire, governed by Herod and other Roman surrogates such as Pilate. The religious, if not the racial, unity of the nation was fractured. The temple still functioned, but it did so with permission. There is nothing to suggest that the perorations of the prophet Malachi in 300 BC against a priesthood that offered blemished animals and a people who despised the covenant given to Abraham, tolerated divorce, and

3 *Martyrdom*, 17.2 (Richardson, 155).

proclaimed evil to be good, saying "everyone who does evil is good in the sight of the Lord" (2:17); nothing to suggest that, apart from those who had fled from the city to refuges like Qumran, a faithless people had been reformed. The Jews were controlled by the fear that rebellion would mean the end of the temple and its worship (John 11:48). The idea of a pleasant land flowing with milk and honey was fading before the prophetic promise of the coming of the Day of God. The power of the religion of Israel was to be found in the prophetic movements, in John the Baptist and communities like Qumran whose members, probably in the last half of the second century before Christ, had distanced themselves from the temple-dominated culture of Jerusalem, with its warrior priesthood, to find holiness in the wilderness.[4]

John the Baptist was part of this last-days movement, dressed in rough camel's hair and eating wild honey, like the Rechabites rejecting urban life and settled agricultural existence, and it was John to whom God gave prophetic knowledge that the one on whom he would see the Spirit descend and remain "is he who baptizes with the Holy Spirit. And I have seen and borne witness that this is the Son of God" (John 1:33–34). Ever distantly respectful of the temple and its sacrifices, Jesus of Nazareth was the teacher and prophet of such a movement, put forward by John the Baptist. He had gained a great following, but he had aroused jealousy and he had violated the great principle on which the religion of Israel was founded: the Lord is One Lord, not a highest creature but He who would be who He would be, dwelling in unapproachable glory (Exod. 3:14). Jesus had made himself the Son of this God.

It is a truism that Christianity is always Jewish. Its sacrament of regeneration, finally a supernatural gift at Pentecost, is rooted in the baptismal practice of the prophetic movement represented by John the Baptist. The sacrament it offers for the journey of life is a transformation of a sacred meal celebrated in Israel for a thousand years, beginning with the Passover twelve centuries before Christ. Its liturgy was rooted in the worship of the

4 D. S. Russell, *The Jews from Alexander to Herod* (Oxford: Oxford University Press, 1967), 164–74; Helmer Ringgren, *The Faith of Qumran: Theology of the Dead Sea Scrolls*, trans., Emelie T. Sander (Philadelphia, Pa.: Fortress Press, 1962).

temple and the synagogue. Its understanding of history, and hence Israel's hope, was the gift of the prophets, who, indeed "invented" history as we know it by their inspired vision of a new world of justice and fruitfulness whose shining reality would give meaning to the familiar, ambiguous historical patterns and events we know. Its morality was a supernatural transformation of the morality of Sinai by Jesus' words: "You have heard it said, but I tell you" (Matt. 5:20, 22). And what Jesus then gave Israel was a seemingly impossible command that their hearts should be perfect and the correlative realization at Pentecost of the gift that would make that rebirth possible, not by the achievement of an ever-greater extrinsic righteousness but by the effusion of the Holy Spirit of transforming love upon God's elect people. The Pharisaic doctrine of the resurrection of the just was the foundation of the Christian doctrine that God's will to give his people life could be defeated by neither their own folly nor the power of Satan; that those he has called he will make perfect and bring into his presence forever.

Underneath all this was the Jewish grasp of the unequivocal goodness of created reality. Ironically, Judaism was always incipiently incarnational; God had called creation good; he had required holiness that from sacrifice to obedience to the law to care for the poor, was to be realized in a righteous life. This is the voice that speaks in the Gospel of Matthew, in which salvation hinges upon care for the poor and oppressed, and the Epistle of James, in which faith without works is dead, a voice that would remain central to the teaching of the Church. The new world that the prophets foresaw was not un-material but a new creation bathed in the glory that belongs to the perfection of God's good creation. This inheritance shaped the bodiliness of Christian life. Baptism regenerated. Holiness was a participation in a transforming mystery, not merely an ideal. The Eucharist was a participation in Jesus' body and blood. Marriage was realized in the making of one flesh. The Church was Christ's body. It was this sense of the intransigent reality and divinely appointed finality of the created order which caused Irenaeus to write that as a principle real things must have a real existence, "not passing away into things which are not but advancing among things that are."[5]

In the wake of captivity, Hellenization, and dispersion Judaism became

5 *Against Heresies* 3.36 (Richardson, 396).

an international religion.[6] The crowd who heard Peter on that first Pentecost was composed of Jews and Jewish proselytes, "devout men from every nation under heaven," all of whom were in Jerusalem, some because Jerusalem was their home, others were visitors from places as distant as Rome (Acts 2:9–10). Luke depicts Pentecost as an event of cosmopolitan significance, the very calling of the Church into existence by the promised Paraclete, and there is no reason to doubt that the great feast of Pentecost, occurring fifty days after Passover, which commemorated the giving of the law of Moses, was the object of pilgrimage for Jews and proselytes from every corner of the empire, from Arabia and Mesopotamia, from Pontus on the Black Sea to Libya on the southern shore of the Mediterranean (Acts 2:5–11, 1 Macc. 15:16–34). It was here that the promise of the prophets was fulfilled by the appearing of the tongues of fire, the miracle that enabled witnesses to tell the Gospel story in many languages and brought those assembled to repentance and baptism (Acts 1:15–2:38).

> This is what was spoken by the Prophet Joel,
> And in the last days I shall be, God declares,
> that I will pour out my Spirit upon all flesh,
> and your sons and your daughters shall prophesy,
> and your young men shall see visions,
> and your old men shall dream dreams;
> Yea, and on my menservants and my maidservants
> in those days I will pour out my Spirit
>
> (Acts 2:17–18, Joel 2:28–29)

The inheritance the Church claimed when it began to write also owed something to the religion of the Gentiles, who were, as Saint Paul observed, "a very religious people," among whom sacrifice, motivated at least in part

6 Alexandria and Rome had large Jewish populations, as did Babylon, where many Jews had remained after the exile of 586. See John P. Bartlett, *Jews in Hellenistic and Roman Cities* (New York: Routledge, 2002). Josephus believed there were 8000 Jews in Rome at the time of embassy of the Jews to Julius Cesar, *Antiquities of the Jews*, 7.11 (*Works of Josephus*, Whiston, trans. 385).

by ideas Jews would have understood, was commonplace (Acts 17:22). When Paul began his mission, he found a people increasingly interested in salvation as much or more than success. Romans knew, perhaps suspected is a better word, that human souls had a future beyond death. Furthermore, while the idea of Incarnation may have been cheapened historically by the behavior and misbehavior of the Olympians, Romans and Greeks were not scandalized by the thought that men shared a common kinship with the gods, "if there is any truth in what the philosophers say of the kindred between God and man."[7]

And although the Gentiles were committed half-consciously to a body-soul dualism, Jews were not afflicted with the pervasive belief that the world is illusion that characterized Persia and the East beyond. The bedrock propositions of Western experience are the axioms that being is good and its corollary that something, some finite being, exists, not as a manifestation of some spirit-world but in itself. Aristotle's *Metaphysics* is given in part to a consideration of "what a thing is," and in the Hebrew Scriptures there is almost no notice of the commonplaces of idealism.[8] Despite the pervasive strain of Orphic-Pythagorean-Platonic thought that Gnosticism would later adapt to its purposes, these considerations always encouraged in the Roman world a practical spirit, fed by the Peripatetic and even the Epicurean traditions where these were known, that was not alien to what might be called Jewish realism.

Finally, the Fathers would come to rely on Greek philosophy as the intelligible under-pinning of their supernaturally given proclamation. One need mention only the word *homoousion,* same-substance, which caused a centuries-long argument and which has been retranslated into English twice in living memory. The vocabulary in which the dogma of the Trinity was expressed depended upon words such as substance, person, and nature that were also at home in philosophical discourse. The Gospel of John and the letters of Paul could not have been written, and would surely have been unintelligible, apart from a texture of vernacular commonplaces, part philosophic, part religious, in which the doctrine of participation, itself essential to the Gospel message, could be located.

7 Epictetus, *Discourses*, 1.9.1 (Hard, trans., 22).

8 *Metaphysics* 1030a (McKeon, 787).

The revealed root would always be God's providential call of Abraham and thus of Israel, his salvific actions in history, and the message of the prophets. Saint Paul's point in Romans is not that Israel is lost, but that it finally will be saved. Paul clearly believes that the time will come when those who stopped their ears at the claim that Jesus is the Messiah of God would repent and believe: "If their rejection means the reconciliation of the world, what will their acceptance mean but life from the dead? If the root is holy, so are the branches" (Rom. 11:15–16). And in another sense Judaism, like Roman religion and Hellenistic philosophy, was saved by its incorporation into the very life of the Church, where the prophets are read, the psalms chanted, where the story of Israel's salvation is sung at the Easter vigil, where Sunday by Sunday an act initiated at Passover time in Jerusalem in the reign of Tiberius is celebrated. The point that divides will always be the answer given to the question, "Who do you say Jesus is?"

Christians, the Apostles, their successors the Apostolic Fathers and their followers the Apologists, heirs of the promised Holy Spirit, wrote in the certainty that Jesus had fulfilled the prophecies, finally satisfied the search for truth so long pursued by the philosophers, revealed the God unknown who lived at the edge of Roman pantheon, and set straight and fulfilled the intimations that marked the poetic vision of paganism at its best.

# Part II
## *Revelation*

> Now we have received not the spirit of the world but the Spirit which is from God, that we might understand the gifts bestowed on us by God. And we impart this in words not taught by human wisdom but taught by the Spirit.
>
> 1 Corinthians 2:13

> For we have not followed cunningly devised fables, when we made known to you the power and coming of our Lord Jesus Christ, but were eyewitnesses of his majesty.
>
> 2 Peter 1:16

The Cumaean sibyl might deliver a message answering a specific question or perhaps offer an ambiguous generality, and the official *augures* might discern the will of the gods from the flight of birds, but these did not offer an account of the nature and destiny of the created order and the human soul. These could not satisfactorily relate the accounts to the past or point to a way of life that ended in the defeat of that old enemy, death. Following the experience of the Hebrews, to whose leader Moses, God had appeared in mysterious, unapproachable majesty and spoken words of eternal consequence at Mount Sinai, the Church taught a new way, explicatory of the cosmos, salvific of the human race, fulfilling God's will to his everlasting glory, that had been revealed to his apostles by Christ risen from the dead.

The Church that was to bear the message revealed and to exercise the power of God given to it was born at Pentecost in the year that Christ died, only to be seen again on the third day alive in glory. Jesus had told his disciples that he must go away so that the Paraclete could come to them (John 16:7). When the Spirit came Peter knew this as the fulfillment of the promise given by the prophets (Acts 2:16), and the apostolic mission, the preaching of repentance and the gift of Jesus presence, was launched. "Go therefore and make disciples of all nations, baptizing them in the name of the Father, and of the Son, and of the Holy Spirit, teaching them to observe all things that I have commanded you, and, lo, I am with you always, to the close of the age" (Matt. 28:19). The apostolic mission was not a merely human enterprise. "You shall receive power when the Holy Spirit has come upon you, you shall be my witnesses in Jerusalem and in all Judea and Samaria and to the end of the earth" (Acts 1:8).

With the great commission of Matthew 28:20 Jesus set the apostolic mission on the road, empowered after Pentecost with the Holy Spirit, as in Acts, which recounts the miracles of Peter and Paul. The apostles had been given power over demons and the ability to heal the sick, yet they were quite literally homeless, always on the road or the sea, and always outside the law, vulnerable as subversive of Roman order. Paul in Second Corinthians recounts his sufferings: "imprisonments, with countless beatings, and often near death. Five times I received at the hands of the Jews the forty lashes less one. Three times I have been beaten with rods; once I was stoned. Three times I have been shipwrecked; a night and a day I have been adrift at sea" (11:23–26). And Paul adds, "And, apart from other things, there is the daily pressure upon me of my anxiety for all the churches." The churches could be reminded by letter, but keeping them steady required the apostolic presence, "frequent journeys, in danger from the rivers, danger from robbers, in danger from my own people" (1 Cor. 1:26). John the Presbyter could challenge rebellion by letter, but he knew that he might be required to go, threatening that if he came, he would bring to order the rebellious Diotrephes (3 John 9).

The task of the apostolic mission was to preach the good news, first to announce the Gospel, then to baptize, to welcome those whom God had called into company of the elect by giving them the gift of faith. Among the adults of the first Christian generations, conversion began when the Spirit-led heart responded to the apostolic proclamation.[1] Their membership in Christ was sealed through the sacrament of baptism and the laying

1 Slaves and children would be baptized at the behest of their master or father, the household or *oikos* being a political unit represented by its head.

on of hands. Those baptized into Christ were then the Church, his spirit-filled body. "As many of you who were baptized into Christ have put on Christ" (Gal. 3:27). The end and purpose of the apostolic mission was the establishing, within the apostolic account of God's revelation, of the sacramental life, which life grew from baptism. John, who had baptized with water in recognition of repentance, had promised that one would come who would baptize "with the Holy Spirit and with fire" (Matt. 3:11). Jesus taught in John's Gospel that mankind was called to second birth: "Unless one is born of water and the Spirit he cannot enter the kingdom of God"; the soul must have a rebirth through the Spirit given in baptism (3:5). The sacrifice of the cross had made atonement for the sins of the world; it had also purchased the presence of the Holy Spirit, who would not be sent in the fullness of his power until the sacrifice was complete: "If I do not go away, the Counselor will not come to you; but if I go, I will send him to you (John 16:7). Jesus said, "I have come to bring fire on the earth, and how I wish it were already kindled. I have a baptism to be baptized with; and how I am constrained until it is accomplished" (Luke 12:49–50).

The fire for which Jesus had longed came upon the earth to those at Pentecost, "tongues of fire, distributed and resting on each one of them," with it the gift of a spiritual language that was universally intelligible, signifying with power the universal mission of the apostles (Luke 12:49). Peter saw that as he spoke, the prophecy of Joel that the Spirit of God would be poured out on all flesh, that promise was being fulfilled (Joel 2:28–32). Charged with the fact that God had sent the Messiah and that he had been crucified by sinful men, those present asked, "What shall we do?" to which Peter replied, "Repent, be baptized every one of you in the name of Jesus Christ, and you shall receive the gift of the Holy Spirit" (Acts 2:38). This creating of the Church was ever the purpose of prevenient grace, the Holy Spirit working to call the elect. Although the apostolic mission was always willing to give reasons for the faith, to tell the story of God's promise to Israel, of the coming of the Messiah and his sacrifice, the planting of the seeds of conversion across the Mediterranean world, from the Phrygian back-country of Asia to Spain, in three decades, in the years between Pentecost and the time in the sixties when Paul and Peter were providentially brought to Rome, was not the fruit of conviction on rational grounds alone but was a testimony to the power with which the

Holy Spirit of God is able to bless witness to the truth. For witness, the announcing of the Good News, was the first apostolic work, and would remain so throughout the ages, ever memorialized in the closing words of every Eucharistic celebration: "*Ite, missa est,*" which means "Go, it is dismissal," but which took on the deeper, extended meaning, "Go, you are sent to be my witnesses."

Over time the witness of the Church would be shaped by books and letters claiming apostolic authority, consonant with the good news preached, but the words with which Peter, Paul, and the other apostles taught in the wake of Christ's appearing to them was the living, largely unwritten tradition that was still preferred at the turn of the century. Paul taught a tradition that he had received, "that Christ died for our sins being of first importance" (1 Cor. 5:3), a tradition that included the recitation of the words with which Jesus had established the "new covenant in his blood," which words would be repeated decades later in the three synoptic Gospels. It was received tradition that every celebration of the Lord's supper set forth or displayed anew the death of the Lord (1 Cor. 11:26).

Knowledge of Jesus' remembered teaching ran through the Church in words evocative of what would be the Gospel of Matthew, and in some part of the Church, in communities distant, in imagination but not in faith, from the Jerusalem tradition represented by Matthew, there were the recollections of what would become the Gospel of Mark, the Gospel of John, and the beautiful, carefully written Gospel of Luke. The apostolic letters, although often written because of difficulties and doubts, were addressed to settled communities of believers. These little churches, hidden in the thickets of pagan practice and Jewish hostility, are the result of the proclamation that Jesus is the Messiah in words the exact content and timbre of which we know only what Acts tells us. The apostles had been instructed by Jesus to go without purse (Luke 10:24), to enter a house with blessing, and to leave if their message was not received. The Gospel was a proclamation and an offer. To Jews the Apostles told the story of God's promise to Israel, as Stephen did in Jerusalem and as Paul did in the synagogue at Psidian Antioch and in Thessalonica. Sometimes as at Iconium there was a riot pitting those who believed against the gainsayers (Acts 14:1–7). At Thessalonica Paul argued from the Hebrew scriptures, "explaining and proving that it was necessary for Christ to suffer," that "this Jesus whom I proclaim to you, is the Christ" (Acts 17:2–3).

Among the newly converted Gentiles, only rarely would the appeal to the Septuagint have apostolic weight. Perhaps Paul's apology before the elders at the Areopagus showed something of the pattern the proclamation to the Gentiles would take when addressed to learned Gentiles, an appeal first to the insights of their poets and philosophers whose writings sometimes echoed Christian doctrine (Acts 17:22–31). The letters of John the Presbyter develop their profound insights without evident appeal to the Septuagint or the history of the promise made to Israel. But whether Jew or Gentile, the preaching of the Gospel would make reference to the human situation. For the Jew, it was enough to testify before the synagogue that they, their own people, had killed the Messiah. It is not farfetched to believe that the exordium of Romans 1:18–32, in which Paul testifies that the rejection of God, despite the evidence of nature to God's power and divinity, has led to the abandonment of mankind to base vice and every kind of evil, was typical of his preaching to the Gentiles, this providing background for the gracious offer of forgiveness and eternal life through faith in Christ and incorporation into his Church through baptism.

The apostolic revelation taught in the post-Pentecostal years was instantiated in the written tradition by a process precise knowledge of which still evades scholarship. The genres of the distinctive literature of the Church were Gospels, stories of Jesus' origin, teaching, and deeds; apostolic letters, and apocalypses, accounts of the pattern of time culminating in the return of Jesus to call the saints to life with him in the new creation. The four Gospels were finally received by the Church in a process that was complete by about 150. Which of the four was written first is not as important as the fact that the four tell the same story, often in the same words. Matthew, originating in Aramaic-speaking Jerusalem, was first, at least in the sense that references to its texts had some currency when Mark and John were still not part of the common literary tradition.[2] The second Gospel tradition, distinctive in its ability to display knowledge of the same persons and deeds described in the Synoptics in different language, treating these from a perspective colored by a Pentecostal presence, is the Gospel of John, which from a standpoint within Synoptic tradition represents a different experience of

2 Papias knew Matthew when its Greek text was still unstable and when Mark was a separate book (*Church History*, 3.39.14–16).

Jesus that is at the same time the theological key to the meaning of Matthew, Mark, and Luke.

Apart from Gospels, the second great Christian genre of the first century was the apocalypse, of which the first two centuries, building upon Old Testament apocalyptic represented by the prophecies of the coming Day of God in Isaiah, Jeremiah, Joel, and Daniel, produced many examples: Apocalypses of Peter, Paul, Thomas, Stephen, and the Virgin Mary.[3] Only one, the revelation given the prophet John on Patmos in the reign of Domitian, after some difficulty gained admission to the canon, providing the received tradition of the unfolding of history toward its fulfillment in the Day of God prophesied by Isaiah.

Over time the words and deeds of Jesus were recollected, recounted, recited, and recorded. Between living memory and the written accounts there would always be a delicate interplay, a process evident in the belief of Christian writers that properly understood, that is understood in the light of the Prophetic Spirit, the Spirit of the Prophets that had been poured out on the Church at Pentecost, the Hebrew Scriptures foretold and vindicated the claims of Jesus of Nazareth.

Between believing and unbelieving Jews the meaning of the Hebrew Scriptures was at issue; what Christians believed the prophets had meant founded the Church, separating the followers of Jesus from the synagogue. Jews believed that if Jesus were the Son of God, he would not have suffered but with his appearance would have brought the perfect and peaceable kingdom foreseen by Isaiah. The upshot was that Christians appropriated the Hebrew Scriptures as their own amidst the protests of the synagogue, and gave the books of the Old Covenant a meaning which the synagogue denied. Inevitably the Church would create a literature, but in the beginning that literature was neither a carefully wrought theology nor a collection of moral precepts nor a comprehensive manual of liturgical instructions, with the result that memory, inspired by the same Spirit that had inspired the prophets, presided over an eclectic field of texts and recollection to form and perpetuate the Gospel and finally to determine which books were to be accepted as representing truly the words and deeds of Jesus and the

3 Quasten, 1:143–50; M. R. James, *The Apocryphal New Testament* (1924; reprint ed., Oxford: At the Clarendon Press, 1966), 33–34, 504–68.

intentions of the Church. Finally, proved by time and usage to reflect the faith of the Church, the Christian literature of the first two centuries would be a rich pattern of Gospels, letters, apostolic recollections, and prophecy that would become part of the very constitution of the faith. Without these writings, understood by the Church as revelation from God, history would be silent regarding the teaching and deeds of Jesus and the moral aspirations and holy hopes of Christians. But first there would be inspired memory.

# One
## *Living Voices*

In the beginning there was memory vivified by the Spirit, understood as the fulfillment of Hebrew prophecy. Jesus had said, "The counselor, the Holy Spirit, whom I will send in my name, he will teach you all things and bring to your remembrance all that I have said to you" (John 14:25). When Jesus stayed with the disciples after the journey to Emmaus he said, "These are my words which I spoke to you, while I was still with you, that everything written about me in the law of Moses and the prophets must be fulfilled. Then he opened their minds to understand the scriptures" (Luke 24:14–15). The apostles knew the Hebrew Scriptures, read week by week in the synagogue, but the task of going into the world to teach and baptize was not given in a book but to the twelve and the other apostles. "And they remembered his words, and returning from the tomb they told all this to the eleven and to all the rest" (Luke 24:8). In the beginning the Gospel was not written in a codex: "You show that you are a letter from Christ delivered by us, written not with ink but with the Spirit of the living God, not on tablets of stone but on tablets of human hearts" (2 Cor. 3:3). This inspired knowledge of the meaning of Jesus had not come suddenly or surely. When Peter and the Beloved Disciple saw that the tomb was empty, "as yet they did not know the scripture, that he must rise from the dead" (John 20:10).

Perhaps reliance on the living voice during the years when many witnesses remembered Jesus' words inhibited the writing of Gospels and apocalypses. During the second decade of the second century, about 110, eighty years after Pentecost, two witnesses, one from Phrygia in the Asian backcountry, the other from Antioch, the cosmopolitan capital of Syria, attested the cautious and critical view some Christians then took of written Gospels. Papias was the bishop of Hierapolis, an important town in upland Phrygia that Paul mentioned and had perhaps visited (Col. 4:13), located about one hundred miles northeast of Ephesus, on the Lycus River, a near neighbor to Laodicea and Colossae, sometimes called Hierapolis Salutaris because of its healing springs. Papias, remembered by Eusebius as author of *Expositions of the Sayings of the Lord,* looked forward to visits from those who knew first-hand the words and traditions of the apostles, whom he names in the order Andrew, Peter, Philip, Thomas, James, John, Matthew, "or any other of the Lord's disciples," a group that would have included the larger number of apostles, men who had not been with the Lord in his pre-crucifixion ministry but who had been sent, beginning with Paul. Such visitors were John the Presbyter, whose letters Papias knew, of whom we know only what can be gleaned from his writings and who arguably might have been the editor and publisher of the Gospel, and Aristion for whom we have only a name. Papias preferred the *viva voce* witness of these visitors to the written Gospels which he surely knew in more than one form. "I did not think I could get so much profit from the content of books as from the abiding and living voice."[1]

This attitude is puzzling save on the supposition that Papias considered the living voice the best of sources, because Eusebius quotes Papias' exegetical work on his knowledge of Mark: "Mark, having become the interpreter of Peter, wrote down accurately everything that he remembered, without, however, recording in order what was said or done by Christ." And also Matthew: "Matthew composed the oracles in the Hebrew language, and each one interpreted them as he could."[2] But in Hierapolis Papias preferred the living voice, the recollections of men like John and Aristion who remembered what the apostles or disciples of the apostles had said, to the written witness of Matthew and Mark.[3]

At about the same time Ignatius, bishop of Antioch, the old Seleucid capital of Syria, a Roman citizen who could not be tried and sentenced in the provinces, was accompanied by a cohort of soldiers, his "ten leopards," as he was being taken as a prisoner of the state from Antioch to Rome, where he would be tried and sentenced to a martyr's death. As Ignatius traveled across Asia, he wrote letters to the local churches: Ephesus, Smyrna, Tralles,

1 *Church History* 2.15; 3.39.2–4 (*NPNF*[2] 1:170–71).
2 *Church History* 3.39.15, 16 (*NPNF*[2] 1:173).
3 Skepticism was not unique to Christians. See Alexander Lovejoy, "The Living Voice: Skepticism towards the Written Word in Early Christian and in Graeco-Roman Texts," in David J. A. Clines. *The Bible in Three Dimensions,* 221–47.

Magnesia, and to Rome. To the church in Philadelphia he wrote: "I have heard certain people saying, 'If I find it not in the written sources I do not believe it is in the Gospel.' And when I said to them, 'It is written,' they answered me, 'That is the question.' But as for me, my source is Jesus Christ; the inviolable source is his cross and his death and resurrection, and the faith through him, wherein I desire to be justified in your prayers."[4]

Here the Greek translated "written sources" means original documents, archives, thus written records. The matter in contest is the content of the Gospel, the written accounts of Jesus' life and words, accounts not always consistent with one another, a difficulty acknowledged by the Church in the years before tradition and inspiration had settled the text and meaning of the Gospel.[5] Like Papias, Ignatius preferred the living memory of the Church, the received tradition of the death and resurrection of Jesus, concerning which there was no argument, at least in the Church that Ignatius called Catholic, the community of the elect possessed of the faith entire. At the turn of the first century the written Gospels were not yet received everywhere as unambiguously representative of revealed truth regulative of "the Gospel" as it was represented by the living tradition Ignatius has received. Ignatius and his unnamed opponents did not lack written sources, for their disagreement is an argument about exactly what has been written, the implication being that there were alternative written traditions, so that to the claim "It is written," the response could be, "That is the question." Written accounts were always bound to be incomplete; the author of John, apologizing for having selected certain signs and narrative elements, wrote, "There are many other things Jesus did; were every one of them to be written, I suppose that the world itself could not contain them." (Jn. 21:25).

4 *Phld.* 8.

5 By the turn of the century the concern caused by differences among the Gospels was addressed in the Muratorian Canon, lines 17–37: "Though various elements may be taught in the individual books of the Gospels, nevertheless this makes no difference to the faith of believers, since by one sovereign Spirit all things have been declared in all." See Charles E. Hill, *The Johannine Corpus in the Early Church*, (Oxford: University Press, 2004), 128–38. See also, Hans Lietzmann, *Das Muratorische Fragment* (Bonn, 1902; 2nd ed., 1933); E. S. Buchannan, "The Codex Muratorianus," *Journal of Theological Studies* 8 (1906–1907): 537–45;

The principal means of the spread of knowledge of the religion of the Jews had been a book, the national literature of the Hebrews, a book written originally in a language that enjoyed very little reach beyond Judea, Galilee, and Samaria. But translated into Greek, according to the traditional account by Ptolemy Philadelphus (BC 308–246), who wanted a copy for his library in Alexandria, it enjoyed popularity among literate Jews in Judea and the dispersions.[6] Called the Septuagint with reference to the tradition that it was completed by seventy scholars in seventy days, the entire compilation, which contained more books than the Hebrew canon because it included other texts written in Greek, such as Baruch, was the work of time, probably completed by BC 132. In the third century AD, when Origen compiled his *Hexapla*, six parallel columns of Hebrew and Greek texts of the Hebrew Scriptures, the Septuagint, existing in at least four versions, had been carried throughout the Mediterranean by the Jews of the dispersion.[7] Whether read in the original Hebrew, as was surely the case when Jesus took up the Isaiah scroll in the synagogue in Nazareth (Lk 4:17), or known in the Greek translation, as it would have been in the Greek congregations Paul addressed, this book was "the scriptures," *hai graphai*, as much as the Hebrew text.[8]

It was to these books, the Hebrew Scriptures in Greek, that exegetical appeal was made by those Christians who preached that Jesus was the Messiah. Paul wrote the Corinthians that he was delivering to them what he had received as of first importance, and what Paul had received was an exegetical tradition that understood Jesus as the fulfillment of prophecy: "That

6 Josephus, *Antiquities* 12 .2.2 (Whiston, 253), is one source of the legendary account, given in a letter to Aristeas.

7 Alexandria and Rome had large Jewish populations, as did Babylon, where many Jews had remained after the exile of 586. See John P. Bartlett, *Jews in Hellenistic and Roman Cities* (New York: Routledge, 2002). Josephus believed there were 8000 Jews in Rome at the time of embassy of the Jews to Julius Cesar, *Antiquities of the Jews*, 7.11 (Whiston, *Works of Josephus*, 385).

8 Origen's *Hexapla* presented, in addition to the second century BC text, three second-century AD Greek versions by Aquila of Sinope, a convert to Judaism who wrote about 130; Symmachus the Ebionite, and Theodotion, who about 150 translated the Hebrew Bible into Greek. Whether he was revising the Septuagint, or was working from Hebrew manuscripts that represented a parallel tradition that has not survived, is debated. In the second century Theodotion's text was quoted in *The Shepherd of Hermas* and in Justin Martyr's *Dialogue with Trypho*.

Christ died for our sins in accordance with the Scriptures, that he was buried, that he was raised on the third day in accordance with the scriptures" (1 Cor. 15:3–4). Paul concludes Romans by ascribing glory to the only wise God, "who is able to strengthen you according to my Gospel, the preaching of Jesus Christ, according to the revelation of the mystery which was kept secret for long ages but is now disclosed through the prophetic writings" (16:25–26). This claim, that Jesus was prophesied by the Scriptures and fulfilled their promise, was at issue between Jews who accepted Paul's interpretation of the prophetic writings and those who considered the claim that Jesus was the promised messiah blasphemous. Acts records the controversy in the synagogue at Thessalonica, when Paul argued for three weeks that the Scriptures proved Jesus was the Messiah and prophesied his death. Some were persuaded and joined Paul and Silas, but the Jews, the unbelieving Jews, were jealous, saying, these men have turned the world upside down, preaching that "there is another king than Caesar" (Acts 17:2–7).

It was prophetic texts, seen as the link between the old covenant and the new, that engaged Christian writers most intensely. Justin, writing about 145, considered the most compelling proof of Christianity to be its character as prophecy fulfilled, the prophecies of Isaiah and Joel and Ezekiel, gloriously realized: "How should we believe a crucified man that he is first-begotten of the unbegotten God, and that he will pass judgement on the whole human race, unless we found testimonies proclaimed about him before he came and was made man, and see that things have thus happened."[9]

When the Church began to write it remembered that Jesus had presented himself in this context. Having read from Isaiah 61 Jesus told the Nazareth synagogue: "Today this scripture has been fulfilled in your hearing" (Luke 4:16–21). The disciples had been slow to understand the prophetic character of the Scriptures until Jesus, on the road to Emmaus, "beginning with Moses and all the prophets . . . interpreted to them in all the Scriptures the things concerning himself" (Luke 24:32). After Pentecost, Spirit-inspired apostolic memory unfailingly located Jesus in the context of the Hebrew Scriptures. In John's account when Jesus cleansed the temple, the disciples remembered Psalm 69:10: "Zeal for thy house will consume me," and after

9 Justin 53 (Richardson, 277).

Jesus was glorified, the disciples remembered that his triumph had been prophesied by Zechariah (John 12:16; Zech. 9:9). At Pentecost Peter proclaimed to those hearing that what they saw fulfilled the prophecies of Joel (Acts 2:16–21) and the words of the Psalms of David (2:34–35). Apollos confuted the Jews in public, showing by the Scriptures that Jesus was the Christ (Acts 18: 24–28). Justin Martyr's *Dialogue with Trypho the Jew* contains an extended defense of the claim that "there existed long before this time certain men more ancient than all those who are called philosophers, both righteous and beloved by God, who spoke by the divine spirit, and foretold events which would take place and are now taking place."[10] Theophilus, bishop of Antioch, writing about 180, attributed his conversion to the "holy prophets, who through the Spirit of God foretold past events in the way they happened, present events in the way they are happening, and future events in the order in which they will be accomplished."[11] Near the end of the second Christian century Irenaeus wrote *The Proof of the Apostolic Preaching*, which included an extensive demonstration that Jesus had fulfilled the prophecies.[12] The place of the Hebrew Scriptures in Christian imagination toward the close of the second century is illustrated by Melito of Sardis, whose beautiful Easter sermon, eight hundred lines, takes the journey of Israel from slavery in Egypt to freedom as prophetic of the Christian journey from death to resurrection, presenting the Passover Lamb as prophetic of Christ, in whom the model became reality:

> For instead of a lamb there was a Son,
> And instead of the sheep a Man,
> And in the Man Christ who has comprised all things.[13]

This preaching, this ongoing Spirit-inspired exegesis of the Hebrew Scriptures, conveyed in a rhetoric that belonged distinctively to the Church,

10 *Dialogue* 7 (*ANF* 1:198).

11 Theophilus of Antioch, *Ad Autolycum* 1.14 (R. M. Grant, trans. [Oxford: Clarendon Press, 1970]), 19.

12 Irenaeus, *Demonstration of the Apostolic Preaching*, trans. J. A. Robinson (London: SPCK, 1920).

13 Melito of Sardis, *On the Pascha and Fragments* (Oxford: University Press, 1979), 5.

was the principal means through which the Gospel was spread across the Mediterranean, beginning in the churches of Achaia, in towns such as Thessalonica and Corinth, and rippling out across the Hellenistic world.

The earliest known written form of the good news of Christ's redemption was not a codex or a scroll, but a simple statement, recorded in a letter, that represented the heart of apostolic preaching, as in Romans: "While we were yet helpless, at the right time, Christ died for the ungodly. . . . Since therefore we are justified by his blood, much more shall we be saved by him from the wrath to come" (5:6–9). And more fully in First Corinthians:

> Brothers, I remind you of the word by which I proclaimed to you the gospel, which you received, in which you stand, by which you are saved . . . . For I delivered to you as of first importance what I also received, that Christ died for our sins in accordance with the scriptures, that he was raised on the third day in accordance with the scriptures, and that he appeared to Cephas, and then to the twelve (15:2).

Proclaiming this message of the saving work of Christ was the work of the herald, the *kērox*, who in Roman official culture was protected by political convention that enabled the herald to carry messages even into enemy territory. Thus Timothy was a herald and apostle (1 Tim. 2:7). The Gospel was not taught in any conventional sense of the word as, for example, a traveling sophist might teach; there was not in the first place a philosophic appeal to intellect or reason. The herald was charged with delivering his message, whether he announced an assembly, a truce, or a victory. The Gospel of Christ was a story of facts and acts that could be believed or rejected, the acceptance of which was not a matter of discursive reasoning alone but of grace, for the elect, upon the witness of apostolic messengers, were called into the Church by the Holy Spirit whose gift of faith made possible belief in the Gospel. "God chose you from the beginning to be saved through sanctification by the Spirit and belief in the truth" (2 Thes. 2:13).

Paul's iteration of the work of Christ, his sacrificial death, resurrection, and return in glory anticipated the development of more concise and complete statements of the faith that over three centuries would, expanded and refined by Ignatius, Irenaeus, and many others, become the Creed of Nicaea. The letters of Ignatius contain such creed-like statements:

> Regarding our Lord, you are absolutely convinced that on the human side he was actually sprung from David's line, Son of God according to God's will and power, born of a virgin, baptized by John that all righteousness might be fulfilled by him, and actually crucified for us in the flesh under Pontius Pilate and Herod the Tetrarch."[14]

By 185 Irenaeus would describe the faith the Church has received from the apostles and their disciples in words that, often phrase by phrase, anticipate the later creeds.[15]

> She believes in one God, the Father Almighty, Maker of heaven, and earth, and the sea, and all things that are in them; and in one Christ Jesus, the Son of God, who became incarnate for our salvation, and in the Holy Spirit, who proclaimed by the prophets the dispensations of God, and the advents and the birth from a virgin, and the passion, and the resurrection, and the ascension into heaven in the flesh of the beloved Christ Jesus, Our Lord, and his future manifestation from heaven in the glory of the Father, to gather all things in one, and to raise up anew all flesh of the human race, in order that to Christ Jesus, our Lord and God and Savior and King, according to the will of the invisible Father, every knee should bow, of things in heaven and things on earth and things under the earth, and that every tongue should confess that to him and that he should execute just judgement towards all; that he may send spiritual wickedness and the angels who transgressed and became apostates, together with the ungodly, and unrighteous, and wicked, and profane among men, into everlasting fire; but may, in the exercise of his grace, confer immortality on the righteous, and

14 *Smyrn.* 1.1 (Richardson, 113).
15 *Against Heresies* 1.10 (Richardson, 360).

> holy, and those who have kept his commandments, and have persevered in his love, some from the beginning of their Christian course, and others from [the date of] their repentance, and may surround them with everlasting glory.

Although the great creeds of Nicaea (325) and Constantinople (381) would finally contain supra-historical claims of a purely theological nature such as the *homoousion*, of one substance, used to maintain the unqualified divinity of Christ, Irenaeus perfects the succession of creed-like statements that, beginning with Paul, contain in fundamental form the elements of the world-renewing, plainly historical story of Jesus' deeds on behalf of the salvation of mankind.

These creed-like summaries, stories in themselves, mirrored the narrative outline that the Gospels would take, moving from the birth of Jesus, though his teaching, to the Passion Narrative, and finally to his return in glory to judge all creatures. Then there was the Lord's own words and deeds, set within the history of a time and place. At first these words were retained in memory, but then at a certain point one of his followers recorded the *logia*, or sayings, which may have included parables and aphorisms, and perhaps the beginnings of a narrative. There is nothing to show that this cannot have happened immediately after Jesus spoke the Sermon on the Mount, but someone, and probably more than one, at a time and place unknown, began to make of Jesus' words and deeds the written tradition which would complement and confirm living memory.

The apostolic letters and the Gospels appeared against a background of controversy. In the first quarter of the second century the Church still sometimes preferred the living voice of apostolic witness, as it was seen as the Spirit-inspired reading of the prophets. Yet by the time Ignatius writes an alternative interpretation of Jesus' meaning emerges, a voice noticed earlier in First Corinthians (15:1–25, 2 Tim. 2:18), the Johannine Epistles (1 Jn 4:2–3, 5:6, cf. Jn 19:35; 2 Jn 7), and Jude 4–6. This voice offered an interpretation of Jesus understood not in the context of the Hebrew prophecy and the apostolic experience of the resurrection, but framed against the background of a common dualism that inhabited Hellenistic imagination like a noxious fog. Irenaeus gave them the name gnostics, those who know or who recognize the truth others cannot see, because the revelation they accepted did not require assent to "what had happened in Jerusalem" but provided saving insight into reality through a system of ideas and images framed around the descent of the divine, "spiritual," knowledge-giving Savior from the *plērōma* or fullness above. Gnosticism, as it was called in later scholarship, would have its great teachers—Valentinus, Heracleon, Ptolemaeus, Marcion, Basilides—who would interpret Christian preaching and Christian books in an anti-incarnational sense. It would have a copious literature of its own: Valentinus' *Gospel of Truth*, commentaries on John by Valentinus, Heracleon, and Ptolemaeus; the *Gospel of Thomas* and the *Odes of Solomon,* works which conflated Christian and Gnostic themes; and over time a plethora of gospels and apocalypses and acts attributed to the apostles. The fourth-century library discovered in 1945 near ancient Chenoboskion in Upper Egypt consisted of sixty-one texts, almost all Gnostic.[16] Characteristically, while the Catholic Church had considered the writings of the prophets the foundation of faith, Gnostics would ignore the prophetic witness, and one of their most influential teachers, Marcion of Pontus, would insist that creation, and the prophetic writings of the Hebrew Scriptures, were the works of an evil god.[17]

It fell to the Apostles and their disciples to preach the Gospel while guiding the Churches away from the discarnate Christ of the Gnostics and from an imperfect interpretation of the Hebrew testimony to Jesus which left Christians bound to the Old Covenant, a not inconsiderable movement represented by the Nazoreans and Ebionites. While Gnosticism resonated with the philosophical preconception of the Greeks, the interpretation of Jesus by Jewish Christians as a god-inspired prophet who became the Son of God, bound as it was to Hebrew literature and religious milieu of Jerusalem, while creating its own books, had little influence outside Jewish congregations. The Gospel According to the Hebrews, written in Aramaic, hovered at the edge of canonicity. Eusebius, citing Clement

16 *The Nag Hammadi Library in English,* ed. J. M. Robinson, 3rd. rev. ed. (San Francisco, 1990). The find included fragments of Plato's *Republic* and Asclepius.

17 E. C. Blackman, *Marcion and His Influence* (London: SPCK, 1948), 66–74.

of Alexandria, believed that Luke had translated it into Greek for the use of the Gentiles.[18]

The propagation and defense of the faith of Paul, Ignatius, and Irenaeus would be achieved by their preaching but also, as the future would show, through their letters and what Justin called their memoirs, the Gospels. These books were believed to be revelation given by God. They instantiated the revelation given the twelve and the other apostles when they saw the resurrected Lord, and made public the experience of conversion that inspired the new heart. None of the Christian literary forms employed by the Church were unique to Christianity, but all, by the time the canon was fixed at mid-second century, were distinguished by the claim that held the Gospels, the apostolic letters, and John's Apocalypse to be the work of God the Holy Spirit. The apostolic letters were like and unlike the letters of Cicero. The Gospels shared something of the biographical character of Plutarch's *Lives* but were written against the background of a hope Plutarch had not known and described the man who was also God. The canonical apocalypse resembled apocalyptic texts from the Hebrew Scriptures, but its author knew the meaning and the end of the story in a way that Isaiah did not.

18 *Church History* 6.14.2 (*NPNF*[2] 1:261); Quasten, 1:112. Jerome's translation was from a text in the library in Caesarea.

# Two
## *Apostolic Letters*

> See with what large letters I am writing to you with my own hand.
>
> Galatians 6:11

Paul's letters are the earliest surviving form of Christian writing. We have at least thirteen, as well as other voices from the first century, three letters from John the Presbyter, two from Peter, and one each from James and Jude. This number does not represent accurately the epistolary efforts of these writers. We can be certain that there were more, for what we have, as Collingwood wrote of the serendipitous survival of manuscripts, is the contents of an old desk drawer, letters written at disparate times and places by apostolic men who can hardly have imagined that a letter addressed on a specific day to a troublesome situation would take its place in a body of literature held by the Church to have been revealed by God, having the authority of Exodus or Isaiah.

The existence of these texts offers artefactual evidence of the power of the bonds of charity, representing apostolic attempts to teach and to encourage the obedience that belongs to love. They were intended to witness and to warn. The letters of Paul, John, and Peter claimed the authority given to those commissioned by Christ, an authority perfected in them by the life-changing experience of the glory of the resurrected Lord. John begins his first letter with the claim that the word of life had been made manifest to him, "which we have looked upon and touched with our hands; We saw it and testify to it" (1:1–4). Paul grounded his authority in the call given him by the encounter with the risen Christ on the Damascus Road. God had revealed himself to Paul "in order that I might preach him among the Gentiles" (Gal. 1:16). Peter remembered the day when on the mountain he saw Jesus transfigured and heard the voice of God say from heaven, "This is my beloved Son" (2 Pet. 1:16–17; Matt. 17:1–8). Pentecost had been a public revelation of the power of God. To the twelve and the other apostles belonged the particular mission born of an experience of Christ risen, of unchallengeable power, personal, intimate: God made Christ risen "manifest not to the people but to us who were chosen by God as witnesses, who ate and drank with him after he rose from the dead" (Acts 10:41). Christ had commanded that they go into all the world (Matt. 28:19, Mark 16:15). To announce and establish this mission the apostles wrote, offering inspired counsel and discipline.

The New Testament letters as we know them were addressed usually to churches; less frequently, as in the letters to Timothy, Titus, and Philemon, to individuals, and delivered by trusted messengers.[1] Often Paul's letters were to be shared among the churches nearby; the letter addressed to the Colossians, after it was read at Colossae, was to be sent to the Laodiceans to be read there. The apostolic correspondence stretched across the empire, attesting to the cosmopolitan character Christianity developed as the apostolic mission engaged the Mediterranean world. Paul wrote to Ephesus, Colossae, and to Laodicea in the Phrygian back country of western Asia, to Thessaly and Corinth and Philippi in Greece, and to Rome. On the evidence of the address of his first letter, the Apostle Peter was in correspondence with churches spread across Asia Minor, in Pontus, Cappadocia, Galatia, Bithynia, and proconsular Asia (1 Pet. 1:1). It may not be accidental that the places to which the two great apostles wrote were geographically contiguous but not congruent; Peter engaged with churches in central and northern Asia Minor and Paul with southwest Asia, Macedonia, Greece, and the Adriatic coast. The book of Acts is careful to tell the reader that when Paul had preached up the Asian coast as far as Mysia, he was prevented by the Holy Spirit from going further northwest, into Bithynia. Then, called by the dream of a man beseeching him to come over to Macedonia, Paul turned west toward Corinth (16:9). From the scanty information we have it would

1 Eldon Jay Epp, "New Testament Papyrus Manuscripts and Letter Carrying in Graeco-Roman Times," in *The Future of Early Christianity. Essays in Honor of Helmut Koester*, ed. Birgit A. Pearson (Minneapolis, Minn.: Fortress Press, 1991), 35–56.

seem that the only territory in which both Peter and Paul preached was Galatia in central Asia Minor. Paul says that he had preached the Gospel from Jerusalem around the Mediterranean as far as Illyricum, modern-day Croatia and Albania, pursuing his ambition "to preach the Gospel not where Christ has already been named, lest I build on another man's foundation" (Rom. 15:20).

Apostolic letter-writing implied paternal authority over those addressed. He reminded the Corinthians, "You have many teachers but only one father" (1 Cor. 5:14-15). The New Testament epistles are never casual. All, with the exception of Hebrews, a profound and well developed interpretation of the history of sacrifice in Israel that had no addressee, and Philemon, written to mitigate the condition of a beloved bond-servant, are exercises in apostolic oversight and discipline. Paul's letter to the Romans is also an exception, for that church was seen as the exemplar of the faith every apostle taught.[2] Paul had no warnings or chastisements for the Roman church. His language implies no claim to authority there; rather Paul thanked God for the Romans' faith, "proclaimed in all the world" (1:8), and then went on not to instruct so much as teach and to explain, enunciating in the lengthy text of his letter those Pauline doctrines that would become foundations of Christian thought and life: the futility of self-justification (4:1–12); the inability of fallen man to live in grace without the Holy Spirit (7:14–25); and the image of a world, damaged fatally by sin, unfolding toward the glory that will be revealed (8:18–25). Hebrews also has something of the form of doctrinal catechesis, although it may have been inspired in part by the author's desire to direct those to whom it was addressed away from the worship of angels (1:5–14).

In contrast, Paul writing to Galatia was "astonished that you are so quickly deserting him who called you into the grace of Christ," rebuking the church there for abandoning the Gospel Paul had preached only to adopt what seemed a synagogue-influenced Christianity that clung to the old law to the derogation of grace-formed freedom in Christ. In his first letter to the Corinthians Paul, using the occasion of their request for advice (7:1), attempting to gain control of a rapidly deteriorating situation, drew

2 Ignatius, *Rom.* 3.1 (Richardson, 104): "You never grudged anyone. You taught others."

upon the plentitude of his apostolic authority. Willing to correct the Corinthians either with gentleness or with the rod as the situation required, Paul threatened a visit: "Some are arrogant as though I were not coming to you. But I will come to you soon, if the Lord wills, and I will find out not the talk of these arrogant people but their power. For the kingdom of God does not consist in words but in power" (4:14–21). The greatest scandal was the toleration by the Corinthian church of immorality not to be found "even among the pagans, for a man is living with his father's wife" (5:1), a situation Paul commanded the church to correct; "you are to deliver this man to Satan for the destruction of the flesh that his Spirit may be saved in the day of the Lord Jesus" (5:3–6), reminding the Corinthian authorities that he would be present in the Spirit.

In the Corinthian church there was too much accommodation to the world, too much friendship with would-be brothers who were idolatrous, avaricious, or drunkards (5:11). It was in this congregation that the future hope of Christ's return, ardently expected but seemingly so long delayed, had been reinterpreted as the doctrine that life in the Spirit was itself the resurrection, so that some denied the resurrection of the body, presumably on the theory that in the renewing and fulfilling presence of the Holy Spirit the resurrection had already taken place (15:12–19). At Corinth the exercise of the gift of prophecy had proved contentious, with some jealous to possess this highest gift, and its disorderly use disturbing the congregation (12:4–12, 14:1–19). It was there that Christians had abused the Eucharist by turning the agape or love feast that was centered around the solemn thanksgiving into a secular banquet (12:21–22). Perhaps Paul's scathing letter accomplished its purpose. Second Corinthians has a much milder tone, but at the same time it announced an impending third visit; Paul kept in touch (12:19).

The three-letter Johannine sequence, while offering along the way profound theological insights, was occasioned by the outbreak among his congregations of the "spiritual" or gnostic interpretation of the meaning of Jesus, the beliefs that knowledge or insight into a dualistic world-system rendered the believer who could say "I know him" sinless (2:4), and that while Jesus had indeed appeared in this world as a divine messenger, he had not come "in the flesh" (4:3, 2 John 7). This brief correspondence, of which we have only John's side, has a special poignancy because, within the limits of our knowledge, John was finally unable to secure either his authority or right doctrine through his letters. Made aware by news from a messenger that there was a right-thinking faction, in his third letter John rejoiced that his children followed the truth, but in fact the church was badly divided. Diotrephes would not even receive John's emissaries, welcome and hospitality being signs of agreement in faith in an age in which Ignatius warns his congregations not even to speak to one who denies the incarnation: "Do not receive him into the house or give him any greeting, for he who greets him shares his wicked work" (2 John 11). The victory had not yet gone decisively to the "spirituals" because there still existed in the church a minority gathered around one Demetrius, whose faith John attests (12). John's third letter was the end of the Presbyter's attempt to maintain his authority by letter: "I have much to write to you but would rather not write to you with pen and ink. I hope to see you soon, and we will talk face to face" (13–14).

The short Epistle of Jude, one of the twelve, perhaps the Judas of John 14:22, like the letters of Paul and John, was written to curtail the destructive influence of a faction that had interpreted freedom in Christ as license: "ungodly persons who pervert the grace of God into licentiousness and deny our only Master and Lord Jesus Christ, blemishes on your love feast they boldly carouse together, looking after themselves" (12). The inroads of what would become when systematically developed the Marcion-like interpretation of Paul left its signs across the first-century Church. It is not surprising that the second letter of Peter concludes with an attempt to gainsay the two failings that infected the Church in the post-Pentecostal decades: despair at the delay of the Lord's return and the misinterpretation of Pauline liberty as license. Those disappointed Christians whom Second Peter addresses ask, "Where is the promise of his coming? For ever since the fathers fell asleep, all things have continued as they were from the beginning" (3:4). It fell to Peter's lot to give the Church's answer. God withholds judgement because "one day for the Lord is as a thousand years. The Lord is not slow but is forbearing toward you, not wishing that any should perish . . . . But the day of the Lord will come like a thief in the night" (3:9–10).[3] And

3 Peter is citing Psalm 90:4. "The thief in the night" is among the popular eschatological aphorisms.

regarding Paul, Peter says simply that Paul preaches the same Gospel "according to the wisdom given him," but that in Paul's presentation there are things "hard to understand and easily twisted" (2 Pet. 3:15–17), so much so that a different version of the Gospel, removed from its broader context, would over time be created, by Marcion in the second century, by the Paulicians in the third, and by Luther, basing his theory of justification by faith alone on Romans 5, in the sixteenth.

It was inevitable that in their exercise of their paternal authority the apostolic letter- writers would teach and encourage the moral principles that shaped Christian behavior. Nothing was more obscure to the Hellenistic world than the new morality of Christians, the teaching that purity of heart, the command not only of extrinsic actions but of the very desires of the heart, was required of those who would enter Christ's kingdom. The apostles wrote as though the essential beginning of holiness for those on the way out of Roman culture was the avoiding of fornication and adultery,[4] not in pursuit of an arid chastity but for the sake of that purity of heart without which no one will see God, and also as part of a larger teaching framed to establish the indissolubility and sacred character of marriage. Paul in First Corinthians had written as though marriage was a concession to human nature (7:1–2), but in Ephesians, based on the belief that the body is the temple of the Holy Spirit (1 Cor. 3:16, 6:19), he would construe an analogy between the indissoluble bond uniting man and woman as one flesh with the indissoluble love of Christ for his Church (5:21–33). Marriage and the bearing and nurturing of children Paul considered a characteristic duty, but not to the derogation of voluntary celibacy "for the sake of the kingdom of God" (Matt. 19:12).

The Epistle of James is a handbook of revealed moral principles, emanating from the Jerusalem church, reminding the reader that trials, temptations, perhaps persecution, allowed by God in a fallen world, are to be expected given his providential desire to bring humankind to himself. James warns against lip service to Christ absent good works, denying the Pauline

4 Paul in Romans 1 teaches that the darkened mind characteristic of impurity is the consequence, indeed the punishment, due those who deny the truths taught by nature, which witnesses God's invisible nature, his eternal power and deity" (18–25).

hyperbole that faith alone fulfills Christian obligation, reminding his readers that teachers will be judged with greater strictness. Restraint of the tongue is taught in the memorable figure: "The tongue is a fire," staining the whole body and "set on fire by hell" (3:6). The apostle warns against the false belief that our lives are our own, that our plans can reach fruition without God's providential help; do not claim tomorrow, it is the Lord's: "Say, 'If the Lord wills, we shall live and we shall do this or that'" (4:13). The Apostle warns against the false claim, "I was tempted by God. God cannot be tempted with evil and he himself tempts no one; but each person is tempted when he is lured and enticed by his own desire. Then desire, when it has conceived gives birth to sin, and sin when it is full-grown brings forth death" (1:13–15). This image of the responsible soul would be embedded in apostolic moral catechesis. James offers no sympathy to those who complain that the battle for holiness is too hard: you have not yet resisted unto blood, that is martyrdom. Fidelity to Christ, denying self, was a battle with a more than terrestrial dimension, for as Paul would teach in Ephesians, we wrestle not with flesh and blood, but against principalities, powers, and world rulers of this present darkness (6:12). In this race for eternal life the soul was required to discipline the body, so Paul will say, I do not run aimlessly, "but I pummel my body and subdue it" (1 Cor. 9:27). And the adventure was for sinners, for every man is a sinner, forgiven by Christ's death and our humble confession (1 John 1:5). It was John the Presbyter who described the difference between sins that impair but do not destroy the bonds of charity, sins which may be forgiven by the prayer of the Church, and those that are mortal or deadly, requiring some greater healing; he established in outline the moral theology that would inform Christian life through long ages. That mortal sins could be forgiven was the matter of an argument that lasted for two centuries, into the age of Callixtus and Hippolytus, the early third century.

The theological glories of the apostolic letters are incidental but profound, being insights that made their way into the catechesis of the Church. Paul's description of the fallen human race, having neglected the evidence of nature and conscience, standing before the impending justice of God in Romans 1:16–22; his description of a the universe of man and nature unfolding toward glory from beneath the corruption of sin (8:18–25); the description of the divided self who does what it does not will as patient of gracious healing by the Holy Spirit; his brilliant exposition of the resurrection body of glory as a putting on of the glory of Christ's resurrection rather than the sloughing off of the irredeemable flesh (1 Cor. 15:12–28, 2 Cor. 5:1–10); the familiar, much loved treatise on charity of First Corinthians 13; Paul's explanation of the relation between the new Israel and the old using the figure of the vine and the engrafted branch (Romans 4); and the cosmic Christ, "the image of the invisible God, the firstborn of all creation, in whom all things were created in heaven and on earth" (Col. 1:15–16), a text that ties Paul's thought to the Johannine prologue; for all these, presented in language that reaches poetic heights as it expounds eternal truths, the Church is indebted to Paul of Tarsus.

Peter's two letters also contain insights that became essential parts of the apostolic patrimony: the teaching that it is the destiny of the elect to share in the very nature of God, which crowned the philosophy of the Stoics with revealed truth (2 Pt 1:4); the beneficent explanation of the delay of Jesus' return as the sign of God's mercy, and with it the promise of a new creation, a new heavens and a new earth as also envisioned by the prophet John (2 Pet. 3:3–10). These glory-clad images and truths, and many others, would be mined by the Church as anchors of revealed truth, their authority persisting not impaired but enhanced into the present. Whether the letters called pastoral epistles are by Paul's hand or the work of a disciple who wrote them in his name, they teach flawless doctrine and offer a picture of the work of the apostolic ministry as it was when the Church took its place in the Roman world.

Two letters addressed to Timothy and one to Titus offer what appears to be advice to a Christian people who have accepted Peter's interpretation of the delay as evidence of God's mercy (2 Pet. 3:9) and who now face the challenge of living in the world while not being of the world. Both Timothy and Titus played a part in Paul's ministry, Timothy having been Paul's companion, fellow-minister and envoy, while Titus was Paul's messenger to the Corinthians.

The author of First Timothy still fervently expects "the appearing of the Lord Jesus Christ, which will be made manifest at the proper time," but now this expectation, always into the present an essential part of the Christian creed, has lost its place as the existential focus of daily life, an exigent consideration in matters of family and career, to become the background against which holiness is pursued. Godliness stands the believer in good stead on that Day, but it is of value "in every way, as it holds promise for the present life and also for the life to come" (1 Tim. 4:8). The return of Jesus had taken its place in the settled hope of Christians as a sign of the creatureliness, the finitude, the radical contingency of the world, a world which relied moment by moment on the will of the Father for its existence and as an awareness that the day would come like a thief in the night, when he would call mankind and nature home. Christians now expected judgment not when Christ appeared like the lightning flashing from east to west (Matt. 24:27) but at their deaths, which was their birth to eternal life with Christ. The cosmic Day prophesied by Isaiah and described by Jesus in Matthew 24 and 25 would surely come, but meanwhile life was conditioned by the coming day when death would open the door to judgment and to life in God's presence. The work of the apostolic mission was no less urgent than when Paul had counseled caution with regard to earthly commitments in the light of Jesus' imminent return (1 Cor. 7:25-31). Paul would still say: "I charge you in the presence of Christ Jesus who is to judge the living and the dead, and by his appearing and his kingdom, preach the word, be urgent in season and out of season, convince, rebuke, and exhort" (2 Tim. 4:1-2). Now the context of evangelical urgency is the stubbornheartedness of a wavering Church and the apostasy of those with itching ears who "accumulate for themselves teachers to suit their own likings and will turn away from listening to the truth and wander into myths" (2 Tim. 3:3–4).

"Myths," or "fables" as *muthos* is sometimes translated, is a code word for the "spiritual" heresies that press everywhere on the apostolic Gospel. First Timothy is aware of the threat posed by the elaborate aetiologies of the Gnostics, by means of which they subtly encourage intellectual pride and curiosity while faith and love are neglected (1 Tim. 1:3–7). Or again the author may have in mind those who perpetuated the error Paul found among the Corinthians, teaching that the resurrection promise has already been fulfilled by life in the Spirit (2 Thess. 2:2, 1 Tim. 1:20, 2 Tim. 2:17), or he may be referring to the proto-Marcionite dualism that despises God's creation and encourages a false asceticism (1 Tim. 1:8–11), which Paul calls the doctrine of demons (1 Tim. 4:1). These systems, as Paul warns in the concluding verse of First Timothy, are "what is falsely called knowledge, *gnosis*, for by professing it some have missed the mark as regards the faith" (1 Tim. 6:20). The demonic attempt to promote an anti-incarnational, illuminist interpretation of Christianity would persist with some tokens of success into the third century and would be steadfastly opposed.

In First Timothy Paul offers advice that is appropriate to a church that faces an indefinite future in a situation in which its doctrines are challenged within and without.

> I urge that supplications, prayers, intercessions, and thanksgivings be made for all men, for kings and for all who are in high positions, that we may lead a quiet and peaceable life, godly and respectful in every way. This is good and it is acceptable in the sight of God our Savior, who desires all men to be saved and to come to the knowledge of truth. For there is one God, and there is one mediator between God and men, the man Christ Jesus, who gave himself as a ransom for all, the testimony to which was borne at the proper time. For this I was appointed a preacher and apostle (2:1–7).

Paul sought for his churches a quiet and peaceable life, inaugurating the tradition of prayers for the rulers that would be echoed in Clement's *Letter to the Corinthians.*[5] There is a Christian way characterized by submission to godly authority and apostolic truth. The Apostle Paul gives this reason: Christians were to be subject to human institutions, to the emperor as supreme, and to governors as sent by him to punish those who do wrong and to praise those who do right not out of servile fear but "for the Lord's sake" (2 Pet. 2:13). Christians were free men, but freedom was not to be used as a pretext for evil. "Live as servants of God. Honor all men. Fear God. Honor the Emperor" (1 Pet. 2:1–17). From the Emperor, who would be required to give an account to the master of the universe, to the bondservant, every man was a servant, properly obedient in heart to what is right and to those to whom obedience is owed. "Let all who are under the yoke of slavery regard their masters as worthy of all honor, so that the name of God and the teaching be not defamed." Those under believing masters

5 Clement 61.1–3 (Richardson, 72).

should serve all the more faithfully, "since those who benefit by their service are believers and beloved" (2 Tim. 6:1–4).

Now, perhaps near the turn of the first century, the Church of the living God, which is the pillar and bulwark of truth (1 Tim. 3:15), planted by apostles, prophets, and teachers, is to be gathered around bishops. This German-derived title translates the Greek overseer (*epi*, over; *skopos*, one who watches or looks out, and was the ordinary word for supervisor, current in public affairs and pagan cults. Celibacy was not a condition of service; the bishop was to have one wife, that is not to be married a second time, keeping his children submissive and respectful, a good manager, not a recent convert.[6] Paul does not enumerate the duties of the bishop, which he assumes the congregation knows, and whom Ignatius would later describe as the center of communion and the chief liturgical officer.[7] Ignatius will write that the bishop should be followed "as Jesus Christ did the Father" (*Smyrn.*, 8.2).

A deacon is one who serves, an office instituted, according to Acts, to assist the apostles "in the daily distributions," presumably of food, for the apostles wished to devote themselves to the more important duty of preaching (6:2–4). Deacons were Church servants who over time would assume certain liturgical and administrative duties. And now these officers are to be recompensed by the Church for "the laborer deserves his wages" (1 Tim. 5:18). Paul cites no Gospel authority for the bishop-deacon governance he recommends because there is no rule to cite other than the faith and prudence that live in the heart of the Church. These offices, borrowed from

6 The marriage bond as in Matthew 19:3–12 and as Paul had described it in Ephesians 5 was held to be unique and permanent, so that it would be the second century before the remarriage of widowers would be tolerated. The failure of this discipline, as in the *Shepherd of Hermas*, was among Tertullian's examples of the abandonment of apostolic standards by the Church of Pope Callixtus. A second marriage likewise barred women from enrollment as widows (1 Tim. 5:9).

7 Ignatius warns against doing anything without the bishop; do not "try to convince yourselves that anything done on your own is commendable. Only what you do together is right. Hence you must have one prayer, one petition . . . ." (*Magn.* 9:7 [Richardson, 96]); Respect the bishop "as fully as you respect the authority of God the Father" (*Magn.* 2.3 [Richardson, 95]).

the pagan world, would be sanctified in use, so that communion with the bishop, seen as the successor of the apostles, meant communion in the faith.

Having blessed the creation of a nascent body of professional Christians, Paul goes on to warn Timothy against clerical avarice, the temptation to use ministry as a source not of sustenance but of wealth, the insidious belief that "Godliness is a means of gain" (1 Tim. 6:6). "There is great gain in godliness with contentment," but those who desire to be rich fall into temptations, into many senseless and hurtful desires that plunge men into ruin and destruction. "Love of money is the root of all evil," and through this "many have wandered away from the faith and pierced their hearts with many pangs." But for Timothy a "man of God" is to aim at righteousness. "Fight the good fight of the faith, and take hold of the eternal life to which you were called." It remains only to warn the mighty of this world not to put their trust in "uncertain riches" but in God, who richly furnishes us with everything we enjoy; to be rich in good deeds, liberal and generous." First Timothy is warning against what the *Shepherd of Hermas* would later condemn as devotion to business rather than to God. From First Thessalonians to the Pastoral Epistles, First Timothy, Second Timothy, and Titus, the apostolic letters trace the journey of the elect from the first formulation of the faith, through the ever more systematic developments of Christian thought and morality, out of the age of eschatological fervor into a settled faith affirming that God is patient, willing all men to be saved, until in time there is a visible body not identical with but partly containing the elect, organized around its officers, ready to teach the faith, witness to the truth with their bodies, resist heresy, and perpetuate the apostolic mission until the end of the age. Without these apostolic letters our knowledge of the making of the Christian mind in its formative period, the years before Ignatius wrote about 115, would be limited to the *Didache* and Clement's *Letter to the Corinthians.*[8]

After the letters of John and Paul's letters to Timothy and Titus, no letter except those addressed to the angels of the seven Churches by the

8 A third first-century document might be the *Epistle of Barnabas*, but consensus would date it later, perhaps in the principate of Hadrian (117–135). See A. Luyken Williams, "The Date of the Epistle of Barnabas," *JTS* 34 (1933), 337–46; Quasten, 1:90–91.

prophet John at the command of Christ would be made part of revelation, but letters would continue to play an important part in the government of the Church, the spread of the Gospel, and the formation of doctrine. It was with a letter that Clement hoped to heal rebellion in Corinth, with a letter that Victor of Rome asked Polycrates of Ephesus to convene a synod, with a letter that Polycrates represented the consensus of the Asian bishops, and with a letter that Victor proposed to excommunicate the Asian churches. On this occasion Irenaeus conferred by letter about this question not only with Victor but with "most of the other rulers of the churches.[9] Letters of Cyril of Alexandria, his second letter to Nestorius, and of Leo, his letter to Flavian, Leo's Tome, were and remain weighty doctrinal authorities, and until the present the Roman bishop has taught and governed through letters addressed to those in peace and communion, as did Clement before the turn of the first Christian century.

9 *Church History* 5.24.8. 9, 18 (*NPNF*[2] 1:242–44).

# Three
## *Paul*

> He was a herald both in the East and in the West; he gained the noble fame of his faith. He taught righteousness to all the world, and when he had reached the limits of the West, he gave his testimony before the rulers and then passed from the world and was taken up into the Holy Place, the greatest example of endurance.
>
> *Clement of Rome to the Corinthians* 5

Clement wrote on behalf of the Roman church as the grateful heir of Paul's witness and preaching at a time when it would have been surprising had there not been those in the Roman church who remembered the venerable apostle who taught in the city for two years in the 60s.[1] Still it is remarkable that only sixty years after Pentecost the importance and universality of Paul's ministry could be cited as commonplace. Paul had taught righteousness to all the world.

Paul's last years are a puzzle. He had written the Roman church that he planned to visit Spain, and perhaps he did visit "the limits of the West" (Rom. 15:24, 28), but the account of his martyrdom near the Via Ostiensis is certified by his relics. By the time Clement wrote to Corinth those who had not known Paul in the flesh knew him from his letters. The First Letter to the Thessalonians, written as early as twelve years after Pentecost, was the first of thirteen, fourteen if Hebrews is included, and is the earliest literary witness to the existence of the apostolic mission commanded by Jesus

1 Traditionally third successor to Peter (*Against Heresies* 3.3.3, *Church History* 3.15). Whether the office of bishop was so named when Clement wrote is unclear.

when, as Matthew remembered, he told the apostles to go into the world, to baptize and to teach, promising them his presence until the end of the age (28:19).

Whether all fourteen are rightly attributed to Paul depends upon one's definition of authorship, for the New Testament implies recognition of more than one kind of apostolic authority: the work of the writer's own hand, those writings dictated by him, and, in keeping with the custom of the day, those attributed to him by a disciple who knew his master's teaching, and whose work, in an age that did not value originality, was not seen as plagiarism but as a gesture of gratitude and honor. Some of the fourteen are Paul's on the evidence of the text; his authorship of the letters to Corinth and Thessalonica, to the Romans, the Ephesians, to the Colossians, the Philippians, and to Philemon is undisputed, and we know that other letters by his own hand are lost.[2] Three letters, two addressed to Timothy and one to Titus, are sometimes thought to have been attributed to Paul posthumously, but the early Church considered them as Pauline as Romans, while Hebrews, as far as the evidence goes, was not considered Pauline until the fourth century.[3]

We know Paul through his letters which, epistolary in form, are partly expositions of the faith revealed, partly flashes of inspired systematic insight, often presented as part of his Gospel in his responses to practical problems. Some, such as Galatians and First Corinthians, have an immediacy born of crises in particular churches. The Corinthian church was rife with liturgical disorder, the abuse of the love feast or agape (1 Cor. 11:17–22); the immorality of an incestuous marriage (5:1), heresy, the denial of the future resurrection (15:12–58), and the misuse of the gift of prophecy (12–14).[4] The Galatians were tempted to defect to a "different Gospel" that rejected salvation through faith in favor of obedience under the law of Moses (1:6). Others, the so-called prison letters, Ephesians, Colossians, Philippians, are more reflective and theologically profound; the Greek is smoother, the ideas

2 Colossians 4:16 implies that Paul had written to the church at Laodicea.

3 Clare K. Rothschild, *Hebrews as Pseudepigraphon: The History and Significance of the Pauline Attribution of Hebrews* (Tübingen, Germany: Mohr Siebeck, 2009).

4 Prophets answerable only to God posed difficulties for congregational order, as in 1 Corinthians 14:9–16 and the *Didache* 12.1–13.7.

larger, and semiticisms, Hebrew (said to be) glimpsed through the Greek usage, rarer, the controversial tone muted. In them doctrine is more highly developed, as in the great image of the cosmic Christ in Colossians 1:15–20 and the depiction of the marriage of Christ and his bride the Church as the model for Christian marriage in Ephesians 5:21–32.

Paul is remembered not only from his letters but from Acts, the last half of which is a semi-official biography, in which, while his dramatic missionary success is not diminished, difficulties between Paul and Peter are resolved (15:1–29) and Paul, after successful missionary endeavors, at the end is brought to Rome a prisoner (28:14), where he would be remembered as sharing with Peter the founding of the Roman church.[5] Paul first appears in Acts at the stoning of Stephen as an agent of the temple, holding the coats of those Jews of Jerusalem who were determined to secure Stephen's death because as he understood the Christian message Jesus had said, "Jesus of Nazareth shall destroy this place and shall change the traditions which Moses delivered unto us" (6:14, 7:58, 8:1). The attempt on Paul's part to stamp out belief that Jesus was the Messiah was no avocation. He would set out for Damascus with letters of the High Priest, commissioned to root out believers in Jesus' messiahship from the synagogues at Damascus and to bring them bound to Jerusalem (Acts 9:1); Paul's was a sacred mission dedicated to the preservation of the pure faith of the Pharisees with its unbending devotion to the law of Moses.

The author of the letters, the converted Pharisee, an effective, though by human reckoning accidental, member of the apostolic mission whose inspired efforts changed the world, was born in Tarsus, a city on the southern coast of what is now Turkey, then the capital of Cilicia, famous for its learning. His father was a Jew of the diaspora in whose household Saul had been educated to be more zealous for the law than many of his contemporaries (Gal. 1:6). This zeal had led him to Jerusalem, where he had "been brought up at the feet of Gamaliel," a master of the Hebrew Scriptures (Acts 22:3), the wise man who had advised the Sanhedrin to leave Christians alone lest they be found fighting God (Acts 5:33–39).[6] Then on a certain day when, full of zeal for Pharisaic orthodoxy, Paul, armed with letters from the temple authorities, was on his

5 Clement 5.3–7 (Richardson, 46).

6 Gamaliel, (BC 15–52 AD), son of Simon ben Hillel.

way to stamp out the Christian heresy among the Jews of Damascus, the one whose followers he sought to dissuade from their allegiance to this heresy appeared to him so dramatically that he was struck blind. Jesus, appearing in a brilliant light, spoke to Saul in a way that transformed him from a persecutor of the Christians into the great apostle to the Gentiles, changing his name from the Hebrew Saul, the name of the first king of Israel, to Paul, which in Greek echoes the word *phaulos*, describing one low or mean or of no account, which would be how Paul ever after saw himself in the light of God's grace.

Paul wrote that he had been called to his apostleship by God before he was born (Gal. 1:15), but there was an immediate background for Paul's conversion. He was well-versed in the Hebrew Scriptures. He was "a Pharisee, the son of a Pharisee," therefore steeped from his birth in the theology of righteousness through strict adherence to the law of Moses; "circumcised on the eighth day, of the people of Israel, of the tribe of Benjamin, a Hebrew of the Hebrews, as to the law a Pharisee, as to zeal a persecutor of the Church, as to righteousness under the law, blameless" (Phil. 3:5–6). He had certainly studied the blasphemous doctrines of a sect he wished to extirpate. He had heard Stephen recite the history of Israel as it was understood in the light of Pentecost, an interpretation which made Jesus of Nazareth the perfect fulfillment of prophecy (Acts 6:8–7:60).

As a Pharisee Paul would have believed in the resurrection, as the Lazarus story shows a common belief among the pious (John 11:24). Although he does not cite any specific source on this question, Paul would have been aware of the apocalyptic accounts that had become common in the Maccabean period. Building on the prophetic anticipation of the Day of God in Isaiah and Ezekiel, a day that brings wrath, judgement, and punishment, comfort, peace, and fruition (Isa. 34–35, 65–66, Jer. 30–31, Ezek. 30–3, Joel 2, Mal. 4); there had grown up a more specific and personal belief in the vindication of the just and the punishment of the wicked, represented in the Hebrew canon by Daniel (1:1–4) and Baruch (4–5) and in the non-canonical apocalyptic literature by *Enoch* and the *Assumption of Moses,* each of which might have been accessible to Paul.[7] This anticipation

7 Some acquaintance with the Old Testament Apocrypha on the part of the apostolic generation is indicated by the quotation in the epistle of Jude (14–15), of Enoch 1:9. The account of the Archangel Michael contending with

of the coming of the Day that had inspired John the Baptist was reflected in the teaching of Jesus in Mathew 24–26 and wholeheartedly accepted by Paul, giving an urgency to his preaching.

Well-educated and well-read, the source of Paul's power and the experience that certified his apostleship was the life-changing encounter with the living Christ as he made his way down the Damascus road. In Paul's words, God "was pleased to reveal his son to me." We have Paul's account of this remarkable event in his own letter to the Galatians (1:12–17) and Luke's account in Acts (9:1–19, 22:6–10, 12–16). At noontime Paul was encompassed in a great light which his companions did not see. But they did hear the voice ask, "Saul, Saul why do you persecute me?" To Saul's question, "Who are you?" came the reply, "I am Jesus whom you are persecuting." In the Acts account blind Paul was led to the house of Ananias in the street called Strait in Damascus where, presumably by baptism and the laying on of Ananias' hands, he was filled with the Holy Spirit (Acts 9:17), his sight was restored and the blindness that had caused him to persecute Jesus healed.

This was Paul's Pentecost; he had been given an experience of the living presence of Jesus that would ever be the foundation of his Gospel. Knowledgeable in the Scriptures, Paul would now understand the text in a new way, not as something learned from men but as a prophetic gift of God (Gal. 1:11–12). Paul located this vision of Jesus in a series of apostolic encounters with the risen Christ by more than five hundred, a series in which Peter stood first and he, the least of the apostles, last (1 Cor. 15:8), but this list can hardly have been complete. The dramatic nature of his own conversion, occurring against the background of his vocation as an agent of the Jerusalem Pharisees, meant that suspicion would pursue Paul, making his establishing of the right relation with the Jerusalem apostles a work of time (Gal. 1:23–24). It would also mean that of all the apostles Paul would

the devil over the body of Moses at Jude 9, although not included in the incomplete Latin manuscript published by Antonio Ceriani in 1861, is attested by patristic sources as belonging to the *Assumption of Moses*. Jude apparently assumed that knowledge of the grounds of Satan's claim, Moses' murder of the Egyptian (Exod. 2:12), as explained in the *Assumption of Moses*, was common knowledge among his intended readership.

have the greatest appreciation of the futility of salvation through the Law and a commensurate deep awareness of the newness and power of salvation through the transforming grace of Christ.

After a time in Arabia, whether in the desert like Anthony or in a village we do not know, Paul returned to the church in Damascus, where he stayed for three years among those who had witnessed his conversion. He then went to Jerusalem to visit Peter, with whom he remained for fifteen days (Gal. 1:18). He left Jerusalem for his first attempt to realize his apostolic vocation in Syria and Cilicia, preaching and writing of salvation through God-given faith that Jesus is the son of God whose sacrifice, summarizing and representing the sacrifice of the Paschal lamb, saves us from the justly-visited wrath of God and renews by the gift of his Spirit.

Paul was a talented and inspired teacher, but his Gospel was not his own; he claimed a certain independence but never originality, speaking always as the representative of the one apostolic tradition. There are the references in the letters to the sacramental and moral tradition Paul had received and in his turn taught (1 Cor. 11:23–26, 2 Thess. 3:6). This would have presupposed the interpretation of the Old Testament as the background which the Gospel fulfilled. Always Paul made a distinction between revelation, what the Lord had given him as revealed truth, and his own opinion, as in the troubling matter of fidelity to an unbelieving spouse (1 Cor. 7:12–16), which he offered on his own authority, while his instruction regarding the celebration of the Eucharist he taught the Corinthians as having been "received from the Lord" (1 Cor. 11:23). When Paul viewed mankind what he saw was the participation of all mankind in Adam's fall: "As in Adam all die, so in Christ all will be made alive" (1 Cor. 15:22). God willed the universal ability of mankind to see in nature the divinity and eternity of God, and had set the stamp of moral obligation as a testimony to his law in every conscience. Ignoring these signposts to faith, universal rebellion had led the Lord finally to abandon mankind to degrading lust and repugnant sinfulness (Rom. 1:18–31, 2:14–15). Before the justice of God both Jews and Gentiles stood guilty, Jews because they had violated the law through rebellion and idolatry, Gentiles because, while having the God-given ability to see the testimony of creation to his invisible nature, his power, and his divinity, they had chosen idolatry, so that God gave them up to darkened minds and to base behavior, issuing finally in unnatural passions (Rom. 1:24–25). But, considering the human family soul by soul, salvation was a gift of grace given by God as he chose; the clay could not question the potter (Rom. 9:21). Regarding those outside, those not yet called by preaching and the Spirit, Paul had nothing to say beyond warning Jew and Greek to avoid the wrath of a just God by heeding the witness of conscience and the evident testimony of nature (1 Cor. 12:15, Rom. 1:20–23, 2:14–16).

Paul's mission was directed to those whom God would call. He was not a salesman but a herald, announcing a Gospel into which the Holy Spirit would call the elect. In that way he pursued his work with confidence, remarkably devoid of any note of anxiety as to its rightness, unconcerned that he and the other apostles would reach so few. The call to repentance was universal, but once delivered its particular effectiveness was the work of God; "those whom he predestined he also called, and those whom he called he also justified, and those whom he justified he also glorified" (Rom. 8:29–30). Paul was untroubled by the awareness that in the vast Mediterranean world the will of God was being realized by only the tiny congregations of Christian believers, because he was convinced that God would save his elect, be they few or many. Peace would come to those deemed worthy by the Spirit, but if the invitation was rebuffed, the apostle should shake the dust from his feet and be on his way (Matt. 10: 14).

Paul lived in a moral world in which sacrifice for sin was an accepted principle in Jerusalem and in Rome, and he knew, on an analogy with the prophetic practices of the Temple, that without the sacrifice of Jesus humankind are lost sons of Adam, ensnared in our first father's disobedience and liable to its effects, of which the summary is death. As hearers of the preached word, our salvation is effected first by faith, with faith itself, along with hope and, superlatively, charity, being gifts of God to his elect, making possible their incorporation in Christ by new birth through the Holy Spirit ministered to us in baptism and the laying on of hands (1 Tim. 4:11), sustained in us by the Eucharist. Humility, the ability to receive the gift, is the key to this salvation; the recognition of our helplessness in the one thing that matters most, being the condition for our receiving at the hands of God, who brings strength out of weakness, those gifts that forgive our sins and join us to Christ. The justice that we have is not ours by right and we cannot attain the right-heartedness that pleases God of our own will and power; it is a gift. Paul's own conversion was a divine footnote to Pentecost, and his preaching invited those God called into the same transforming friendship with God in Christ that had been given in Jerusalem on the first Pentecost through repentance and baptism.

Paul preached the necessity of conversion against the background of cosmic drama, for Christianity always presumed to know the origin and cause as well as the destiny of the created, natural order. With his knowledge of Hebrew Scriptures, understood in the context of his vision of God's Glory and majesty and his indefeasible will for redemption, Paul developed a theology that saw both the moral and natural histories of the world, themselves necessarily complementary, as the providential remaking of a fallen world after the rebellion of angels and men had afflicted nature and human nature. Mankind like creation will enjoy a providential transposition from corruption to glory, with death, the last enemy, overcome by the resurrection of Jesus and the fruition of indwelling grace, in which all believers, joined to him by faith and love in this life, will participate to some just degree when he returns in glory to judge the living and the dead. Nature itself will then be free of corruption. "I consider that the sufferings of this present time are not worth comparing with the glory that shall be revealed in us" (Rom. 8:18). Creation is full of expectancy, waiting for the sons of God to be made known. Christ and those who belong to him, resurrected in glory, are the meaning of creation. Created nature has been condemned to frustration; not willingly, but for the sake of him, that is for the glory of God, who condemned it, through no fault of its own, but by reason of him that made it subject in hope. For nature in its turn will be set free from the tyranny of corruption, into the glorious freedom of the sons of God. For we know that every creature groans and travails in pain even until now. We ourselves do the same . . . waiting for the redemption of our bodies (Rom. 8:20–23).

Paul sees clearly that there are two ways: Spirit-given right-heartedness leading to life and finally to glory, and self-willed disobedience leading to corruption and finally to death. Paul the realist knew that the problem of life, beyond the various insufficiencies of existence, is death, and, genius that he was, he knew that the dreadful process of corruption leading to death, afflicting man and nature, was rooted not in nature as it came from the hand of God but in sin with which our first parents had afflicted it. Christ was and is the consummate sign of loving obedience leading to life and finally to glory.

The sign through which Christ conquered was his resurrection. Thus Paul's anger with those in Corinth who believed one might have life in the Spirit without the resurrection of the body, or as Paul would name it, of the flesh (1 Cor. 12–14). The flesh will be wayward until the end because of the waywardness men and angels inflicted upon it through their rebellion. But it too has been redeemed by the flesh of Christ who suffered in his body and was raised in his body, although the restored glory of creation, like the glory of the resurrection, must await his return. By his sacrifice and resurrection, which purchased for us Pentecost, Christ then gave our bodies a new living principle in baptism and gave us not only his teaching but his person, present to us in the showing forth of his death in the bread and wine that joined believers to him (1 Cor. 11:23–26).

And the end, the fulfillment, is glory in God's presence: "This slight momentary affliction is preparing for us an eternal weight of glory beyond all comparison" (2 Cor. 4:17). Glory is a word difficult to define but essential to the very meaning of Paul's Gospel. Just as sin leads to corruption and death, righteousness leads to life and glory. The divinely given destiny of man and the world is glory, that realm possessed of every perfection, every beauty, every truth, that surrounds God's throne. Paul describes glory as having weight and solidity (2 Cor. 4:17). Glory is not "spiritual" in the sense assumed by Platonic-gnostic dualism; it is the quality of the supernatural, that which lies above and beyond nature shining through the natural order not with a steady light but in resplendent glimpses. The realm of glory is more real than this present world, not less. Creation groaned and travailed, having been subjected by God to the result of rebellious angels and men not willingly, but in hope, so that the promise of a creation free from bondage, with death defeated and the elect resurrected in glory, might be fulfilled (Rom. 8:19–24). Paul's gospel is framed by a view of the situation of man in the world that the apocalyptic themes of the post-exilic centuries had made commonplace. Christians wrestled not with flesh and blood "but against the principalities, against the power, against the world rulers of this present darkness, against the spiritual hosts of wickedness in the heavenly places" (Eph. 6:12). In this arena Satan, cast out of heaven at the birth of Jesus, might appear as an angel of light (2 Cor. 11:14, Rev. 12:7, 12).

Paul undertook his mission with what he would have conceived as a natural constituency, for he began with the conviction that every Jew in

Jerusalem and in synagogues scattered throughout the Roman world was called to find the fruition of faith in obedience to the preaching that proclaimed Jesus the fulfillment of the prophecies. This hope would be frustrated. The pattern that would be reiterated is illustrated in Acts. Paul and Barnabas entered the synagogue in Antioch on the Sabbath, asked to be recognized, and presented the good news. "When the meeting of the synagogue broke up, many Jews and devout converts to Judaism followed Paul and Barnabas, who spoke to them and urged them to continue in the grace of God." Success brought the whole city together to hear Paul on the next Sabbath. This provoked jealously. "When the Jews saw the multitude they were filled with jealousy and contradicted and reviled Paul." The apostles, acknowledging that it was necessary that the good news first be spoken unto the Jews, turned to the Gentiles, reciting Isaiah: "I have set you a light to the Gentiles, that you may bring salvation to the uttermost parts of the earth. And when the Gentiles heard this they were glad and glorified the word of God, and as many as were ordained to eternal life believed" (Acts 13:4–52).

The success, power, and persistence of the Church in the age of Tiberius, Caligula, Nero, and Claudius is a testimony to the power of Pentecost, apart from which Christianity would have been no more than a reforming movement and would surely not have survived the tension and perplexity caused by the delay of Jesus' promised return among a people who longed for that day. When Paul wrote, belief in the return of Jesus was vivid and life-inspiring, and indeed would remain so, although the dramatic urgency of the first post-Pentecostal years would over time fade into a conventional, if no less real, conviction that affirmed the radical contingency and ultimate fulfilment of the created order by God's intervention to bring his saints into his presence in a renewed creation. Always on Paul's mind is what Isaiah and Jeremiah called the Day of God, which Jesus calls simply "the day" in Matthew 24 and 25, and which for Paul is the Day of the Lord, which will come as a thief in the night when least expected (1 Thess. 5:2). Standing firmly in the tradition of Isaiah and Ezekiel, as mediated through the rich body of Apocalyptic from the Maccabean period, Paul writes elsewhere and often of the wrath of God that is coming upon the earth (Rom. 1:18, Eph. 5:6, Col. 3:6). Judgment is at hand. Paul wrote against a background not so much of the desire for personal salvation or even against the background of the high psychology represented by Augustine's image of the restless heart, but against the canvas of cosmic reality according to which the world and mankind in it would soon pass under the scrutiny of the divine judgment. His readers believed they were living in the last days, as have all Christians in all times. Jesus had said that he would return, and that soon, at which time God would exercise judgment, displaying his wrath against unbelievers, and welcoming those who believed, who were in Christ, into his kingdom.

Yet if life and faithfulness had depended simply upon the more or less immediate realization of that future hope, blessedly psychological in nature, Christianity might well have suffered the fate of other messianic sects, disappearing under the weight of great promises unfulfilled. But from the first it was the experience of Christians that the body of elect was a supernatural creation, called into existence by the Prophetic Spirit whose presence, promised by Jeremiah (31:31–34), by Ezekiel (11:19, 18:31), by Joel (2:28–32), and by Jesus himself (John 14:15–18, 16:4–15), enabled them through the same Spirit to share in the life of Jesus and so in the life of the Father in this present. There is a logic-straining language that permeates Paul and John which presupposes a deep coinherence or indwelling of God in Christians and the Church. Paul could confidently say that to be in Christ is to be a new creature (Gal. 6:15), reflecting the teaching of Jesus in the Gospel of John: "I am in the Father, you in me, and I in you" (John 20:14). This belief may have been rendered plausible in a natural sense by the philosophical commonplaces of the day that assumed a kind of participation of finite beings in a transcendent pattern of thought and reality, but the Pauline (and Johannine) teaching is far deeper, born of the renewing experience of the indwelling of the Holy Spirt in the life of every Christian, the first-fruits as Paul would name it (Rom. 8:23), yielding joy and courage and peace. Christians were "sealed with the promised Holy Spirit, whose presence is the guarantee of our inheritance, until we acquire possession of it" (Eph. 1:14).

The first gift that the experience of Christ in the Holy Spirit sponsored was the gift of faith, which was the lynchpin of the newness of life that Jesus had brought. Faith enabled the belief that the account of things the apostolic preaching offered is true: that Jesus is the son of God, who by his actions, his sacrifice, an act of unwarranted, unanticipated mercy and love, has established our right relation with God by making atonement for our sins and joining us to Jesus. Faith is a word rich in connotations. To be justified not by works but by faith meant believing God as Abraham had believed God's promise (Gen. 15:6), believing truths proposed to intellect and rooted in the heart, that Jesus is the Messiah, the King of Israel, the Son of God. It meant accepting the gracious act of Jesus, God's only Son, as the foundation of Christian lives, and this meant laying aside the pride of *autokratēs,* that perfect command of the soul to which noble pagans aspired, that self-won virtue to which Cicero aspired, in favor of humility. In humility's wake comes hope, belief that God's promises will be fulfilled for us and in us. And the perfection of faith and hope is love, which unites us to Jesus and the Father, assuring us that we are able to love him because He first loved us and enabling us to love our neighbors (1 Cor. 13:13, 1 John 4:9–10).

Judaism was itself an exhortation to justice based on love for God and neighbor, with love understood not so much as a supernatural union but as the reverent ordering of life in the light of God's law. Paul had been a Pharisee of the Pharisees, among whom conformity to the Law of Moses was salvation. Judaism was realized in behavior, although this is not to suggest that the religion of the Pharisees and the pious, the Hasidim, lacked depth and devotion; they had first been commanded to love the Lord their God single-heartedly (Dt. 11:1). But the focus of Pharisaic Judaism was not on interior renewal or conversion but on obedience. Jesus had taught: You have heard it said in the Law of Moses do not kill, but I tell you do not hate. You have heard "An eye for an eye and a tooth for a tooth," but I say "love your enemy and pray for those who despitefully use you" (Matt. 5:17–30). The Gospel offered a new law made effective by the gift of the new heart prophesied by Jeremiah (31:31), a renewal made possible by the Holy Spirit whose presence in the life of the baptized had been purchased by Jesus' sacrifice. John the Baptist had prophesied that the one who was coming would baptize with water and with fire (Matt. 5:11). This was the fire Jesus longed to see kindled, which would descend on the apostles at Pentecost (Luke 12:49). Paul would answer the fact of human weakness with the gift of the promised Spirit, who formed Christ in the baptized, believing soul (Rom. 7:13–8:11).

That gift was purchased by sacrifice, and that sacrifice was perpetuated in the life of the Church, for the solution to judgement and death for Paul was sacrifice, not the sacrifice of the temple, not the sacrifices familiar from the streets of Tarsus and Ephesus, but the one summary sacrifice of Jesus, God's Messiah. Christ our Passover is sacrificed for us (1 Cor. 5:7). "Being found in human form he humbled himself and became obedient even to death" (Phil. 2:8); "You who once were far off have been brought near by the blood of Christ" (Eph. 2:15), the sacrifice displayed or made evident in the Eucharist (1 Cor. 11:24, 26). Whether Paul was the immediate author of Hebrews or not, he knew that without the shedding of blood, without the offering of life itself, there is no remission of sin (Heb. 6:22). "He has appeared once for all at the end of the age by the sacrifice of Himself" (Heb. 9:26). The center of the apostolic mission was the story of Jesus' death and his resurrection; initiation into Christ was accomplished through baptism. Christians were joined to his death in baptism, from which waters a Christian emerges with the promise of eternal life. "We were buried therefore with him by baptism into death so that as Christ was raised from the dead by the glory of the Father, we too might walk in newness of life" (Rom. 6:4).

The life of the elect of God was fed by the sacrifice of the Son of God. Christians were not only joined to this sacrifice by participation in ideas, although this had its own necessity, but just as Israel was joined to God by the blood of the oxen sprinkled on both people and altar (Exod. 24:6–8), just as the blood of the Passover Lamb was placed on lintel and doorposts and the lamb then eaten by the people, just so Christians were brought into the sacrifice by their sharing in Jesus' very life, his own body and blood. The bread which we break is a participation in the body of Christ; the cup of blessing is a participation in the blood of Christ (1 Cor. 10:16). The bodiliness of Christianity is omnipresent in Paul's doctrine that the Church is the body of Christ, which is found again in his doctrine of baptism, in the Eucharist, which enables believers to share in Christ with a reality that names unworthy participation profanation of the body and blood of the Lord (1 Cor. 11:27), and in his understanding of marriage, through which man and woman become one flesh in Christ. Paul teaches that the union between Christ and Christians is so complete that sins against the justice of marriage may be seen as the impossible act of joining Christ to a prostitute (1 Cor. 6:15–16).

Paul's work was evangelization; "Christ did not send me to baptize but to preach the Gospel" (1 Cor. 1:17). Paul was not given to the stable life of a teacher or presbyter around which churches, with their routine of baptisms and celebrations of Jesus' presence, were built; he remembered that he had baptized only Crispus, Gaius, and the household of Stephanas (1 Cor. 1:14). It was Paul's vocation to give an account of the justice, the glory, and the providential love displayed in God's mercy toward Israel, providing by his preaching an opportunity for the Holy Spirit to open the hearts of his hearers to the promise of new life in Jesus that would issue not only in the regeneration of the spirit but in the resurrection of the body.

Paul's letters are testimonies to a life dedicated despite great personal difficulties and persecution to preaching this good news; imprisoned, beaten, stoned, often hungry and thirsty, a life of sleepless nights and, above all, the pressure of anxiety for all the churches (2 Cor. 11:23–29). He was not an imposing presence; he knew the Corinthians said, "His letters are weighty and strong, but his bodily presence is weak and his speech of no account" (2 Cor. 10:1). But those weighty letters and the teaching they embodied reached beyond the occasions that had caused them to become regulative for the Christian faith in the age of Clement and Ignatius, when there was no canon, when the Gospel of John was apparently unknown in Rome. Perhaps Paul's popularity then and now is due in part to the awareness that he was one of us, running a race, struggling in a contest to overcome sin, longing to please God but sometimes doing the very thing he did not want to do (1 Cor. 9:24, Eph. 6:12, Rom. 7:15–20), afflicted meanwhile with some weakness of body or soul that the Lord had refused to heal or remove (2 Cor. 12:7).

The writers of all the letters in the New Testament were theologians in the sense that they did more than recite dominical commands and traditions, but presented aspects of the Gospel in their theological, historical, and spiritual implications. Paul was a theological genius of the stature of John, the author of the three epistles. He taught and developed an understanding of participation, a half-theological idea he found in Hellenism, so that to live was not merely to obey Christ's teaching, but to share in his very life, to have a mind formed by his mind (Phil. 2.5). And Christ himself was not only the person who lived in Galilee and died under Pontius Pilate, but was the cosmos made personal, which found its fulfillment and perfection not in a political resolution, nor in a historical process, but in a person, human and divine, son of God, son of man, through whom the worlds were made. It is among the glories of the faith that the fulfillment of every destiny is found not in a political or economic condition but in that person. Underlying the thought of Paul in his maturity was the image of Christ in whom all nature and the elect subsist and find their meaning; for Paul to live was Christ, the person in whom the cosmos found its perfection. Jesus is the Messiah sent to Israel, but he is also the fulfillment, now and in the future, of the life of every man and of all nature:

> He is the image of the invisible God, the firstborn of all creation. For in him all things were created, in heaven and on earth, visible and invisible, whether thrones or dominions or principalities or authorities—all things were created through him and for him. He is before all things, and in him all things consist. He is the head of the body the Church. He is the beginning, the first-born from the dead, that in everything he might be preeminent. For in him all the fullness of God was pleased to dwell and through him to reconcile all things on earth or in heaven, making peace by the blood of his cross. (1:15–20)

This is Colossians 1:15–20, in which one hears the great Johannine preface: "In the beginning was the Word . . . All things were made through him." And in Ephesians Paul wrote that the father "accomplished his great work when he raised him from the dead and made him sit at the right hand in the heavenly places far above all rule and authority and power and dominion and above every name that is named, not only in this age but in that which is to come, and he has put all things under his feet and has made him head over all things for the Church which is his body, the fullness of him who wills all in all" (1:19–22). The polished letters of the fifties—Colossians, Ephesians, and Philippians—with their overarching image of the cosmic Christ, are primarily interested in supernatural life in Christ as the present reality of Christian profession and display little anxious concern for the approaching Day, but Paul still looks forward to the resurrection of the body (Phil. 3:11) and the letters to Timothy look forward eagerly to the appearing of Jesus (1 Tim. 5:14, 2 Tim. 4:8).

It was a particular gift of Christianity that history, which for the Romans had had no transcendent purpose, following prophetic tradition,

Jesus' words in Matthew 24–25, and the great vision of the prophet John, now had a fulfillment and an end, a cosmic fulfillment in which every person called into the Church was destined to participate because life itself had a purpose: to live in Christ so as to share in the glory and the promises. Every life was now not only a moral challenge, as it would have been for the best pre-Christian Romans, but a moral adventure lived out in Christ's company and presence. Paul was born into a waiting world that did not dare to believe. He and his fellow apostles left a world in which the seeds of hope they had planted would bear fruit until the end of the age, when Christ will return from heaven in glory with the sound of the trumpet. It is judgment, the judgment of God, that gives meaning to life, paying to the sons of Adam the supreme compliment that they alone of every creature may by grace-filled obedience be made worthy of the promises of Christ. The judgment to which Christians looked forward was "Come you blessed of my father; well done good and faithful servant, enter into joy" (Matt. 25:21).

We know from Romans that Paul intended to visit Rome, although he did not foresee that he would come a prisoner, guarded by one Julius of the Augustan legion (Acts 27:1). Having brought Paul to Rome, Luke leaves him living at his own expense, preaching the kingdom of God and teaching about the Lord Jesus Christ quite openly and unhindered (Acts 28:30). The authorities did not long ignore Paul's teaching about the Kingdom of God. By universal tradition Paul's life ended when he was beheaded, probably in his sixties, at a site now marked by the little church of Saint Paul at the Three Fountains on the Via Laurentina and buried on the estate of a Christian woman Lucia on the Via Ostiensis. There Constantine built the great basilica of Saint Paul's outside the Walls, which was expanded by Theodosius I in 386, and there in 2006 Paul's sarcophagus was re-discovered.

After the Church became an imperial institution, Paul always appears with Peter, their earnest discussions of the relation between law and grace long past, sharing with the Prince of the Apostles the honor of founding the Roman church. He is there at Santa Pudenziana at the foot of the Esquiline in 397 representing the Church of the Gentiles, and subsequently in the apses of a hundred churches, with his brother apostle Peter, welcoming Christ as he returns with the sound of the trumpet and the archangel's shout (1 Thess. 4:16). In the forecourt of Saint Paul's outside the Walls, and before Saint Peter's on the Vatican hill he stands, holding the sword by which he won the crown of martyrdom. The fresco of Paul's face in the recently discovered catacomb of Saint Thecla, his small pointed beard and bald head, may preserve something of the memory of his unimpressive appearance.[8]

Paul had a hard life, always explaining himself, always defending his call to apostleship, contending with those who claimed to be apostles but were not, aware that he was never quite free of suspicion, for as the Second Letter of Peter warned, there were things in his gospel that were not easy to understand and which could be twisted (3:15–16). So intense did the hostility of the Jews become that on Paul's last trip to Jerusalem more than forty pledged themselves before the high priest not to taste food until they had killed Paul (Acts 23:12–16). It was in the midst of this difficulty that Paul was given the vision: "As you have testified about me at Jerusalem, so you must bear witness to me at Rome" (23:11). And twenty or thirty years after his martyrdom at the Tre Fontane, Clement praised Paul as the teacher of righteousness to all the world. His letters have ever formed and inspired the Church for which he taught and suffered, being as they are not only the first written formulation of the Gospel but the literary bridge to the written tradition of Jesus' life and teaching.

The magnificent structure of Paul's thought that was achieved in the prison letters of the fifties was the flowering of a mission undertaken in the forties, of which the first literary evidence is the First Letter to the Thessalonians, a document usually dated to 51, and about as long as the First Letter of John. Paul had preached the Gospel to the Thessalonians, establishing the church. Out of anxiety for their welfare he had sent Timothy from Athens, and when Timothy returned bearing the good news of their steadfastness, Paul wrote First Thessalonians (2:13. 3:1, 6). That church had become very dear to him, indeed his glory and his joy (2:19). He reminded

8 Fourth-century images of Paul, Peter, and Andrew are stereotypical; dark-haired Paul, white-haired, white- bearded Peter, large-bearded, hirsute Andrew. There is no reason to doubt that these conventions preserve characteristics of the great apostles. In June 2009 *L'Osservatore Romano* reported the discovery of the image of Paul in the Catacomb of St. Thecla on the Via Ostiensis, which Reuters published on 22 June 2010. Paul is the figure with the bald head and pointed black beard.

the Thessalonians that he had come to them as one who had suffered for the Gospel at Philippi, that his motive had been disinterested love; that he had taught with gentleness, not demanding the respect due an apostle (2:6–7).

At the same time, at the very beginning of his ministry, Paul claimed that the Church was not the result of his initiative and preaching, but of the call of God and the gift of the Spirit; the Thessalonians had accepted the word of God not as the word of men but as what it really is, "the word of God." What Paul and the other apostles accomplished was not a human work. Our Gospel came upon you "not only in word but also in power and in the Holy Spirit with full conviction." "You became imitators of us and of the Lord, for you received the word in much affliction, with joy inspired by the Holy Spirit, so that you became an example to all the believers in Macedonia and Achaia" (1:7). The Gospel not only claimed conviction but changed hearts. "You learned from us how you ought to live and please God. This is the will of God, your sanctification." Believers were to control their bodies "in holiness and honor," not "in the passion of lust like the heathen who do not know God" (4:1–5). Neither Paul's preaching nor the belief of the Thessalonians was the work of man. Faith was a transforming gift that was realized in holiness. Conversion was a supernatural event. The Church had accepted Paul's Gospel as the work of God; the Thessalonians were converted "with joy inspired by the Holy Spirit," and now "they wait for his Son from heaven, whom he raised from the dead, Jesus who delivers us from the wrath to come" (1:6, 10). They are now "to lead a life worthy of God, who calls you into his own kingdom and glory" (2:12). The letter is full of that note of holy subjectivity rooted in the second great commandment that urges appreciation (for pastors) and sympathetic engagement with fellow Christians (5:11–14).

First Thessalonians, perhaps the earliest of Paul's letters to have survived, is noteworthy for what it does and does not address. There is reference to the opposition Paul had encountered at Philippi and the suffering this shameful treatment had caused, perhaps a reference to the opposition of the synagogue or perhaps a reference to injuries inflicted by an enraged pagan mob because Christians no longer sacrificed to the gods, for which they were counted atheists. This would be the case in Ephesus (Acts 19:23–41), when preaching by Timothy and Erastus depressed the sale of silver images of Artemis. Paul noted that Christians of Thessalonica had "turned to God from idols, to serve a living and true God" (1:9), again suppressing the profitable sale of tokens and images on behalf of what was considered an uncivil and superstitious cult. Perhaps because the church at Thessalonica consisted of converted Greeks, there is no mention of failure of the law to justify. In none of his letters does Paul seem dismayed that the universal Gospel he preaches has not been universally received, for his success, such as it may be, is presently the will of God.

Paul foresees in First Thessalonians day-by-day challenges. Like every other Christian writer Paul taught that fruition of the Spirit is holiness of soul that permeates the desires and makes the body worthy of incorporation into Christ. "For this is the will of God, your sanctification, that you abstain from immorality, that each one of you know how to control his own body in holiness and honor, not in the passion of lust like heathen" (4:3–4). There is the Christian admonition regarding work. First Thessalonians presages the reminder of other Pauline epistles that Christians are to avoid idleness: "Work with your hands . . . so that you may command the respect of outsiders and be dependent on nobody" (4:13). Finally, there was also difficulty caused by what came to be seen as the long delay of Christ's return. The background for the Gospel Paul preaches is the apocalyptic urgency assumed by John the Baptist, by Jesus himself. In this letter Paul addresses a church that looks forward eagerly to Jesus' return, some of whose members had already fallen asleep. These too, he assures the Thessalonians, will go out with those who are alive to meet the Lord when he returns. That day will come like a thief in the night, when peace and security seem to abound (4:13–16). But this hope is set within and guaranteed by the Christian experience of the sanctifying power of the Holy Spirit.

The text of First Thessalonians 4:13–18 will ever be a reference point for faith no less significant than Romans 8 or First Corinthians 13, setting in a high key Paul's fundamental theme that Christ's return will mean wrath to unrighteousness but joy to the elect of God. That there are two ways, the way of life and the way of death, was implicit in Jesus' teaching in Matthew 25, and would be the theme of such first-century Christian writings as the *Didache* and the *Epistle of Barnabas*. Paul wrote in First Corinthians that the Day would bring a purifying fire which would test the works even of the elect (1 Cor. 3:13), but the end is Christ, and Paul's image of the end of the age, Christ descending from heaven with a cry of command, with the archangel's call, at which the dead in Christ will be resurrected to join with those living to meet the Savior in the air, would ever inhabit Christian imagination.[9] "And so we shall always be with the Lord" (1 Thess. 4:17).

9 The image of Christ returning, welcomed by Peter and Paul who go out to meet him in the air, is the central image in the apse of Roman churches of the period 400–1100. A secondary image developed from this theme is Christ reigning, having returned, as at Santa Pudenziana, and by the twelfth century Christ reigns with his mother, as at Santa Maria in Trastevere. Always the theme is the realized reign of Jesus; the Church is the new Jerusalem or heaven realized in Christ's presence in the Eucharist.

# Four
## *Gospels*

> The Word, the Artificer of all, He that sitteth upon the cherubim, and contains all things, He who was manifested to men, has given us the Gospel under four aspects, but bound together by one Spirit.
>
> Irenaeus, *Against Heresies* 3.8

Gospels are a distinctively Christian literary form that had by mid-second century replaced the "living voice," for by that date anyone who, like John the Presbyter and Ariston, remembered the words of those who had known the apostles had fallen asleep, and the Church was a cosmopolitan institution held together not only by revealed faith but by published sources. By 150 Justin would write that the memoirs of the apostles as well as the prophetic writings were read at the Eucharist.[1] Irenaeus knew by about 185 that there were too many Gospels, some spurious or of heretical provenance; he was adamant that there were four Gospels, no more and no less, although his typological reasoning—because there are four winds, four corners of the earth, and four great living animals in the Apocalypse—does not now seem compelling.[2]

The word Gospel is Old English, originally good + spell, meaning good tidings, later taking the form God + spel meaning God's discourse or story. Exported to the Teutonic areas of northern Europe by English and Irish missionaries, there Gospel met the Latin *bona adnuntiatio* and *bonus nuntius,* good news. German adopted *evangelium* from the Old Latin and Vulgate *evangelium*, which was the Greek *euaggeliov,* the word meaning good,

1 Justin 67 (Richardson, 287).
2 *Against Heresies* 3.11.8 (*ANF* 1:428).

*eu*, as in eulogy or euphony, plus the Greek *aggeliov*, message, good news or glad tidings. The angel, the *aggelos,* God's messenger, appeared to the shepherds to announce the *euaggeliov* (Luke 2:8). "Gospel" is distinctively English. In its original form the Gospel was both God's word proclaimed by his heralds and the written account of Jesus, his teaching, his actions, by which he set mankind free, purchasing through his death the reconciling forgiveness of sins and the gift of his Spirit, through whom the Church would be formed.

There were surely written Gospels by the turn of the first century, but what then made up the Christian canon was less obvious than it seems in retrospect to have been. The Church-wide reception of what had been written remained a difficulty. Eighty years after Ignatius reminded the Ephesian Christians that inspired memory might be more reliable than the written word, Irenaeus was still combating those who, "when they are confuted by the Scriptures . . . turn around and accuse these same scriptures as if they were not correct, nor of authority, and [assert] that they are ambiguous, and that the truth cannot be extracted from them by those who are ignorant of tradition."[3] Irenaeus did not dispute the existence of tradition, indeed of more than one, for he knew the Valentinians and Marcionites had their own, but he brought forward a tradition that was founded on apostolic authority commissioned by Jesus, resonant in the heart of the elect, and taught by the twelve, that still spoke with the apostolic voice from Jerusalem, Ephesus, and Alexandria and especially from Rome. Irenaeus wrote, "Every church must be in harmony with this Church," which is "that very great, oldest, and well-known Church, founded and established at Rome by those two most glorious apostles Peter and Paul."[4]

By 185 the living voice that Ignatius and Papias preferred had become the idea of tradition, coordinate with Scripture, which proved but did not establish the faith of the Church. Now, in the age of Irenaeus, the living voice was stabilized by a public literature, originating for the most part in the first century, enjoying with some few exceptions Church-wide recognition, of distinctively Christian character: always the apostolic letters, but now also four Gospels that told the story of Jesus and his divine message,

3 *Against Heresies*, 3.2.1 (*ANF* 1:415),

4 Ibid., 3.3.2 (*ANF* 1:415–16).

and an Apocalypse that, by bringing the prophetic view of history taught by Jesus (Matt. 24–25), the belief that this world's long centuries open upon judgment and joy, into the intellectual mainstream of the Church, unveiled the meaning of history.

At the same time that Irenaeus offered his beautiful creedal summary of the Catholic faith in his *Refutation*, about 185, when he recorded the existence in the Church of four and only four Gospels, representing these as the literary foundations of faith, Irenaeus knew the nugatory facts of Gospel origins. He knew that Luke was dependent on Paul (3.14.1), and he is probably the author, or at least the authoritative popularizer, of the identification of the eyewitness of John 18:35 as the Beloved Disciple, the apostle John. Generally, Irenaeus sees the Gospels as sources for proof texts to establish the Catholic faith and put down Gnosticism. Unlike paganism, perhaps in imitation of Judaism with its sacred books, Christianity appears early as a community of writers and readers, burdened with the necessity of giving accounts that were more than mythic, telling what Jesus had said and done at a specific time and place.[5] There would always be an interplay between writings and the living voice, and although great witnesses like Ignatius and Papias preferred the living voice to writing, they were aware near the turn of the first century that written recollections existed and that appeal was made to them.[6] Inevitably, there would come a time when memory would fail, accounts would become confused, interpretations alien to the teaching of the apostolic mission would be composed, and the stability of the written word, books recognized as the authentic memoirs of the apostles to use Justin's words, would be preferred.[7] Then as the principal source of historical memories of Jesus gradually faded—characteristically a man of twenty-five who might have known an apostle in his old age would not survive far into the third decade of the new century—the apostolic letters and memoirs would

5 Brian J. Wright, *Communal Reading in the Time of Jesus* (Minneapolis, Minn.; Fortress Press, 2017) makes the case that public reading of Biblical texts was common practice in the early Church.

6 Ignatius wrote as one familiar with writings that claimed authority (*Phld.* 8.2), and Papias even as he preferred the living voice knew of Mark and proto-Matthew (*Church History* 3.39).

7 Justin 67 (Richardson, 287).

begin to be quoted as having an authority not unlike the authority of the writings of Moses and the Prophets recorded in the Septuagint. By about 150 Justin links reading from the prophets with reading from the memoirs of the apostles at the Eucharist.[8]

Oddly, from a twenty-first-century point of view, Irenaeus displays no interest in that feature of Matthew, Mark, and Luke that modern scholars find most interesting, their respective characters as synoptic, literally seen together, the apparent tendency of three of the Gospels to imitate or quote one another. The word synoptic, used with reference to the Gospels, does not come into English vocabulary until the 1840s. Irenaeus seems unaware of the synoptic problem. The Gospels are held to be of apostolic origin and authority although of the four canonical Gospels only one, Matthew, certainly bears the name of one of the twelve. Luke was the friend and traveling companion of Paul. The Gospel of John may or may not bear the name of the son of Zebedee. Irenaeus was among the first plausibly to identify the disciple who witnessed the Lord's death on the cross as the author of the Gospel of John. It may bear the name of the great presbyter who wrote the three canonical epistles bearing John's name and is based on the testimony of several Galileans among whom the apostle Andrew, the disciple who brought Peter to Jesus (1:40–41), is prominent, probably as the beloved witness who had witnessed Jesus' death (John 19:35). Since the mid-second century, and Matthew long before, the four have been accepted as true accounts of the life and teaching of Jesus, the differences between them, typically no more than among the several biographies of any historical figure, reconciled as being congruent accounts written under the authority of the same Holy Spirit, each representing an aspect of the Gospel truth.

In print the four canonical Gospels in a widely-used English translation occupy just over one hundred pages, but they are the narrative foundation of the kingdom of Christ. The order of the Gospels could plausibly be understood as determined loosely by the place of origin of each. Among the Gospels the tradition of Jerusalem represented by Matthew stands first, then the Roman tradition of Mark, and the Asian tradition of John, inserted within the witness of Paul, Luke, Acts, and the Pauline Epistles, and again with the other, non-Pauline letters, in the order of place: first the witness

8 Ibid.

of Jerusalem (James) then of Rome (the Petrine letters), then the witness of Asia—perhaps Jude, the three Johannine letters, and the apocalypse of John. This can be no more than suggestive, and there is another order, Matthew, John, Luke, Mark, that is witnessed early.[9]

Over the years that separated Paul and Papias of Hierapolis, between 60 and 110 or 120, by a process of which we have no record, or perhaps only brief sketches in the Muratorian or Anti-Marcionite accounts of the writing of John,[10] the creed-like recitations of Jesus' saving actions, reflected in a narrative outline, would be complemented by historical accounts that included in the Gospels such recollections of his words as the Sermon on the Mount, his parables, and the discourses remembered in the Johannine circle. To these would be added over time other apostolic recollections that reached back to the days when John baptized in the Jordan near Bethany and forward to the empty tomb. These first accounts, sayings, and parables may have been written in Aramaic, the vernacular language of Syria and Palestine, or possibly in Hebrew, the literary and sacred language of the Jews, which was often written using the Aramaic alphabet, as may have been the case with Matthew.[11] When the apostolic mission moved into Asia the language of evangelization would be Greek, but when it moved east, into Syria and Mesopotamia, the Church would speak and write in Aramaic or the more scholarly Syriac, creating a literature of which the Peshitta, the Aramaic Bible, and the Tatian's Gospel harmony, the *Diatessaron*, are representative. Later, because what was written before about 130 either lacked publicity or common acceptance, it would seem evident, as Irenaeus would

9 Matthew, John, Luke, Mark is witnessed by Codex Bezae of the fifth century and by the Old Latin.

10 Muratorian Canon, Metzger, *Canon of the New Testament*, 306; Lietzmann, lines 9–17. The canon is contained in a Latin manuscript of the seventh or eighth century discovered by Ludvico Antonio Muratori in the library at Bobbio and published in 1740. Dated between 170 and the fifth century, the manuscript contains a refence to Pope Pius I (140–54) and assumes that the *Shepherd of Hermas* is popular among Christians while warning that it is not to be read in Church.

11 During the Babylonian captivity of the sixth century BC Hebrew letters were replaced by square Aramaic letters with Hebrew becoming a liturgical and theological language.

write, that the apostles had first preached and then had written,[12] although writing in the form of letters exchanged had accompanied the apostolic mission as early as the age of Paul, who probably wrote First Thessalonians in the forties.

According to Eusebius the written tradition recording Jesus' words and deeds was the subject of exegesis or explanatory commentary by the first decade of the second century, by which time Papias of Hierapolis, whose testimony to the existence of Matthew and Mark as quoted by Eusebius looms large in the history of the canon of Scripture, had written his five books or chapters titled an *Explanation of the Sayings of the Lord*, with sayings being *logia*, the plural of *logion*, a variant of *logos* (word) which meant oracle or divine communication. When Papias wrote he included brief comments on the origins of two Gospels, and there is a plausible suggestion that Papias' text may also have included an account of the origin of John which Eusebius omitted from his *Church History*.[13] Quoting one of his sources, whom he describes as "the presbyter," Papias writes, "Mark, having become the interpreter of Peter, wrote down accurately, although not indeed in order, whatever he remembered of the things said or done by Christ." Papias goes on to apologize for Mark, claiming Mark had no first-hand knowledge of the Lord, that he wrote with the needs of his readers in mind, and with no intention of giving a connected account. After Papias' testimony the standard account of the origin of Mark would always be consonant with Papias' evidence given in Eusebius' *Church History:* Mark wrote down the preaching of Peter. Papias, although still preferring the living voice of those knowledgeable visitors who came to Hierapolis,[14] felt compelled to defend Mark from the charge that his account differed, presumably from some better-known account available to Papias and his readers, and that standard must have been the tradition represented by Matthew or

12 "The Gospel has come down to us, which they did at one time proclaim in public, and, at a later period, by the will of God, handed down to us in the Scriptures. . ." (*Against Heresies* 3.1.1 [*ANF* 1:414]).

13 The Anti-Marcionite Prologue makes Papias in his *Five Books* the source of the information that the Gospel was written by John while still alive, with Papias his amanuensis. See B. W. Bacon, "The Latin Prologue of John," *Journal of Biblical Literature* 32 (1913):194–217.

14 *Church History* 3.39.15 (*NPNF*[2] 1: 172–73).

proto-Matthew, a work in Greek that translated the Hebrew or Aramaic Matthew.[15] As Papias knows these sources about 110, Mark is not part of the work attributed to Matthew; the Markan and Matthean texts then stood alone.[16] Papias of Hierapolis, who probably wrote within eighty years of Pentecost, had received the tradition that "Matthew set in order the sayings, the *logia,* in Hebrew, and everyone translated them as he was able."[17] Papias' language suggests that there may have been more than one translation of Matthew's sayings, but he failed to indicate the Matthew he considered authentic. Later the *Gospel According to the Hebrews,* written in Aramaic but with Hebrew letters, found a place among the Ebionites and Nazarenes, whose historical interest was centered on the Jerusalem church with James as its head (Gal. 2:9–12). A copy of this Hebrew Matthew existed in the library at Caesarea when Jerome wrote his work *On Famous Men* in 393.[18] The Gospel according to the Hebrews was cited by Origen, Jerome, Epiphanius, and other sources.[19] Epiphanius, writing about 377, noticed that the sect of the Ebionites used the Hebrew Matthew and no other.[20] The exact relation between the text Jerome cites and the text Epiphanius knew and the version known to Papias remains speculative, but Epiphanius' evidence is enough to make Papias' report that Matthew was first written in Hebrew plausible. The Matthean tradition as Papias knew it was reliable but still somewhat fluid, since everyone translated the Hebrew as he was able. The name of the translator whose text became the Greek Matthew, says Jerome, has been lost.

15 *Church History* 3.24.13–14 (*NPNF*[2] 1:153).

16 See John M. Rist, *On the Independence of Matthew and Mark* (Cambridge: Cambridge University Press, 1978), 104–07. "There is no evidence in the texts themselves which necessitates literary dependence of Mark on Mathew or of Matthew on Mark" (107).

17 *Church History* 3.39.16 (*NPNF*[2] 1:173).

18 "He who translated Matthew into Greek is no longer known with certainty. Further the Hebrew Text itself is still preserved in the library at Caesarea, which the martyr Pamphilus collected with great care. The Nazaraeans of Beroea, a city of Syria, who use this book, also permitted me to copy it." Jerome, *De Vir Illustribus*, 3.

19 Quasten, 1:111–12.

20 Epiphanius, *Panarion* 30.3.7 (*The Panarion of Epiphanius of Salamis, Book I*, trans. Frank Williams, 2nd ed. [Atlanta, Ga.: SBL Press, 2009]), 133.

After Papias' serendipitous evidence, dating from the first or second decade of the second century, there will be no references to the existence of any written report of Jesus' words or deeds until about 150, when Justin in his *First Apology* writes that the memoirs of the apostles' *apomnēmoneumata*, recollections, were read at the Sunday Eucharist.[21] After Justin there will be other evidence, the account given in the Muratorian Canon of the origins of Luke and John and the witness of the Gospel Prologues called the Anti-Marcionite Prologues. The dates of the Anti-Marconite Prologues and the Muratorian account are much contested, but it would be difficult to find an authority willing to date either earlier than Justin's *First Apology*, about 150. With respect to external evidence favoring the existence of any Gospel, the thirty-year period between Papias and Justin offers only silence, not only the silence of external evidence but the absence of the testimony of any text.

The principal means by which the very existence of Gospel texts can be shown to exist is citation by the Apostolic Fathers and Apologists, and as the extant evidence suggests, it was Matthew that would be the text preferred by first- and second-century Christian writers, exemplifying as it did the literary form called Gospels, which while they were sacred biographies were much more, typically including a collection of sayings and parables. Because we have no Gospel manuscripts, only small fragments, before the third century, the citation of Gospel texts by Christian writers of the first and second centuries is the best evidence of their existence and their contents, and even then we have no very precise knowledge of the text these writers are quoting, for the thought that the texts of Matthew and Mark known to Papias about 110 were identical to the texts of these Gospels as they existed at mid-second century is an assumption. When the *Didache* was written, probably no later than 75, perhaps earlier, the author prefaced his advice with a moral catechesis drawn from what he calls "the gospel," texts which were or would be Matthew 5, the Sermon on the Mount. When Clement wrote to the Corinthians, although he knew Romans and believed Paul's First Corinthians had been written "with true inspiration,"[22] he based his argument mostly on the Septuagint,

21 Justin 67 (Richardson, 287).

22 Clement, 47.3 (LCL 1:90–91).

but Clement also knew Gospel material later attributed to Matthew, the Beatitudes (13), the parable of the sower (24), the warning that those who corrupt the little ones will be cast into the sea (46), and the apocalypse of Matthew chapters twenty-four and twenty-five. But remarkably, Clement, writing from Rome, cites no text that is unique to Mark as we have it. This pattern of apparent reliance on Matthew is also found in Ignatius, who certainly knew of a written tradition; when he said, "It is written," the reference was to a text close at hand.[23] Ignatius writes as though "the Gospel" is the word preached or proclaimed; the Gospel texts Ignatius quotes will later be found in Matthew.[24] Although Justin Martyr, the author of the important *First Apology* addressed to Antoninus Pius about 150, knows some Gospel material that might be drawn from Luke, the preference for Matthew persists, and so close is the relation between the texts of Matthew and Luke that it can rarely be said that references that seem Lukan are uniquely from that source. In the period 1867–1885 the *Ante-Nicene* editors found in Justin's writings sixty-two citations of Matthew, nineteen of Luke, and three to Mark, although one or more of these three may also be found in substance in Matthew, and although the citations to Luke may find parallels in Matthew.[25] The relative neglect of Mark was not much different by 185 when Irenaeus wrote his work against the Gnostics. In that longer work the same editors found 270 citations of Matthew, seventy identified as belonging to Luke, although these Lukan texts often echo Matthew, and nineteen to Mark. Of course, as Irenaeus had the texts, Matthew was longer than Mark. But this pattern of the neglect of Mark and preference for Matthew will continue into the third century, and can hardly be explained apart from the fact that there was early a written document, bearing a close relation to the Gospel we

23 *Phld.* 8.2. Ignatius' Matthew is an early use of the "western" text, the popular Greek text of the second century. His citations are loose, suggesting that Ignatius may have cited Matthew from memory. See Rist, *On the Independence of Matthew and Mark,* 104.

24 Burnett Hillman Streeter, *The Four Gospels: A Study in Origins* (London: Macmillan and Co. 1930), 271–90.

25 Vincent Taylor in *The Gospel According to Mark* (London: Macmillan and Company, 1957), claimed only three of the possible citations of Mark by Justin as convincing (4).

know as Matthew, that enjoyed a certain priority, or at least a certain popularity, due to its apparent accessibility, its acknowledged antiquity and authority and its completeness, while, about 150 Mark was less well known if at all, and the Gospel of John not yet part of the common literature of the Church.

A rough survey of Christian writers through Irenaeus shows that some ninety percent of their citations display the same characteristic pattern, an obvious reliance on Matthew, with Mark cited never or rarely. When the editors of the *Ante-Nicene Fathers* combed the texts of the Apostolic Fathers for citations of the Gospels they found that these were most often taken from Matthew, or from Mathew including those texts shared by Matthew and Luke but absent from Mark. Granting that the editors' analysis was not as carefully critical as was the work of the Oxford Historical Society in their efforts in 1905 to catalog uses of New Testament texts by the Apostolic Fathers, or the further study of Andrew Gregory and Christopher Tuckett in their *Reception of the New Testament in the Apostolic Fathers* in 2005, although unscientific, the analysis of the *Ante-Nicene Fathers* editors has more than anecdotal weight.[26] This pattern of quotation would be difficult to explain on the thesis that Ignatius, or Clement, *Barnabus,* or *Diognetus,* had before them all three of the Gospels that would later be called synoptic, Matthew, Mark, and Luke, Gospels "seen together" (*syn*=together or simultaneously and *optikos*=seen) because their texts as we have them reiterate and parallel one another, always telling much of the same story, often in the same or similar words.

This failure of the writers before Justin to quote material unique to Mark and their preference for the Matthew-Luke parallels is especially puzzling since we know from Papias of Hierapolis that Mark, recording the preaching of Peter, existed not long after the turn of the century.[27] This avoidance of Markan material is especially difficult to explain because on the assumption that the Synoptics were in something of their present form, the reader of Matthew's 1071 verses would have had before

26 *The Apostolic Fathers in the New Testament* (Oxford: At the Clarendon Press, 1905); Andrew Gregory and Christopher Tuckett, *Reception of the New Testament in the Apostolic Fathers*, 2 vols. (Oxford: University Press, 2005).

27 *Church History* 3.39.15 (*NPNF*[2] 1:173).

him 500 of the 661 verses of Mark, constituting about half of Matthew's Gospel, while Luke in its 1151 verses contained 250 verses parallel to Markan texts. If Ignatius, to take an obvious example, had possessed Matthew, Mark, and Luke he would have had before him Mark itself, then (substantially) Mark in Matthew and about a fourth of Mark in Luke. That Gospel texts unique to Mark are very seldom quoted by Christian writers before Irenaeus suggests that if Mark existed it was local and comparatively unknown, as indeed was the Gospel of John. It suggests further that before about 150 Markan content was not part of the Aramaic Mathew that Papias knew, Matthew as we now have it being the result of a process of assimilation that took place between Papias and 150.[28] It is at least incautious to hold that Mark was the first Gospel, with "first" implying both chronological priority and evangelical preeminence, when the Gospel of Mark is first mentioned by Papias in the second decade of the second Christian century and does not come into common use until after Justin. Until 150 the Church behaved as though the Gospel was Matthew, although the exact form in which Matthew was known is unclear.

The Church always displayed an interest in the origins of the four and there are abbreviated references to their origins current about 200. Not only are there Eusebius' citations of Papias, but there also exist brief sketches of the origins of the three Gospels in the Anti-Maronite Prologues, often dated as early as the late second century although this early date is much contested.[29] The prologue to Mark relates that Mark the "stubby-fingered"—a detail that must have been rooted in local memory—wrote down the preaching of Peter, presumably in Rome, and the prologue to Luke makes his Gospel the work of the Syrian physician, a follower of Paul. while the roughly contemporary Muratorian Canon includes sketches of the origins

28 Martin Hengel, The *Four Gospels and the One Gospel of Jesus Christ* (London: SCM Press, 2000)*:* "The sources from this most obscure period in church history are particularly sparse." (61).

29 The Anti-Marcionite Prologues entered scholarly debate with the publication of Dom Donatien De Bruyne's "*Les plus anciens prologues latins des Évangiles*" in *Revue Bénédictine* 1(1928), 192–214. The early date assigned by De Bruyne, 160–80, was contested by Engelbert Gutwenger in "The Anti-Marcionite Prologues" *Theological Studies* 7:343–409 and remains controversial.

of Luke and John.[30] The Anti-Marcionite Prologue's references to the origins of Mark and Luke have never been considered obviously untrustworthy nor has Papias' report that Matthew was written in Hebrew and translated as the reader was able. At the least, whether written in the second century or later, these historical accounts, Papias and the Prologues, attest the interest of the pre-Nicaean Church in the historical origins of the life-giving Gospels, an interest evident as early as 110–120, when Papias recorded in his *Five Books* what must have been the received account, current in Asia, of the origins of Matthew and Mark, and perhaps also of John.[31] Modern scholarship has never found reason to doubt that Mark records the teaching of Peter, a tradition made plausible by Peter's First Letter (5:13); that Luke was the work of a physician, the companion of Paul; or that an early version of Matthew was written in Aramaic.

Christian interest in the origin of the Gospel of John—and such evidence as exists suggests this was a burning question—was confirmed by an early third-century controversy about Johannine origins that engaged broad interest.[32] About 185, about the time Gaius of Rome argued that the Johannine

30 The text, showing line numbers, is in Hans Lietzmann, *Das Muratorische Fragment* (Bonn, 1902; 2nd ed., 1933). See also E. S. Buchannan, "The Codex Muratorianus," *Journal of Theological Studies* 8 (1906–1907): 537–45; Eckhard J. Schnabel, "The Muratorian Fragment: The State of Research," *JTS* 57 (2014):231–64; Hill, *Johannine Corpus*, 128–38.

31 *Church History* 3:39:14–16 (*NPNF*² 1:172–73).

32 The Johannine Epistles show that John the Presbyter was much engaged with those who considered themselves Christians while denying that Jesus had come in the flesh, that is, in his letters we are witnessing the separation of the "spirituals" from what would become Catholic orthodoxy. Given this circumstance, and given the involvement of the great gnostic teachers with the Gospel text, the argument of Gaius of Rome that the Gospel was vitiated by gnostic associations is not quite implausible. The anti-Montanist Roman presbyter Gaius, who wrote against the Montanist prophet Proculus, Tertullian's *Proculus noster*, was also the object of Hippolytus' *Heads Against Gaius* and *On the Gospel of John and the Apocalypse*. This latter work was known to Epiphanius in the 370s when he wrote of the Alogi, those who denied the logos doctrine of the Johannine preface (*Panarion* 4.26.3.1–4.5, trans. Frank Williams, Books II and III; De Fide [Atlanta: SBL Press, 2013], 27–28). For the extant citations of Caius see Hill, *Johannine Corpus*, 178, 201. Dionysius of Alexandria, writing about 235, denied the Johannine authorship of the Apocalypse on lin-

literature had gnostic antecedents, Irenaeus had written his great anti-gnostic work in which there was a running assumption, never made quite explicit, that the author of the fourth Gospel was the Apostle John, who was at the same time the witness of John 19:35, thereby giving the Gospel of John an orthodox genealogy that would recover it from the gnostic context in which it sometimes appeared.[33] Irenaeus' theory was popular at the time. Whatever Irenaeus wrote in defense of the orthodox origins of the Fourth Gospel was written with an eye to the pressing necessity for providing the Gospel with an orthodox context and history, for "the followers of Valentinus . . . make great use of that according to John to demonstrate their conjunctions."[34] The earliest commentaries on the Gospel of John were the work of the popular gnostic teachers Heracleon, Ptolemaeus, and Valentinus,[35] with Valentinus implicitly claiming John as authority for his system in his *Gospel of Truth*.[36]

Although there is no reason to believe that his information was derived from the *Refutation*, Polycrates, bishop of Ephesus, writing in about 190 during the episcopate of Victor of Rome, seems to second something of the Irenaean account; he assumes that John who slept in Ephesus had been "both a witness and a teacher, who reclined upon the bosom of the Lord, and being a priest wore the sacerdotal breastplate."[37] That a younger disciple

guistic grounds, citing as well its use by the heretic Cerinthus (*Church History* 7.25.2 [*NPNF*² 1:309]). Tertullian calls Proculus "our own Proculus, the model of chaste old age and Christian eloquence" (*Against the Valentinians* 5 [*NPNF*² 3:506]).

33 James Patrick, *Andrew of Bethsaida and the Johannine Circle: The Muratorian Tradition and the Gospel Text* (New York: Peter Lang, 2013), 17–31.

34 *Against Heresies* 3.7 (Richardson, 382).

35 Elaine Pagels, *The Johannine Gospel in Gnostic Exegesis: Heracleon's Commentary on John* (Society of Biblical Literature, Monograph Series, 1973), 17; Extant gnostic commentaries on John are in Grant, *Gnosticism*: Ptolemaeus, 182–83, Heracleon, 195–208.

36 *Against Heresies* 3:11.9 (*ANF* 1:429).

37 *Church History* 3.31.3 (*NPNF*² 1, 1:163). One who had served among the numerous Jerusalem priesthood before 70, and who is widely held to have knowledge of Jerusalem, might well live to recount his knowledge of Andrew and others of the Twelve for Papias in Hierapolis about 110. That the person Polycrates remembers wore the high-priestly breastplate, served as high priest before the destruction of 70 AD, complicates Polycrates' claim.

of Jesus who had stood by the cross might have lived into the reign of Domitian, when John saw his great vision, and even beyond is barely possible, but that a native Hebrew speaker, the author of the Apocalypse, his imagination steeped in the images of the Hebrew Scriptures, could have been the author of the Gospel and Epistles is doubtful to the point of incredibility.

What we know about the Gospel from its text is that John from the viewpoint of the Synoptics was an outlier, having a distinctive vocabulary, significant references displaying an interest in four Galilean disciples, three of whom, Andrew, Thomas, and Philip, play little part in the synoptic narrative. John is organized in its last chapters, the Passion Narrative of 12–20 and the appendix or afterword of chapter 21, around the role of an unnamed Beloved Disciple, emphasizing his relation to Peter and having no easily discernible linguistic relation to the Synoptics but a compelling similarity of style and vocabulary to the three letters written, as the address of the Second Epistle states, by John the Presbyter. This apparent relationship, reinforced by the shared titles, while it does not support unambiguously the identity of authorship among the Gospel and the three epistles, is impossible to disregard. John the Presbyter was the much-valued witness to the living voice which Papias preferred to written accounts, and we know from the three letters that their author was engaged in a bitter struggle with self-confident, assertive, incarnation-denying Gnostics, all of which suggests that his letters can plausibly be located nearer the time of Ignatius than the time of Paul.[38]

The question of Johannine origins would have appeared in the reign of Constantine in a light very different from that shed by centuries of settled assumption, reinforced by the authority of Pius IX in his Syllabus of Errors, that the son of Zebedee was the author of the Fourth Gospel. A century earlier, about 200, a late second-century Christian, should he have wished to take up the question, would have had before him not only Irenaeus' recently published theory, but two accounts that may be roughly contemporary with

38 Hengel, *Four Gospels and One Gospel,* 67: "The guarantor of this tradition 'John the Elder' is identical with the 'elder' of II and III John, and probably also the author of I John and the Gospel," and, "The presbyter John, . . . in my view, [is] the author who stands behind the Fourth Gospel and is the guarantor of Papias' tradition. . . ." (75).

Irenaeus' *Refutation*, but which do not bear the Irenaean mark. The Anti-Marcionite Prologue to the Fourth Gospel, so named because it mentions John's refusal to admit the opinions of Marcion, makes the Gospel a revelation given to the churches with Papias as John's amanuensis and references Papias' then popular, now lost, exegetical work:

> The Gospel of John was revealed and given to the churches by John while he was still in the body, as Papias, called of Hierapolis, a dear disciple of John, related publicly, that is in the last of the *Five Books*. He wrote down the Gospel accurately while John dictated. But the heretic Marcion, since he had been condemned by him because he was opposed to his views, was expelled by John. In fact, he had brought writings or letters to him from the brothers who were in Pontus.[39]

The Muratorian canon, often dated to the late second century, contains the following.

> The fourth of the Gospels is that of John, [one] of the disciples. (10) To his fellow disciples and bishops, who had been urging him [to write], (11) he said, "Fast with me from today to three days, and what (12) will be revealed to each one (13) let us tell it to one another." In the same night it was revealed (14) to Andrew, [one] of the apostles, (15–16) that John should write down all things in his own name while all of them should review it. And so, though various (17) elements may be taught in the individual books of the Gospels, (18) nevertheless this makes no difference to the faith.[40]

39 See above, note 27.

40 The text, showing line numbers, is in Hans Lietzmann, *Das Muratorische Fragment* (Bonn, 1902; 2nd ed., 1933). The Latin is: quarti euangeliorum iohannis ex decipolis [11] cohortantibus condescipulis et eps suis dixit [12] conieiunate mihi odie triduo [13] et quid cuique fuerit reuelatum alterutrum nobis enarremus [14] eadem nocte reuelatum andreae ex apostolis ut recogniscentibus cuntis iohannis suo nomine cuncta discriberet.

Again the Gospel is described as having been revealed, the result of inspired recollection on the part of a Pentecostal assembly of bishops, their work authenticated in the Muratorian text by the witness of the absent apostle Andrew, with publication under the name of John *ex discipulis*.[41] The Anti-Marcionite Prologue to John has a special interest because it offers insight into the historical context, arguing that the author was indeed John, alive at the time of writing, making Papias of Hieropolis John's amanuensis, and dissociating John from Marcion.[42] These two accounts reflect a common tradition; they also, with the reference to Papias' *Five Books*, raise critical questions that cannot be answered with the evidence at hand.[43] The

41 In context, John the Presbyter.

42 The existence in the early twentieth century in European libraries, Madrid, Rome, and Stuttgart among them, of sixteen manuscripts, most dating from the tenth century, containing one or more of the Anti-Marcionite Prologues, indicates their broad popularity. The Latin is: Euangelium iohannis manifestatum et datum est ecclesiis ab iohanne adhuc in corpore constituto, sicut papias nomine hierapolitanus, discipulus iohannis carus, in exotericis, id est in extremis quinqué libris retulit. Descripsit uero euangelium, dictante iohanne recte. Uerum marcion haereticus, cum ab eo fuisset inprobatus eo quod contraria sentiebat, abiectus est ab iohanne. Is uero scripta uel epistulas ad eum pertulerat a fratribus qui in ponto fuerunt. The text's insistence that John was alive (*aduc in corpore constituto*) may reflect an awareness of the tension caused by the popular belief that John was an apostle and at the same time a contemporary of Marcion. However one translates the Latin, *in exotericis, id est in extremis quinque libris*, "the last of the Five Books," a phrase which has generated its own critical literature, it is calculated to refer the reader to what the author considers a commonly available text in which an interested reader could verify the evidence offered.

43 Papias' five books on *The Explanation of the Lord's Sayings* was cited by Irenaeus (*Against Heresies* 5.33.4) and by Victorinus of Pettau about 280 (Quasten, 2:412) and by Eusebius (*Church History* 3.39.1). Papias was also cited by Andrew of Caesarea in the sixth century and by Maximus the Confessor and Anastasius of Sinai in the seventh. Papias' work existed in cathedral libraries as late as 1218 at Nîmes and 1341 at Stams (Edgar J. Goodspeed, *A History of Early Christian Literature* [Chicago: University of Chicago Press, 1942], 164). The extant fragments and English translation are published in J. B. Lightfoot and J. R. Harmer, *Apostolic Fathers* (Grand Rapids, Mich.: Baker Book House, 1962), 261–71. In his chronology to 940, Agapius of Manbij, a Chaldean or Melkite Christian, wrote: "At this time [the reign of Hadrian,

claim to the presence of Andrew as the authenticating apostolic witness is not unique, for according to Clement of Alexandria, "they say that Peter the apostle, when he had learned through a revelation of the Spirit what had been done [the writing down of his preaching by Mark] was pleased and approved the work."[44] And the reference to Andrew recalls the unique account of the Gospel itself that makes Andrew, if he is indeed the Beloved Disciple, the means through which his brother Peter knows Jesus (John 1:40–42).

And it can be said on behalf of the Muratorian account, with its reference to the authenticating approval of the Apostle Andrew, that, Irenaeus' account set aside for the moment, the text of the Gospel can be read to support the claim that the author, or editor, of the Fourth Gospel was John the Presbyter whose name the Gospel bears, and the apostolic authority Andrew, the first-called, who brought his brother Peter to the Lord, seconded by the other Galilean disciples.[45] With its date and provenance warmly contested, the Ante-Marcionite Prologue to John, the Muratorian account, and certain other echoes of the Muratorian and Anti-Marcionite accounts, notably Jerome in his *On Famous Men,* represent the existence of an account of the Gospel of John that makes it the work of an assembly of bishops who, filled with the Holy Spirit, recited the traditions they knew.[46] These recollections, cross-checked by common memory, were

98–117] there lived at Menbidj [Hierapolis in Syria] an eminent scholar (Papias), author of several treatises. He composed 5 treatises on the gospel. He records the following in a treatise which he composed on the gospel of John" (*Universal History*, trans., Roger Pearse, Ipswich, U. K., 2009). Agapius was mistaken in his belief that Papias lived and wrote in Syrian Hierapolis, but that naïve error does not discredit his reference to the five books. His testimony that the Gospel of John was the subject of one of the five books reinforces the testimony of the Anti-Marcionite Prologue that Papias had given an account of the writing of John.

44 Eusebius (*Church History* 2.15.2) citing the eighth book of Clement of Alexandria's lost Hypotyposes "and with him agrees the bishop of Hierapolis named Papias."

45 Patrick, *Andrew of Bethsaida,* 55–61.

46 The Muratorian account had currency in the Church. Jerome, writing from the East, Antioch or Chalcis, perhaps in the 390s, knew it, perhaps from his years in Rome, when he composed his *On Famous Men.* Jerome unreflectively

published under the name of John the Presbyter, one of the disciples, and authenticated by the witness of the absent apostle Andrew.

Although the Gospel of John, with its distinctive history, its promise of the Paraclete (16:1–11), the unforgettable image of the good Shepherd (10:1–21), its promise of eternal life to those who eat Christ's flesh and drink his blood (6:22–72), and its revelation of the divine humility (13:1–17), would later become the best-loved of the four, until the third quarter of the second century John does not find an uncontested place in the literature of the Church. The first more-than-allusive citation of its text is probably to be found in Theophilus of Antioch about 186.[47] The difference between the probable date of its composition, not long after the turn of the century as may be attested by Papyrus Beatty 52, which some date as early as 100–110,[48] and the broad acceptance of the Gospel of John as part of the public literature of the cosmopolitan Church at mid-second century, is to be explained at least in part by the difficulty encountered in dissociating the Fourth Gospel from the context of Gnostic exegesis and argument represented by Valentinus' *Gospel of Truth* and the *Gospel of Thomas,* in which Johannine allusions appear.[49] The

conflates the Irenaean account that establishes the apostolic authorship of John with a remembered "historical tradition" that echoes the Muratorian account. "At that time John was compelled by nearly all the bishops of Asia and delegations from many churches to write more deeply concerning the divinity of the Savior, and to break through, so to speak, into the Word of God, through a boldness that was not so much audacious as blessed. This is the source of the Church's historical tradition that when he was compelled by the brothers to write, he answered that he would do so if a universal fast were proclaimed and everyone would pray to the Lord. When this had been carried out and he had been abundantly filled with revelation he poured forth the heaven-sent prologue: 'In the beginning was the Word and the Word was with God and the Word was God. He was in the Beginning with God'" (*On Famous Men*, trans. Schenk, 54).

47 Theophilus of Antioch, *Ad Autolycum* 2.22 (R. M. Grant, trans., 63); Charles E. Hill's *Johannine Corpus in the Early Church* (Oxford: Oxford University Press, 2004) is a welcome attempt to overcome "the predominantly negative evaluation of the extent and quality of the second-century evidence pertaining to the origins of the Johannine works"(2).

48 Recent paleographical analysis has dated $P^{52}$ nearer 200.

49 Elaine Pagels, *Beyond Belief: The Secret Gospel of Thomas* (New York: Vintage Books, 2004), 50–73.

apparent delay in the acceptance of John may also have been the result of the local nature of its composition; although Ephesus and Syria are suggested, the location of the church in which the Gospel was written and of those to whom it was addressed is still unknown. Augustine believed the Johannine Epistles were addressed to Parthia. It is noteworthy that the Gospel of Mark, written surely not long after Peter's martyrdom in the sixties, came into popular use at about the same time as did the Gospel of John.[50]

In the relative absence of outlying forms and fragments, the stability of the Matthean and Markan traditions, as far as the evidence supports, suggests that knowledge of Jesus' words and deeds within the tradition, written or remembered, was very early on determinate and reliable. One of the difficulties is the imprecision that must accompany the attempt to date the Gospels. It would seem that, with the exception of Luke, the text of the Gospels, while representing stable traditions, written and remembered, may not have been fixed until mid-second century. Although it is contrary to received scholarship regarding the usual treatment of the Synoptics, which typically posits three more or less finished documents dating from well within the first century, that position is weakened by the uncontested difficulties. First, such texts are not known to exist in the first century, and again it is impossible to find the unequivocal use of Mark prior to 150, while the Greek Matthew as Papias describes it was in 110 still a somewhat fluid, although popular and commanding, tradition.

The suggestion that best answers the facts is the existence of a movement toward assimilation and comprehensiveness among the Matthean and Markan traditions as living memory failed, between 125 to 145. This movement, carried out during a period in which there is so little literary evidence to the church's use of Gospel texts, would have produced a stable Matthew and Mark that in the name of accuracy and comprehensiveness might have borrowed from one another and a Gospel of Luke that incorporated Matthew and Mark as well as the results of Luke's research. The rumor the pagan critic Celsus recorded about 178 may have been rooted in the recollection of this process: "I have even heard that some of your interpreters, as if they had just come out of a tavern, are onto the inconsistencies and, pen in hand, alter the original writings three, four, and several more times

50 Vincent Taylor, *Mark*, 1.

over in order to be able to deny the inconsistencies."[51] The similarities among the Synoptics as these existed in the age of Irenaeus seems too self-conscious to have been anything other than deliberate at some stage in their composition, while the differences among them, rooted as each was in a discrete community and a particular geography, continued in the second century to pose a worrisome but not critical apologetic problem.

One response to this perceived difficulty was the Gospel harmony, a weaving together of the texts of the four of which the most famous example was the *Diatessaron*, or through-the-four, composed probably between 150 and 160 by Tatian, perhaps in Syriac, so carefully designed that only fifty-six verses found in the texts of the four were not included. The *Diatessaron* was read in Syriac until the fourth century. Undergirding every apologetic line was the theological argument:

> Though various elements may be taught in the individual books of the Gospels, nevertheless this makes no difference to the faith of believers, since by one sovereign Spirit all things have declared in all: concerning the nativity, concerning the passion, concerning the resurrection, concerning his life with his disciples, and concerning his two-fold coming, he first in lowliness when he was despised, which has taken place, and the second in royal power, which is still in the future.[52]

Whatever the process of their composition may have been in detail, these books, at least Matthew, Mark, and Luke, were by about 150 received across the Church as the inspired, divinely given, accounts of Jesus that preserved memory and anchored faith in time and place. However incomplete written Gospels may or may not have been in the age of the *Didache*, as they emerged or became publicly recognized as the literature of the Church at mid-second century, written Gospels were finally a stable form shaped by the memory of Jesus' life, his words and deeds. In the most

51 Celsus, *On the True Doctrine*, trans., R. Joseph Hoffman (New York: Oxford University Press, 1987), 64; cited in a toned-down version and a different context by Origen, *Against Celsus* 2.27 (*NPNF*[2] 4:443).

52 Muratorian Canon, Metzger, *Canon of the New Testament*, 306.

historically engaged and complete version, which Matthew in its published Greek form exemplifies, not only must there be an account of Jesus' origin as securing his claim to Kingship (Matt. 2:2, 27:37, Mark 15:12, Luke 1:32, John 23:3) his divine sonship (Matt. 3:16–17, John 3:18) but there must also be a texture of references that demonstrate Jesus' fulfillment of the prophecies, including, and especially, the prophecy of his death and resurrection in a passion narrative. There must be the story of his betrayal, trial, death, and resurrection, a passion narrative, a triumphant consummation of the Gospel account, which in John occupies almost half the text. There must be references, as in the proto-creeds of Ignatius, to a historical framework that assumed the secular history of Judea and Galilee in the days of Herod and Pilate (Matt. 2:1, Luke 1:5), and also appeals to Old Testament history, for the readership will know the story of Noah (Matt. 24:37) and will know that Moses handed down God's law (Luke 20:37). There must be demonstrations of Jesus' royal power over Satan and the demons (Matt. 4:1–17) and over disease and death. There must be images of grace at work in life, such as the parable of the workers who came late to the vineyard (Matt. 20:1–17) or unprepared to the King's feast (Matt. 22:1–14), or who won out by persistence or failed by lack of it as in the parable of the talents, as well as commentary on the situation of Christians in the field that is the world (Matt. 13:24–32), all this usually offered not apodictically but in parables and similes. And all this must be cast in the light of the Christian hope that looked forward to the Day of God and Jesus' return in glory to execute judgement (Matt. 26:64), rewarding the faithful and punishing sinners, so there must be an ending that looks to the future, when the apostles have gone into all the world, or, in John, when those who have not seen believe, and when the Church looks forward to the appearance in the sky of Christ returning to judge the world, welcoming the just into his kingdom (Matt. 24:27, 29–51, 25:31–46). And above all there must be the recollection, immediate or remote, of Jesus' words as remembered in Matthew 5:21–48, with its teaching of the morality of the new heart, purity, forgiveness, and the willing bearing of wrong.

As the Church began, perhaps fifty years after Pentecost, to use its written recollections, it would not be John, or Mark and Luke, to which writers would appeal but to the text that later would be chapters five and six of Matthew or a Matthew-like document, later called the Sermon on the

Mount, containing the Beatitudes and Jesus' dramatic transformation of the law. A text or reliable tradition called "the Gospel" surely existed when the *Didache* was written, and it was Matthew or proto-Matthew.[53] Later the Church possessed securely the fourfold Gospel. By 200 there were many Gospels; the Valentinians, Irenaeus said, had too many.[54] Irenaeus, in his spirited defense of the apostolic authority of John, nudged the Church toward the hard and clear distinction between the four Gospels that would be considered canonical and the great number of other gospel-like writings: Gospels such as the *Gospel of Thomas*, which although gnostic in tenor and intent contained texts parallel to those found in the Synoptics; gospels so frankly "spiritual" and often fanciful as to have no relation to the canonical four; and Gospels and Acts that were fictional romances, sometimes attributing magical deeds to the apostles.

Irenaeus taught that there were four and only four and that these were complementary, each representing an aspect of the fourfold Gospel. "The pillar and ground of the Church is the Gospel and the spirit of life; it is fitting that she should have four pillars, breathing out immortality on every side, and vivifying men afresh." Irenaeus' proofs, which involved arguments from the analogies of the four winds, the four zones of the earth, and the four faces of the cherubim, served to fix in the mind of the Church the fact that there were only four, that these four were canonical or constituted a list of books that proved the rule of faith.[55] It was in this passage that Irenaeus identified each of the four Gospels with one of the four living creatures of Revelation 4:6–11; the eagle with John, the ox with Luke, the creature with a face like a man with Matthew, and the lion with Mark, identifications that would inhabit Christian imagination into the present, although the fathers would differ as to the identification of the four with the great living creatures.

After the living voice failed in the second and third decades of the second Christian century, the written Gospels stabilized the teaching of the Church and ever after have remained sources of encouragement to faith

53 *Didache* 1–8 comments on Matthew 5 (Richardson, 171–72).

54 James, *Apocryphal New Testament*, 1–18; Quasten, 110–29; *Against Heresies* 3.11.9 (*ANF* 1:429).

55 *Against Heresies* 3.11.8 (*ANF* 1:428).

and means of conversion, whose undiminished power is a scandal to the all-too-knowing world but good news to those who believe. When in the third century the Church began the systematic collection of its writings, Gospels were grouped together, as in the great uncials, Codices *Sinaiticus, Alexandrines, Vaticanus,* and *Freerianus,* texts beautifully written in small Greek capital letters. In the liturgy as it was to be gradually regularized, a process the beginning of which is evident in Justin, the Gospel reading was the climax of the first part of the Eucharistic celebration and would later be accompanied by a procession with lights and incense, the Gospel book held high. As the pattern of the liturgy was stabilized in the West, and even after sitting for parts of the Mass became common in the era of two-hour-long sermons, the sixteenth century, the congregation always stood for the reading of the Gospel, which was greeted with the acclamation: "Glory be to Thee, O Lord." And from about 1200 to September 1965 John 1:1–14 was read as the last Gospel, with priest and congregation genuflecting at the *incarnatus est*: "He was made flesh." The Gospel Book as containing the word of God is still always carried in procession and censed at solemn liturgies. The veneration in which the Gospels were held provided an impetus for the art of illumination so that from at least the late seventh century there exist beautifully illuminated Gospel books, as in the painstakingly wrought Lindisfarne Gospels (698), the Book of Kells (*c.* 795), and the Grimbald Gospels (*c.*1020).

Before Constantine, Gospels and Gospel books were always liable to destruction by pagan authorities, who considered them the literary sources of an anti-social sect. For almost three centuries the imperial inquisitors, who knew that the new religion was fed by writing, often demanded that Scriptures be handed over to be burned, with refusal to do so the first step toward prison and perhaps martyrdom.[56] The Gospels remained the unquestioned authorities until post-Renaissance skepticism (Matthew Toland, Matthew Tindal) declared their words to be mere natural wisdom: in 1778 Gotthold Ephraim Lessing in the *Wolfenbütel Fragments* pronounced them merely the work of self-interested human invention; in 1859 Charles Darwin offered an alternative scientific explanation of the origins of species; in *Literature and Dogma* (1873) Matthew Arnold declared them to be poetry;

56 *Church History* 8.2.4 (*NPNF*[2] 1:324).

and until the basilisk eye of scholarship rendered them merely time-bound artifacts subject to historical and critical dissection, offering theories themselves insightful and exegetically helpful but often narrowly technical. In the great world the Gospels are now, as in the beginning, often considered a scandal to intellect. In fact they speak from before, above, and beyond scientific and literary theories for, as the Church that bred them witnesses, their author is God,

The Roman authorities knew that much of the power of the Christian movement came from its books, so that Diocletian and Galerius in the last great persecution of 303–311 commanded not only that churches be razed to the ground but that "the Scriptures be destroyed by fire." When the mayor of Thibiuca in Africa was commanded, "give up the books so that they can be burned," he replied, "It would be better for me to be burned than the divine scriptures; for it is better to obey God than man."[57]

57 Quoted in A. H. M. Jones, *Constantine and the Conversion of Europe* (London: Hodder & Stoughton, 1948), 50.

# Five

## *Matthew: The Making of the New Heart*

> A new heart I will give you,
> and a new spirit I will put within you.
>
> Ezekiel 18:31

> For I tell you, unless your righteousness exceeds
> that of the scribes and Pharisees,
> you will never enter the Kingdom of Heaven.
>
> Matthew 5:20

Matthew was the Gospel. When early Christian writers turned to a source of Jesus' words and deeds it was to Matthew, or what became Matthew, that they turned. And within Matthew, their pattern of quotation suggests, they turned first to chapters five through seven, containing the Beatitudes and the dominical transformation of the law from the propositions of the Mosaic law as these were understood by the observant Jew to an interior, life-forming participation of the heart in the will of the Father.

Jesus sat down, opened his mouth, and taught them. Thus began the Sermon on the Mount. Luke knows something of this text (6:20–49), but neither Mark nor John contains obvious parallels. Jesus' words in Matthew 5–6 as he transforms the Mosaic law held a hope for the regeneration of the human heart greater than the virtuous life Aristotle had taught in his *Ethics* and Cicero in his *On Duties.* The opening verses, the eight Beatitudes, are at the center of the moral vocabulary of Christian mankind, although on any showing they are challenging at first sight. They are not prescriptive but descriptive, proposing no course of action but promising beatitude or blessedness to those possessing the right state of soul or, as in the seventh and eighth, able to bear persecution. In this way they are truly kerygma or preaching, a proclamation describing the blessedness that accompanies those on the Christian way. The Greek *makarios* is sometimes translated "happy," but "blessed" is better, for happiness is a subjective state of contentment or well-being, while blessedness is the state of being fulfilled by God at his will and in his presence.

Blessedness is not a virtue, not a natural virtue that the best efforts of man can achieve at least episodically, or even a supernatural virtue given silently at baptism, but a gift following upon that supernatural infusion of grace, life lived in the Christian way, the steady result of day by day, charity-inspired cooperation with the Holy Spirit. They are echoed in what Paul knows as the fruits of the Spirit: love, joy, peace, patience, kindness, goodness, faithfulness, gentleness, self-control (Gal. 5:22). In this Matthean text Jesus does not tell the disciples how to seek blessedness; he does not, as elsewhere, urge repentance. The Beatitudes are gifts, and they are proleptic, looking forward to the coming of the Kingdom. Blessedness will come at Pentecost, when hearts will burn within and the question will be "Brethren, what shall we do?" Jesus is waiting: "I came to cast fire on the earth, and would that it were already kindled" (Luke 12:49). But now, on the threshold of the last day, is the time to prepare the disciples for the new life that is coming, to give them words that they will remember when Jesus' first great promise, "I will send the Holy Spirit, the Advocate or Counselor," is fulfilled.

This is the life prophesied by Jeremiah:

> Behold, the days are coming, says the Lord, when I will make a new covenant with the house of Israel and the House of Judah, not like the covenant which I made with their fathers when I took them by the hand to bring them out of Egypt. . . . I will put my law within them, and I will write it on their hearts, and I will be their God and they shall be my people. And no longer shall each man teach his neighbor, and each his brother, saying "Know the Lord," for they shall all know me from the least to the greatest (Jer. 31:31–34).

And Ezekiel: "A new heart I will give you, a new spirit I will put within you. And I will take out of your flesh the heart of stone and I will give you a heart of flesh. And I will put my spirit within you and cause you to walk in my statutes and be careful to observe my ordinances" (11:19). When Peter stood up at Pentecost he declared the descent of the Spirit to be the fulfillment of the prophecy of Joel: "And in the last days it shall be, God declares, I will pour out my Spirit on all flesh, and your sons and daughters shall prophesy" (Acts 2:17–18, Joel 2:28–32). In that Day they all will possess the Prophetic Spirit. But the new way must possess the mind as well as the heart; the gift will be fulfilled in those who have been taught: "Go, baptize, teach."

The best of the Greeks and Romans had known that the good all men seek is not some possession extrinsic to the self but a state of soul. Aristotle's *Ethics,* with a spirit echoed in Justin's day by the stoic Epictetus, begins by asking what it is that all men seek for its own sake, not as an instrument leading to something greater such as wealth or wisdom, which we may desire because they promise happiness. Rather, happiness itself, *eudaimonia*, is what all men desire for its own sake. But quickly Aristotle turns to the observation that happiness is not possible without goodness. So the Philosopher does not, as Epicurus would later, propose happiness as the complement of pleasure, but as the best state of the soul in the righteous man. And this, famously, is to be achieved not through the appropriation of *theoria*, not through the exercise of intellect, but through the practice of the moral virtues—justice, temperance, prudence, and courage—and that not in a world-pleasing way, but as a good man might practice them. The means was the natural capacity of the self-commanding man to become virtuous.

Aristotle's *Ethics* is the high summary of the best of Hellenism's moral proposals. Yet it neither elevated the eye of the soul above the realm of nature, which Aristotle would have considered impossible, nor purified the will. When after Pentecost Christians looked at the world around them, they saw the ravages of the flaw that would be called original sin, ignorance and that deformation of the will called concupiscence, which five centuries of the best of Greek and Roman moral advice had not been able to repair. Against this was set the moral proposals and the moral power of Jesus. Christ came not only with good advice but with the ability to change hearts. And first came the revolutionary ideas found in the fifth chapter of Matthew's Gospel, the prophetic descriptions of the Christian life called the Beatitudes or blessednesses, a reward attached to each, and then the transformation of the law from divinely given rule to the very form of the redeemed heart.

Given the classical expectation regarding happiness and virtue, Aristotle's *eudaimonia* or good-spiritedness as the result of natural virtue, Jesus' words in the Beatitudes disappoint; many would find them puzzling, some would find them impossible, for the heart of natural man does not reach out to embrace poverty of spirit and mourning, to say nothing of persecution. Yet the Beatitudes are signposts along the royal road that leads citizens of a fallen world to the vision of God, to sonship, and to citizenship in the kingdom of heaven, a description of the realm of Our Father that stands contrasted with the kingdom of the earth. Humility, sorrow for one's sins, gentleness, desire for God, mercifulness, purity of heart, peacemaking, acceptance of persecution for Jesus' sake; Jesus is describing God-given dispositions of the heart that may or may not always be evident to the world in actions. Indeed to the degree that any Beatitude excites public notice, it is in danger of betraying its divine purpose; humility and piety displayed already have their reward (Matt. 6:1). Later, in the series of dominical sayings beginning with "You have heard it said but I tell you," there will be specific teaching that tells the blessed heart how to live in the world (Matt. 5:21–7:29).

The Beatitudes have been the subject of commentary by great teachers, but generations lacking scholarly insight have also understood his words as they walked in the way. Jesus, who knew what was in mankind (John 2:25), begins with the counsel that one who would be blessed will be humble, which means seeing oneself as one really is: a creature, clay in the Potter's hands, helpless in the one thing that matters most despite possessing many impressive competencies, reliance upon which as justifying before God is always deceptive (Is. 29:16, Jer. 18:6, Rom. 9:21). "Blessed are the poor in spirit." God is forever ordering the moral universe by putting down the mighty from their seat and exalting the humble (Luke 1:52). Jesus reminds his followers to seek the lowest place, assuring them that the order of this world is not the order of the kingdom of heaven; there many of the first shall be last and the last first (Mark 9:35). He opposes the proud but gives grace to the humble (James 4:10). "He has scattered the proud in the imagination of their hearts . . . and exalted those of low degree" (Luke 1:31–32). God's opposition to the proud is a lesson humankind must repeatedly re-learn, rooted in the very nature of God, in whose sight a lie cannot stand, and who while summary of power and majesty, expresses his life in Trinitarian self-giving, the divine Son humbling himself for our sakes, "who being in the form of God did not count equality with God a thing to be grasped" (Phil. 2:6). To fail in humility and to cultivate pride is to fail to see things as they are; a broken and contrite heart God does not despise (Ps. 51:17).

This was the great lesson given Job, a good man, whom God never accuses of sins, but a man "wise in his own conceits" (37:24), clinging in the most subtle and unrealistic way to his own rightness before God, redeemed only when, having had his ignorance and littleness demonstrated by the Almighty most dramatically (38–41), he falls silent before the gift of the vision of God: "Now my eye sees Thee . . ." (42:5). So the Beatitudes open by declaring blessed one who is *ptōxoi* in spirit, a word for which the least dramatic definition is "poor in spirit," but connoting a deeper range of meanings that include "crushed, beggarly, mean or low." The reference is clearly not to lack of this world's goods, but to that abandonment of self which opens upon the faith of the elect. There was a reason for Saul's having changed his name from that of the great king to Paul, which resonated with the Greek word for mean, of no account.

The central psychological mystery of the religion Jesus taught is the necessity for that reordering of the soul that sees one's self in the order of reality as of no account in the light of God's glory, as deserving his wrath in the light of his justice. The self-deception called pride is the natural defense of every man from this truth. Enjoying justly some human esteem, avoiding public shame, capable of good deeds—God never accused Job of moral failure—mankind will find it easy to ignore that fact that our decency is fragile, our self-interest perfect, our thirst for something other than the righteousness of God ever-present. There is a sweetness in reality, always hard for the sin-encased soul to see, and perhaps especially hard to see in an age when self-esteem is considered a cardinal virtue. But it is the locating of one's self rightly in God's just order that is a sign of blessedness, and this awareness of who we are is the basis of every other Beatitude and the ground of every gratitude. The poor in spirit are blessed because theirs is the kingdom of heaven. The interior greatness of every human action on earth is rooted in the acknowledged littleness of every man before the glory and majesty of God.

This humility, this poverty of spirit, has as its companion the reality of sorrow for sin and sinfulness (5:5). "Blessed are those who mourn; they shall be comforted." Christians are never encouraged to ruminate on past failures; we are ever to be putting behind us the past with its failure and looking to the future, "forgetting what lies behind, pressing forward and straining forward to what lies ahead" (Phil. 3:14). But for the burden of our actual sins, forgiven but perhaps still bearing the debt of undischarged penance, our weakness and instability in the face of temptation, not despair but holy sorrow is the medicine for the soul. The great spiritual writers seem inhumane when they counsel against light-mindedness and denounce hilarity as being inappropriate to the pilgrim, but life is in the end no laughing matter. To have holy sorrow is to begin to hate that to which we have been attracted. This is the happy sorrow that is blessed. God, we are promised, will wipe away every tear from our eyes (Rev. 21:4), but to enjoy that supernatural friendship there first must be tears of sorrow.

The word translated meek (*praus*) in the third Beatitude is equally well, or better, translated "gentle." Jesus will say, "Learn from me, for I am gentle and humble of heart, and you will find rest for your souls" (Matt. 29:11). And again Jesus quotes Isaiah: "Your king comes to you, gentle, seated upon an ass, and upon the foal of an ass" (Matt. 21:5, Is. 62:11). It is these, the meek, the gentle, who, contrary to the claims of power, will inherit the earth when it is God's earth again. The adjective used in Matthew 5 occurs only four times in the New Testament, but as the abstract noun "gentleness" Paul includes it among the fruits of the Spirit in Galatians 5:22. To be gentle is to refrain from using power rightly possessed to achieve a purpose that, while it may be just, reads out the moral requirement of the second commandment, love your neighbor as you love yourself, by imposing one's own just will without mercy.

Jesus assures his followers that it is not the grasping and aggressive but the gentle who will inherit the earth. The divine ground of Christian gentleness is the Lord's willingness to show us just so much of himself as we can bear, to enwrap his power in his humility. He did not cling to his divine nature in a way that prevented his display of that divine gentleness that is the unvarying companion of his majestic justice. The images of Jesus with the woman at the well, calling little children to himself, not condemning Peter and the twelve when they cannot watch for one hour, and washing his disciples' feet, have always engaged the Christian heart. Gentleness is the choice of reserve rather than rashness; in its most common form it is the gentleness of politeness, standing aside for another, not claiming the highest place, that will find fruit in the gentled civilization founded upon the Beatitudes. What inheriting the earth means is surely that these will inherit the new creation when Christ returns, but it may also mean that even now the gentle will know the good life of the soul as it belongs to this present age.

The fourth Beatitude describes the blessed soul as one who hungers and thirsts for righteousness. Jesus is not speaking of the desire to be righteous as the Pharisees on a certain day might have understood righteousness, but of the desire to be in communion with God, to be right-hearted in relation to the creator and redeemer, which disposition has itself a justifying power. This is the desire, itself a gift of grace, that shapes life in Christ. Whether the words belong to the playwright Robert Bolt or to a contemporary account, we are told that when Saint Thomas More mounted the scaffold he tipped the executioner with the words, "Do your work quickly for you send me to God," to which the cleric standing by replied, "Are you so certain Sir Thomas?" More replied, "He will not refuse one who is so blythe to come to him." Those who hunger for righteousness will be satisfied. This blessed hunger, this holy restlessness, made ever memorable by Augustine's words, "Our hearts are restless until they find their rest in Thee," is the gift to every person who will listen, for we will in the end achieve what we have desired. If our wills are formed to the neglect of God who is reality, the end may be darkness and waste. But for those who can grasp just one of the rays of glory that God has scattered across the world, who can long for something other than themselves, there is the promise of satisfaction, of the fullness of which the world offers a thousand intimations. This hunger for God leads through the trials of life to our sharing in the great banquet that every Eucharist foreshadows.

"Blessed are the merciful for they shall obtain mercy." The Christian call to mercy is founded in God's own mercy to us. That mercy, rooted in his justice, began in his will never to abandon his rebellious creation but rather to heal it through long ages. In the fullness of time his plan was perfected in the merciful gift of his Son who brought regenerating life with water and the spirit, giving those he called the white robe of justification at baptism (Tim. 1:4–7, Rev. 7:9). At the sixteenth-century Council of Trent when, Luther's advocacy of justification by faith alone having raised the issue, the question arose as to whether, having been made righteous once and perfectly through the gift of baptism, the wayfarer at life's end, having marred the robe of baptismal purity, required and would be offered a second justification by the merits of Christ's passion, the conciliar conclusion was in the negative. Christians are assured that, while called to be perfect, "If we say we have not sinned we deceive ourselves and the truth is not in us. If we confess our sins he is faithful and just and will forgive our sins and cleanse us from all unrighteousness (1 John 1:8–10). For our post-baptismal sinfulness the Church offers the repentant the mercy of true forgiveness, sealed by the power of the keys (Matt. 16:19, John 20:19–23). And for the still imperfect heart, marked with holy sorrow and freed of any note of rebellion, there is the merciful fire of purgatory, a state imagined differently in different ages but one whose end is certain: the fruition of life in the vision of God. This is the ultimate mercy promised by the fifth Beatitude: the merciful will obtain mercy. This greatest mercy, this perfecting love, rooted in God's own mercy, is the hope of Christians, shining down the days of every life and inspiring the gentling of the world by those who have been shown mercy. The apostle James writes, "So speak and so act as those who are to be judged under the law of liberty. For judgment is without mercy to one who has shown no mercy; yet mercy triumphs over judgement" (2:13). Since Paul wrote to the Corinthians of the necessary purification of the elect by fire, it has ever been the teaching of the Church that those faithful in whom love exists but which has not found full fruition will by the mercy of Christ be perfected in holiness after death (1 Cor. 3:10–15). But pure in heart we all then will be. This mercy is then the ever-present background for the making of the pure heart which has as its purpose and reward the renewal of that conversation which sin interrupted in the garden. This is the mercy of the love that will not let us go until we are fit for the innumerable company of angels, the spirits of just men made perfect, and God who is the judge of all (Heb. 12:22).

"Blessed are the pure in heart for they shall see God." The creation of the clean heart is ever the master-work of the apostolic mission, a work which while it begins with the proclamation of the Gospel is effective in the sacraments, with the elect, God's chosen, being perfected by those means to the holiness Jesus purchased with his death, when the Holy Spirit came with his regenerating gift of baptism and with forgiveness and communion that light the Christian way. The heart sees; it has an eye which, sin-clouded, cannot behold its maker. Purity of heart is a way, a *praxis*, that requires more than emptying the soul of evil like the demon-cleansed house in Matthew 12:43–45 that soon was to be filled with demons more vicious than the first. Purity of heart requires that the house of the soul be filled with the light of grace by the Holy Spirit; the human heart cannot be purified of sin without being filled by God, and then, the eye of the soul wiped clean, we will see.

Peacemakers, says the seventh Beatitude, are the sons of God, whose will is that peace of the kingdom that Augustine calls the order of tranquility. The rhetoric of the world has as its underlying purpose incitement to strife, to emulation, to aggression, to self-pity, grievance, and ultimately to perpetual warfare. God's sons, his children, bring peace into the world by bearing rather than striking, by walking the extra mile when one has already walked as far as justice requires, by giving more than is just. The presence of evil in the world is never mitigated until it is borne.

Those who enjoy the blessings of the first seven Beatitudes will be rewarded with citizenship in the kingdom of heaven, and inevitably will be persecuted by that mystery of evil called the world.[1] For the first three centuries, and even now, faithfulness might mean death. But presently in the West that persecution will not often be with rack and rope; it cannot be resisted with any violence, only with patience and finally suffering, but it will nonetheless be real. Christians living through modernity know what it is, if not to be reviled publicly, to be held in gentle contempt and on a certain day to be thought an enemy of all that is best by one's neighbor. Less obvious is the persecution inherent in the world that while it assaults the senses allures with the enchantment of technology's transcendence over

1 God loves the world he created with an everlasting and salvific love, but since the rebellion in the garden the world has been open to the soul-destroying enterprise of Satan and his angels. With his resurrection Jesus has overcome the world as it exists in opposition to God (John 16:33), but the devil and his angels roam, seeking whom they may destroy, until Christ returns (Rev. 12:12, 17).

nature, offering comforts that often seem to render restraint and discipline pointless. This new war with the world does not threaten with the executioner's fire and lions, but with the subtle luring of the soul into self-willed pusillanimity. Bearing the cross and denying oneself in a culture whose ignorance of the true dimensions of life makes such actions meaningless, may seem harder to bear than the inquisitor's fire. Yet living a life that bears witness when one can never know the world is listening makes Christians part of that great company who, beginning with the prophets whom Israel despised and persecuted, have been a light in this world, and who have ever been rewarded with the presence of God.

Jesus' description of the gift of blessedness to the soul is followed by the images of salt and light that establish the character of Christian witness in the world. Christ's followers are the salt of the world, and in that sense a gift to it, but if the salt has lost its savour, "what is there left to give taste to it?"[2] It is Christian witness that lifts up the world in hope. This witness is a light that is not to be put under a barrel but lifted high, set on a lampstand so that the Christian way can shine brightly before men who see its good works and glorify our Father in heaven.

Having described the blessedness that belongs to the kingdom, its consequences for believers, persecution, and the necessity of their witness in the world, Jesus turns to the question raised persistently by the charge of the Pharisees that he and his disciples have no regard for the Law of Moses. His disciples pluck grain from the fields on the Sabbath (Matt. 12:1); he eats with sinners, and without ritual purification (Matt. 15:1). So Jesus will assure the Pharisees of every age: "Think not that I have come to abolish the Law and the Prophets; I have come not to destroy the law but to fulfill them. For truly I say to you, till heaven and earth pass away, not an iota, not a dot will pass from the law until all is accomplished," until the holy ones who are the citizens of the kingdom are called and fulfilled. And then the warning and the promise to teachers: "Whoever relaxes one of the least of these commandments and teaches men to do so shall be called least in the kingdom, but who obeys them and teaches them shall be called great

2 This text (Matt. 5:13) may be read as referring either to the loss to the world of the savouring effects of belief or as a warning to Christians, beware lest you lose your savour.

in the kingdom." And the new standard: Unless your righteousness exceeds that of the scribes and Pharisees, those whose whole work is fulfilling the propositions of the law while leaving the heart in shadow, you will never enter the kingdom of heaven.

And how is this to be achieved? By entering perfectly into the love of the Lord through the door to that interior castle, the will. Hardly a new idea: "You shall love the Lord with all your heart, soul, and mind." But what Jesus does not reveal in this place is the fact that this new law will require a new heart which can only be formed by his Pentecostal gift his death will bring. Six times the phrase "You have heard it said" is repeated, to be followed by "But I tell you." What has been said by men of old is the Law of Moses. What Jesus teaches those listening is the new law of the heart that places moral weight not in good deeds, although these will follow, but in the renewed will. It is not what goes into a man that defiles him, the working of the world upon us is to be borne. What makes the man is that expression of the heart that forms our words and actions (Matt. 15:11). The renewal Christ commands surpasses the righteousness of the Pharisees for it will make men and women of a flawed and fallen world citizens fit for eternal life in the kingdom of the new heart.

The first contrast between what has been said and the new law teaches that the death and destruction that characterize life and history begin with contempt, anger, and insult, which can only be amended by the willingness to ask forgiveness, perhaps even when just grounds for anger are present. Be reconciled to your brother before you offer your sacrifice. Litigiousness and contentiousness unlamented lead to prison from which you will not escape until justice has been fully served (5:25–26). It is not enough to refrain from adultery; one must reject from the heart the desire for the pleasurable possession of one not yours but another's, for the settled desire is as good as the deed done (27). There is then the new law of language: abjure hyperbolic claims that presume a power you do not have. Jerusalem is not yours but is the city of the great king; you cannot make one hair of your head white or black (5:33–36). And do not take refuge in ambiguity; let your pledged word be sealed with a yes or no (37). This means that in the kingdom of the new heart the duty of the *rhetor* and the author, of every man as he speaks and writes, is to be ever obedient to the reality of the thing, whether it be an object or an idea or an emotion.

And as for revenge, give it up, putting it away with the willingness to bear something, to do more than the importunate or the would-be oppressor asks. And this turns upon the extension of the second great commandment to include not only the neighbor, but the neighbor who wishes you harm (5:43–48). "An eye for an eye and a tooth for a tooth" had been at the heart of justice as the Old Covenant commended it. It was a principle of Greek morality that revenge was the justifying motive of morality, but among Jesus' followers, something is to be borne.

Of the six contrasts through which Jesus teaches, the most shocking to his hearers was surely the abrogating of divorce, which had been allowed, as Jesus would tell his disciple in the nineteenth chapter of Matthew, because of the hardness of men's hearts, but which now was to be done away with in obedience to God's will as expressed in the primordial unity of man and woman in the Garden; "It was not so in the beginning" (19:8). This renewed vision of marriage would be developed by Saint Paul with the analogy of the relation of husband and wife to the indissoluble union between Christ and the Church (Eph 5:25). But in the context of Matthew 5, Jesus only teaches that, assuming the divine justice of the Edenic disposition to be true, putting a wife away inevitably sends her into another household and to another husband, if not into the street, and by doing so makes both her and the head of the household into which she may have been taken adulterers. Jesus' teaching on divorce would be put forward fully in chapter 19:3–12, where divorce would be seen as a violation of God's will that "the two shall become one" (5). The disciples answered for fallen mankind: "If it is this way between a man and woman, better not marry." This might have been said of the entire body of Jesus' teaching in the Sermon on the Mount. If it is this way; forego revenge, love your enemies, abjure contempt and insult, walk the second mile, achieve purity of heart, who can bear it? But the divine teaching of Matthew 5 does not consist of moral maxims addressed to the world but to citizens of the kingdom of the new hearts that Pentecost will bring.

These six recastings of the law in Matthew 5 offer the clear outlines of the new way of life that marks the kingdom. They are redolent of the nobility of the faith and presuppose the humility the giver of the new law displayed on the night he was betrayed (John 13:1–17). Jesus' sermon on the mountainside was the foundation, laying down the principles of the way that would blossom from his words after his sacrifice made the new heart a possibility and a reality through the gift of the indwelling Advocate and Comforter at Pentecost. "I tell you the truth: it is to your advantage that I go away; the Counselor will not come to you, but if I go, I will send him to you" (John 16:7). The Spirit comes with power to confirm memory and to lead into all truth, to comfort, to convict, and to convert, and to give the peace the world cannot give, and finally, our work done, to bring us to himself. The Holy Spirit redefines the meaning of life and of history. Sin is now not simply a violation of the law but failure to believe Christ's words and to accept the gifts that make for holiness. Righteousness is rightness of the heart formed by faith and by participation in Christ through his sacramental gifts so as to become a new creature.

Mankind is made for the holiness that pleases God, enabling the sons of Adam at last to enter the conversation that was forestalled when our first parents chose the serpent's way. The entire Pentecostal faith, with its promise of forgiveness and the reward of communion introduced the waiting world to the great adventure that gave every man the possibility of becoming a new creature. Thus it would be that when Christians began to write they would turn to this text, to Matthew 5 and 6, to discover the foundations of the kingdom of the new heart. Other Matthean texts would be cited by writers of the post-apostolic age, the apocalypse of chapters twenty-four and twenty-five would find a permanent place in Christian faith, and the Gospel parables have never ceased to form Christian conscience and imagination: the wicked servant who, having been mercifully forgiven his debt, grasps his fellow servant by the throat demanding payment of the small debt owed him (18:20–35); the householder who gave those who had labored little as much as those who had labored long because it was his to be gracious as he chose (20:1–16); the king who gave a wedding feast to which many refused to come, and one who did was cast out as not being properly attired (22:1–14); and the parable of the talents. These would always engage and teach, but it was the words of chapters 5 and 6 that rippled out from a mountainside in Galilee to make a new world.

The teaching of the new way issued in a new piety, with prayer, almsgiving, and sacrifice; things not to be done in order to be seen by men or to earn their approval, but privately and without calculation (6:1–15). Jesus' followers do not need to storm heaven with many words, for they do not like the prophets of Baal need to arouse God with their shouts. Christian prayer is made in the knowledge that Our Father in heaven knows what we and every other creature needs this day, for the new heart beats within its living relationship to the ever-providential God who made it. The first petition of the great prayer recognizes with praise that God's name, that is his being, is holy, asking that his will, reigning gloriously in heaven, may soon be perfected in the Church and in the world. The words "Give us this day our daily bread" have been variously understood because the word for "daily" may be understood to mean "supersubstantial" rather than daily in the ordinary sense, so that the prayer for daily bread refers as well to Eucharistic bread. There follows the petition that our debts or transgressions may be forgiven as we forgive others, a reference to both the fifth Beatitude above and to 6:14–15 below. "If you forgive men their trespasses, your heavenly father also will forgive you."

Always considered the first Gospel, Matthew, with the Beatitudes and Jesus' perfecting of the law, "You have heard it said of old, but I tell you," laid the foundation for the life of the new heart that his sacrifice would bring to the world, accomplishing in the elect the perfect virtue that the philosophers and Pharisees had foreseen but which the fallen could never accomplish apart from the cross of Christ and the regenerating Pentecostal gift he bought. When Jesus sat down on a hillside in Galilee to teach, his words made a new world.

# Six
## *That You May Believe: The Gospel of the Beloved Disciple*

> Filled with revelation he poured forth the Heaven-Sent prologue.
>
> Jerome, *Commentary on Matthew*

> Blessed are those who have not seen and yet believe.
>
> John 20:29

It is arguable that after the Sermon on the Mount the text that has most influenced the making of the Christian mind is the Gospel of John, with its heaven-sent prologue, its dramatic gift of Christ's body and blood (6:35–59), and its promise of the coming of the Counselor, the Holy Spirit (15:5–15). The Gospel of John is not, like Luke, an attempt to write an "orderly account" (1:3), but presents signs culminating in the Passion Narrative, itself about half the book, chapters 13 through 20. The authorial voice, occasionally speaking in the first person (1:14,16, 19:35, 21:24), John from the title given the Gospel, writes relying upon the historical memories of a group of disciples—Andrew, Phillip, Nathanael and Thomas—whom Synoptic tradition neglects.

John, the author, was a writer of great literary ability and profound theological insight; his life changed when he beheld Jesus in glory (1:14), able to express ideas in simple Greek using a limited vocabulary. The linguistic similarities among the Gospel and the three Johannine Epistles are of sufficient density to support the theory that the four are in some way the work of one author, and to give John the title Presbyter from the address of the second and third Epistles. Central to the Gospel's claim to knowledge of the incarnate Jesus is the testimony of the Beloved Disciple who stood by the cross with Jesus' mother, and who saw water and blood flow from the side of the Messiah (19:26–27, 35).

If one begins with Matthew and reads through the Synoptics, the Gospel of John takes the reader by surprise because it is unlike the other three, Matthew, Mark, and Luke, the texts of which the Johannine author would seem not to have known. The Johannine sources cannot have known a collection of Matthew-related sayings or the Sermon on the Mount or the parables of Luke 15–19 and yet have failed to display the direct influence of any of these. The Gospel of John does not recount the temptation in the wilderness, nor does it know the Sermon on the Mount with its Beatitudes. While it provides in Jesus' discourse following the feeding of the multitude the most dramatic testimony that the Eucharist is Christ's body and blood (6:35–59), it omits the institution narrative, Jesus' words, "This is my body, this is my blood," that were received tradition when Paul wrote First Corinthians in the 50s, and which are common to Matthew, Mark, and Luke (1 Cor. 11:3–26, Matt. 26:26, Mark 14:22, Luke 22:19).

Luke, for all its spiritual power, might have been written in the author's study, a work of inspired but calm historical reflection. The Gospel of John is alight with the presence of the Holy Spirit. The Synoptics write a story which is patterned to time; John was written from a standpoint within the experience of Pentecost, looking back upon the ministries of John the Baptist and Jesus. The Johannine Gospel had been written "in the Spirit," for its author had been subject to a divine call no less compelling than Paul's; he too had seen the glory of the Word Incarnate: "We beheld his glory, the glory as of the only begotten son of the Father" (John 1:14, 1 John 1:1–2). The Church has always believed that the Gospel of John was composed under the immediate presence of the Spirit, the Paraclete, the Advocate or Counselor, whose coming the Gospel promises. From what may be the earliest account in the Muratorian Canon, before 200, to Jerome in the fourth century there had persisted the tradition that the Gospel was composed at the insistence of many after fasting and prayer, when John, filled with revelation, poured forth that heaven-sent prologue. The authority of these sources may be contested, but such a process is plausibly implied by the Gospel itself.

The Gospel of Christ burst into history in two ways: the dramatic testimony of the Holy Spirit at Pentecost was the great public event, witnessed by those from every part of the empire (Acts 1:9–11), that made confident apostles of what had been an uncertain group of disciples; but this confidence presupposed the appearance of Jesus, living after death, to those who would be his witnesses. Saint Paul gives a list that was current in the Church: Cephas (Peter), the twelve, five hundred brethren at once, James, all the apostles, and finally Christ's appearance to Paul (1 Cor. 15:6, Gal. 1:15–15, Acts 9:4–5), who saw the Lord perhaps years after Pentecost. Paul's list is not precise, and he may not have been the last in time to see the risen Christ.[1] But it can be said with certainty that, whenever it occurred, the author of John and the three Johannine Epistles had also seen the Lord in glory, and that this encounter inspired his witness (1John 1:1–2; John 1:1–14), just as the vision and voice on the Damascus road made Paul an apostle.

In the Gospel of John, the fruit of Christ's passion is the gift of the Counselor, the Paraclete, this last being a near transliteration of the Greek describing one called to stand by the accused in a court of justice. Jesus must go away, he must make the great sacrifice, so that sins may be forgiven but consummately so that the Holy Spirit may come upon his disciples. The Counselor touches the heart of the world with the gift of repentance: "If I do not go away the Counselor will not come to you go, but if I go I will send him to you. And when he comes he will convince the world of sin and of righteousness" (16:8–11) The Counselor establishes the disciples, and hence the apostolic mission, in truth: "The Counselor, the Holy Spirit whom the Father will send in my name, he will teach you all things and bring to your remembrance all that I have said to you" (14:26). The Counselor unfolds the meaning of history: "When the Spirit of truth comes, he will guide you into all truth; for he will not speak on his own authority, but what he hears he will speak, and he will declare to you things that are to come. All that the Father has is mine, therefore I said that he will take what is mine and declare it to you" (13–15). The Johannine text reflects a

1 Paul's recitation is formulaic, part of the tradition he had received; Paul knew at first hand that Peter, and James and John, sons of Zebedee, were among the twelve (Gal. 2:9).

confidence born of the realization of Jesus' promise that the Paraclete had come; that promise has been fulfilled. John remembers that when Jesus was risen and glorified, his first action was to breathe on the disciples giving them power to forgive sins, "Receive the Holy Spirit," the power that would be the apostolic lifeblood of the Church as it moved through time (20:19–23).

The great prologue of John 1:1–18 is the first of five sections or movements in a carefully conceived schema that includes, second, the recognition of Jesus by John the Baptist and the call of Johannine disciples. Then follows, third, the Book of Signs in 2:1–11:44, the Passion Narrative of 11:45–20:30, including the resurrection accounts, and finally the appendix of chapter 21. The Fathers, Clement and Jerome, called the opening verses "the heaven-sent prologue" and Clement described John as a "spiritual" Gospel; it was instrumental in the conversion of Saint Augustine, who wrote that he had heard of the Word but that the Word became flesh he had never heard.[2]

The subject of these first eighteen verses of the Gospel is a theological cosmology, philosophic in its underpinnings, inspired in its implications, developed around the Word who was with God and who was God and who became flesh. To this is attached a natural theology or anthropology which asserts that the Word is "the true light than lightens every man" (1:9). The reach of the Logos, the eternal reason, is such that the Word is God who with supernatural condescension becomes flesh or incarnate is at the same time the Word that is the light that causes and informs conscience and intellect, lightening every man coming into the world.

Justin Martyr had the theology of the Johannine prologue, if not the text, in mind when he wrote: "Whatever has been uttered aright by any men in any place belongs to us Christians." But there was this distinction: "The seed and imitation of a thing, given according to man's capacity is one thing; far different is the thing itself, the sharing of which and its representation is given according to grace."[3] In a few words John's Gospel

2 Augustine, *Confessions* 7.19; Thomas Shenk, trans., *St. Jerome Commentary on St. Matthew* (Washington. D. C.: Catholic University Press, 2008), 54; Clement, quoted in *Church History* 6.14.7.

3 Justin, *Second Apology* 13 (Bettenson, 5).

proclaimed the supernatural origin of the Word who is with God and who is God, while at the same time precluding forever the possibility that Christianity might become a cult by positing the participation of every man coming into the world in the eternal reason, creating a commonality that, however attenuated, however obscured by sin, unites the human family. In its highest term the intelligible world is held together, as Paul writes in Colossians 1:16, by a supernatural act of divine condescension causing whatever exists to subsist in the Word. The Word became flesh and dwelt among us and by natural or created participation every man shares in the light that is also the Eternal Word. He is the light that lightens every man coming into the world (John 11:9).

The origin of this image of God, majestic and condescending, who, even as he gives form to every creature enters his own creation in fulfillment of his indefeasible will that humankind should at last know him, is rich and complex. It surely owes much to the Old Testament concept of the *dabar Yahweh*, the word of God that never returns empty but always accomplishes God's purpose, the word spoken into the world thereby causing its existence and determining its course (Isa. 55:11). And this in turn recalls the Wisdom of God, that "breath of the power of God . . . a pure emanation of the glory of the Almighty . . . a spotless mirror of the working of God . . . [who] while remaining in herself renews all things . . . passes into holy souls and makes them friends of God, reaches mightily from one end of the earth to the other, [and] orders all things well" (Wis. 7:25–8:1). Scholars will find suggestive parallels to John's prologue in the Hermetic literature of Egypt, Philo of Alexandria, Rabbinic Judaism, and in Gnosticism.[4] It was a great principle of Stoicism that nature is permeated by *logos;* John's prologue focuses and perfects the theology of the logos that is scattered cross the intellectual landscape of the first century. Saint Paul wrote in Colossians: "He is the image of the invisible God, the first-born of all creatures, for in him all things were created, in heaven and on earth. . . . He is before all things and in him all things hold together" (1:15–17). The author of Hebrews wrote that in these last days God had spoken to us by a son, "whom he appointed heir of all things, through

4 See the exhaustive survey of possible sources in C. H. Dodd, *The Interpretation of the Fourth Gospel* (Cambridge: Cambridge University Press, 1958), 10–132.

whom also he created the world. He reflects the glory of God and bears the very stamp of his nature, upholding the universe by his word of power" (1:2–3). Nor should the great figure of Christ the Logos from Revelation 19:11–16, there presented in the image of Christ the knight leading the armies of heaven, be forgotten.

The Johannine prologue intersperses world-making theological assertions with discrete historical claims. Verses 6–7, with verse 15, locate John the forerunner, who was not the light but came to bear witness to the light, and in whose company the first-called disciple Andrew is to be found as the, admittedly sketchy, narrative opens (1:35–40). Verses 10–11 rehearse the rejection of the light by the Jews. The inspired writer proclaims the truth upon which the faith rests: the Word was in the beginning with God, that the Word was not an emanation or a manifestation but was God, all things were made through him; without him was not anything made that was made, in him was life, and the life that was in him is the light that shines in the human heart, and this light shines in the darkness of this world, but the darkness has not overcome it.

Verses 10–15 of the prologue summarize the revealed meaning of Jesus' incarnate life. He was in the world, and the great fact is that the world although occupied territory was not, as Valentinus or Marcion might claim, the work of a demiurge or another God, but was his own. The man who walked the streets of Jerusalem and the roads of Galilee was at the same time the Creator, upholding the world by the word of his power. He came to his own; to Israel. The Son of Man is sent to the lost sheep of the house of Israel (Matt. 10:6). But they did not receive him. This is a persistent theme of this Gospel, whose author looks back from a standpoint in a Hellenized world on Jesus' death in Judea, the rejection of the Messiah by those to whom he was sent. But some did receive him, and to these he gave the power to become the sons of God, that is to those who believe in his name, those believers being those for whom the Gospel was written, it being the particular purpose of John that those who have not seen might believe. These are they who are or who will be born again, of water and the spirit (3:5); born not of blood, their sonship is not of natural inheritance as was the case in Judaism, nor of the will of the flesh, that is of human desire, nor of human will, but of God, born anew of a supernatural gift of grace.

The prologue concludes with the recapitulation of the master theme:

"The Word became flesh and dwelt among us." And then the author's claim: "We saw his glory, the glory that belongs to the only Son of the Father, full of grace and truth. And of His fullness we have all received grace upon grace. The law was given through Moses; grace and truth came through Jesus Christ." The meaning of history and fulfillment of creation is not an experience or a principle but a person, this divine-human person through whom all things were made or, Paul says, in whom all things were created in heaven and on earth (Col. 1:16). So captivating was the Johannine Prologue that in the West it was read at the conclusion of every celebration of the Eucharist for eight centuries.

Following upon the prologue, the great curtain-raiser to this five-part drama, in 1:19–28, Jesus is identified by John as the Messiah. John is baptizing at Bethany beyond Jordan, not in the village but at a nearby stream in the wilderness country. John represents the prophetic tradition, which bears and expresses the promise of the coming of the day of God, found in Isaiah, Jeremiah, Joel, and Ezekiel. It is the promise of the Messianic King and the Messianic Kingdom, of the New Covenant through which the Holy Spirit will be poured out on all flesh. John the Baptist knows that one is coming who will baptize with the Holy Spirit, who is the spirit of the prophets and of prophecy, and he knows that this will fulfill the promise of Jeremiah 31:31: "I will make a new covenant with the house of Israel and the house of Judah. . . . I will put my law within them and I will write it upon their hearts"; and of Joel 2:28: "I will pour out my spirit on all flesh, and your sons and daughters shall prophesy." The prophetic tradition which John the Baptist represents is not the Pharisaic tradition of righteousness under the law, not the accommodationist tradition of the Sadducees, not the revolutionary project of the Zealots, but is the living tradition of Israel, the prophetic root from which the Kingdom of Heaven will grow. John the Baptist epitomizes that prophetic tradition, the prophets being in the Hebrew Scriptures those, almost alone, to whom the Spirit of God is given without measure.[5] The prophet John came dressed in rough camel's hair, eating locusts and wild honey, like the Rechabites and like the Essenes, abjuring the temple-centered city in favor of the wilderness, which,

5 There were exceptions; Bezalel was filled with the Spirit of God to enable his building the tabernacle (Exod. 31:1) as sometimes were anointed kings.

from the Exodus to the divine provision for the Blessed Virgin (Rev. 12:6) to Paul's sojourn in Arabia, is where God may be found.

That Jesus is the Son of God has been made known to John the forerunner by the voice of the Holy Spirit and the descent of the dove: "I saw the Spirit descend as a dove from heaven, and it remained on him. I myself did not know him; but he who sent me to baptize with water said to me, 'He on whom you see the Holy Spirit descend and remain, this is he who baptizes with the Holy Spirit.' And I have seen and have borne witness that this is the Son of God" (1:31–34).[6] This text points forward to 3:5. Nicodemus must be baptized with water and the Spirit, within the Johannine narrative an ahistorical reference because the baptism that regenerates awaited Pentecost. But this is the promise of Jesus' dramatic proclamation on the last day of the Feast of the Tabernacles: "If any one thirst, let him come to me and drink. He who believes in me as the scripture has said, 'Out of his heart shall flow rivers of living water.' Now this he said about the Spirit, which those who believed in him were to receive, for as yet the Spirit had not been given because Jesus was not yet glorified" (7:37–39).[7]

Now confident that Jesus is the promised Messiah, John next makes his revealed knowledge of who Jesus is public by identifying Jesus for two of his own disciples, Andrew and one other, unnamed, as the Lamb of God, a title that points back toward the Passover and forward toward the cross and the Eucharistic Sacrifice, and which is fixed in Christian imagination by the image of the Lamb standing as though slain at the heart of the Blessed Trinity, surrounded by the rainbow who is the One, with the sevenfold Spirit proceeding, in Revelation 5:6–8.

Andrew and another of John's disciples will follow Jesus to the place where he is staying. In that late afternoon in Bethany Andrew came to believe; he found his brother Simon and brought him to Jesus with the words, "We have found the Messiah." It is now that Jesus names Peter the rock (1:42). Andrew will keep "finding" Jesus for Peter throughout the Gospel

6 In the Hellenistic world the title Son of God has extensive connotations; emperors are sometimes sons of god. The Jews of Jerusalem understood that the title meant more as in John 19:7.

7 Ignatius, *Rom.* 7.2: "the water living and speaking within me saying, Come to the Father."

in the sense that it will be Andrew who enables Peter's ministry and Andrew, as the Beloved Disciple, who stands as faithful and perceptive, exemplary of the humility that must mark Jesus' followers, in contrast with Peter's blindness and obtuseness. Jesus then went to Galilee, presumably to Bethsaida, where he found and called Philip and then Nathanael. The Johannine author displays a marked geographical interest. He will not let us forget that the native place of the four disciples who have significant roles in the narrative is Galilee. The reader is told twice that Philip was from Bethsaida (1:44, 12:21), the native place of Andrew and Peter (1:44), the town on the east bank of the Jordan at the northern boundary of Galilee with Gentile territory. Nathanael is also a Galilean, from Cana, which the text assures us was in Galilee (12:21).

These disciples are not Judeans or "the Jews" whom the Gospel writer remembers as not only foreigners but as the temple establishment who crucified the Messiah.[8] In John Galilee is always Jesus' home. At the feast of Tabernacles in Jerusalem, his Galilean loyalty was charged against the popular claim that he might the Messiah (7:41), for although the prophetic tradition determined that the King of Israel be born in Bethlehem in Judea (Mic. 5:2), Jesus was reared in Nazareth and Galilee was his adopted place. Matthew remembered that Jesus had assured his disciples: "After I am raised up, I will go before you to Galilee" (28:10), and in John Jesus meets the disciples at the Sea of Tiberias, the Sea of Galilee (21:1). This pointed interest in Galileans, Andrew, Philip, and Nathanael, who have little or no part in the Synoptic narrative, establishes the local and particular character of the Gospel of John, which while it unmistakably tells the same story that the Synoptics tell, displays no direct influence of the Synoptic text. Andrew and Philip are Greek names.

The *dramatis personae* introduced and located, there then follows the third great movement in the story, the narrative of Jesus' ministry in chapters 2–11, then the Passion Narrative of John 12–20, and the afterword or appendix of chapter 21. Almost half the Johannine text is given to the Passion Narrative, the trial, death, resurrection of the Lord, with its great discourses of chapters 13–17. Overlaying this five-movement structure is a

8 In the United States before 1800 the citizens of other, often nearby, counties were sometimes called foreigners.

pattern of *kairoi,* times of dramatic significance, that marks a movement toward the sacrifice of the cross that is determined by the coming of "the hour." At the wedding feast at Cana Jesus tells his mother, "My hour has not yet come" (2:4). The hour is extensively the manifestation of Jesus as the Son of God and King of Israel; it is also and more specifically the hour of the sacrifice of the Lamb of God, the decisive moment at which the purpose for which Jesus came into the world is accomplished, marked with his cry from the cross, "It is finished" (19:29). Jesus also looks forward to the consequences of his sacrifice. The hour is coming when God will be worshiped neither at Mount Gerizim, the shrine of the Samaritans, nor Jerusalem but in spirit and in truth (4:21, 23). "Truly, truly I say to you the hour is coming, and now is, when the dead will hear the voice of the Son of God and those who hear will live" (5:25). "The hour is coming when all who are in the tombs will hear his voice and come forth" (5:28). "No one laid hands on him because his hour had not yet come" (8:20). But as the Passover draws nearer Jesus will say, "The hour is come that the Son of Man should be glorified" (12:23). "Shall I say, 'Father save me from this hour?' For this purpose I have come to this hour" (12:23–27). Jesus' death will be the defeat of Satan and the liberating of the cosmos from his power: "Now is the judgment of the world, now shall the prince of this world be cast out" (12:31, Rev. 12:8, 12, Luke 10:18). "I will not now speak many things with you for the prince of this world is coming and he has no part in me" (14:30). This Johannine sense of crisis reflects the New Testament conviction that the advent of Jesus marks a time of decisive cosmic import in God's plan for the salvation of mankind.

With chapter 2 the Book of Signs begins. These the Gospel's author describes as a selection from the things Jesus did, which "were every one of them to be written, I suppose that the world could not contain the books that would be written" (21:25). The Gospel of John then recounts seven signs: the miracle at Cana (2:1–11); the conversion of the Samaritan woman through Jesus' gift of prophecy (4:1–30); the healing of the lame man at the pool by the Sheep Gate on the Sabbath (5:2–18); the feeding of the multitude (6:1–14); the encounter with the woman taken in adultery (8:1–11); the healing of the man born blind (9:6–41); and the raising of Lazarus (11:1–45).

Each of the signs exemplifies Jesus' power over nature because nature is his; "all things were made through him and without him was not anything made that was made." Often Jesus' signs overcome some evil or imperfection, directing nature toward the fulfillment that belongs to the future kingdom, making present in time the first-fruits of that fulfillment. The elevation of the water into wine does not overcome any evil, but it supplies a homely deficiency with an abundance that is a sign of the kingdom. There is no necessity that the guests be supplied with fine wine beyond the providence of the householder, whose embarrassment Jesus forestalls, but Christ effects not only those signs that signal the defeat of evil, the overcoming of sin through forgiveness, the healing of diseased limbs and blind eyes, hunger, and death, but his kingdom brings joy of which a sufficiency of good wine is the apt image. And beneath the Cana image is always the foretaste of a natural order that will be raised to the glory of the supernatural.

The complex image of Jesus' encounter with of the woman at the well (4:1–30) displays the universality of Jesus' mission, to Samaritans as well as Jews, revealing the nature of the worship that is coming, "in spirit and in truth," but also establishes Jesus' place as a prophet and makes his claim to be the source of "water welling up to eternal life." When the woman says, "I know the messiah is coming," Jesus replies "I am he." This gift of life, more than healing or feeding, is the great sign.

Jesus' signs are often related to and often introduce a specific teaching, The feeding of the multitude opens upon the necessity for that great supernatural feeding, eating the flesh and drinking the blood of Jesus if one would have life (6:25–59). The healing of the man born blind points toward the recognition that evil, which is not the result of his sins, or of his parents' sins, is permitted in a fallen world so that God's glory may be revealed (9:1–5). And then the dramatic raising of Lazarus from the dead prophesies Jesus' role as the Lord of life.

Jesus' summary mission is not merely to heal, not only to supply the grace of life, but to defeat death and to bring to fruition God's plan, frustrated in Eden, that his creatures should have life in his presence. Jesus might have offered Mary of Bethany comfort, building upon her recitation of the common teaching that the dead would rise on the Day of God. But his command that Lazarus come forth establishes the truth that Jesus is himself "the resurrection and the life" (11:25). In these signs there is a rough progression, moving from Our Lord's gift of abundance and pleasure at the wedding feast and plenty at the feeding of the multitude toward the ultimate gift of life eternal which is given to those born again of water and the Spirit (3:5) and fed by his body and blood (6:51–53). These signs mark out the development of the Johannine narrative which ends with 12:20–22, the appearance of the Greeks who wish to see Jesus. These Gentiles apply to Philip, who brings them to Andrew, who takes them to Jesus, an order reflecting the Johannine hierarchy.

Apart from the signs Jesus does, there are also teachings that do not seem to be directly related to any sign, as for example, famously, the proclamation that God loves the world so much that he sent his son, not to condemn the world but to save it (3:16). This list would include the teaching that while the Son does not claim equality with the Father they are one (14:11, Phil. 2:8). The Father is always with the Son and the Son with the Father (8:28–30): "He who sent me is with me; I always do what is pleasing to him." "I and my Father are one" (10:30). "I am not alone, the Father is with me" (16:22). "He who has seen me has seen the Father" (14:9). The Gospel's exposition of the relation between the Father and the Son and the Holy Spirit will provide proof texts for the revealed dogma of the Blessed Trinity as this is developed in the pre-Nicaean period (14:11, 25; 16:27, 32; 17:56). Echoing the Trinitarian pattern of the self-giving of Father and Son is the offering of life as the way to life. "No man takes it from me, I lay it down of my own accord" (10:18). "Unless a grain of wheat falls into the earth and dies, it remains alone, but if it dies it bears much fruit" (12:24).

To John belongs the persistent contrast between those whom the Father has called into life in Christ and "the world." Jesus is the way to the Father, the only way (14:6). In the figure of the sheepfold there is one shepherd, and to attempt to enter through another gate is to play the thief. When the Son of Man is glorified, when the great sacrifice is made, the prince of this world is by that action, which undoes the rebellion and restores mankind to the friendship of God, judged (John 16:11). Jesus will judge the world. "The Father judges no one, but has given all judgment to the Son, that all may honor the Son even as they honor the Father" (5:22). "As the Father has life in himself, he has granted the Son also to have life in himself and has given him authority to execute judgment" (5:26–27). Among these interlarded discursive passages the most memorable is perhaps the teaching of chapter 6 that fixed in the Church's memory the truth that to share in the Eucharist is to share in the person of Jesus and thus to have life in him.

The words "Now before the feast of the Passover, when Jesus knew that his time had come to depart out of this world" announce the Passion Narrative (13:1). It was during the Passover supper that he said the words that his disciples would remember and imitate forever, but John does not record these words, choosing instead to make Jesus' washing the disciples' feet the centerpiece of his account. "Knowing that he had come from God and was going to God," he rose from supper, laid aside his garments, and began to wash his disciples' feet. Jesus' dramatically simple action of kneeling before his disciples to wash their feet illustrates for his disciples who he is and who they must be. It is God who in Jesus condescends in order to lift up. "Taking the form of a servant . . . he humbled himself and became obedient unto death" (Phil. 2:6). This is in stark contrast with the conventions of Roman society, which at its best, often with a note of nobility, is ever about honor and the assertion of the self, and with the temper of Judaism, whose finest adherents might on a certain day proclaim their righteousness on street corners.

This text is often interpreted, rightly, as being about service, or sharing in the necessities of others, but it is about much more. It is about the qualification of power by love as we touch the lives of other persons, the removal of the note of domination in even those relationships that justly require obedience. "You know that the rulers of the Gentiles lord it over them. It shall not be so among you; but whoever would be great among you would be your servant" (Matt. 20:25). "If I then, your Lord and teacher, have washed your feet, you ought also to wash one another's feet. I have given you an example" (13:15). The new commandment of love (13:34) is not a new commandment, for Israel had always been taught to love the Lord their God, but a commandment newly vivified by the indwelling Paraclete and linked by Jesus to the teaching that humility is the ordering root of love. The Second Commandment requires the magnificent subjectivity largely absent from the Hellenistic world; thinking of the other person as one's self. This moderation of one's own way, the denial of self on behalf of some higher good, ultimately God, perfected in the cross, will be the defining characteristic of Christian brotherhood and of a gentled, unafraid civilization that bears the marks of Christ. Jesus' washing of the disciples' feet is propaedeutic to his giving of himself, the hour toward which the Johannine narrative steadily moves.

The Gospel of John does not teach through parables; there is nothing of that engaging "once upon a time" narrative form that offers the reader the examples of the barn-builder, the prodigal son, or the guest who came unprepared. The Gospel of John presents Jesus to the reader through his deeds, the signs he offers to faith, and through unforgettable images such as the Good Shepherd (10:1–18), the vine and its branches that illustrate the living relation between Christ and those who live in him (15:1–11), and the grain of wheat that dying gives life (12:24–26). Often there are symphonic assertions of themes such as light that are interwoven throughout the text. Jesus says "I am the Light of the world" in 8:5, 9:12, and 12:46, and these refer back to the Prologue: "In him was life and the life was the light of men. The light shines in darkness" (1:2–3). Jesus is "the true light that lightens every man coming into the world" (9). Similarly, "life." The light was the life of men. He came that we might have life in his name (20:31). Those who hear the voice of the Son of God will live (5:26). "The bread I will give for the life of the world is my flesh" (6:5l).

Beneath the literary structure of the Fourth Gospel is the ever-challenging, ever-fascinating figure of the Beloved disciple, who is the indispensable witness to the reality of the incarnation. "He who has seen it has borne witness." He is the great witness to the humanity of Jesus, the one who could bear witness that blood and water flowed from Jesus' side as he hung on the cross (19:35), evidence essential to right belief at a time when the faith of John was challenged by those who denied that Jesus had come in the flesh (1 John 4:2–3). To him Jesus commits his mother from the cross, at the same time making Mary the mother of the Beloved Disciple and hence of every disciple, that is of the Church (21:20, 24). Although the word Church (*ekklēsia)* does not occur in John, the Gospel is as sure as Paul that there is a body of the chosen comprised of those whom the Father has called out of the world "that you should go and bear fruit and your fruit should abide" (15:16).

The writer of the Gospel considered his work done with chapter 20, but then the consternation caused by the death of the Beloved Disciple among congregations who believed that Christ had promised that their beloved witness he would live until the Parousia would occasion the writing of the last chapter of the Gospel (21:20–23). Throughout its text the Gospel persistently construes a contrast between the perceptiveness and faithfulness of the Beloved Disciple and the blindness and spiritual ineptitude of Peter, who always depends upon the disciple Jesus loved for his own knowledge of the Lord, while in his anonymous humility, reflective of Jesus' actions in the night in which he was betrayed, the Beloved Disciple makes Peter's role possible. For the text presents Peter as the Church would ever know him, as the one who professes that Jesus is the Holy One of God (6:9), and as the first witness to the resurrection (20:5–6), which is made possible by the humility of the Beloved Disciple, who stands aside so that Peter can be first to enter the empty tomb (20:4–6), imitating in his life the great example Jesus had given on the night he was betrayed.

This pattern is repeated throughout the Passion Narrative. Peter must learn the betrayer's name through the Beloved Disciple, who is closest to Jesus at the supper (13:22–24). The Beloved Disciple, who is known in high-priestly circles, gains access to Jesus' trial for Peter, who stands outside to betray the Lord three times (18:17, 25, 26–27). The Beloved Disciple stands by the cross with Jesus' mother while Peter is nowhere to be found (19:25–27), and on the morning of Jesus' resurrection reaches the empty tomb first but stops short to allow Peter his place as first witness (20:3–8). Here we are told that the Beloved Disciple believes, while the text is silent regarding Peter's faith. At the Sea of Tiberius it is the Beloved Disciple who must identify the Lord for Peter (21:7).

Andrew, Peter's brother, fulfills the role of the Beloved Disciple in John 1: 43, for it is Andrew who is first to believe, who finds his brother with the announcement, "We have found the Messiah," and who brings Peter to Jesus, so that from the beginning Peter's access to Jesus is mediated. Andrew, with his townsman Philip, then dominates the sketchy narrative John 1–12, only ostensibly to disappear from the Passion Narrative, where his role as the one who mediates Jesus to Peter is given to the Beloved Disciple, a title used in the Passion Narrative to soften the contrast which, had the name Andrew appeared where "Beloved Disciple" stands in the Passion Narrative, would have been a disqualifying departure from Synoptic tradition and a violation of the Beloved Disciple's characteristic humility.

The relation of Peter's consistent "firstness" in the Johannine tradition to the spiritual excellence of the Beloved Disciple is a question answered in chapter 21, an answer prompted by the death of the Beloved Disciple in the face of the mistaken belief that he would remain until the Lord's return

(John 21:22–23). The appendix begins with the appearance of the Lord to the disciples at the Sea of Tiberias, the Sea of Galilee, when Peter had said "I am going fishing." As day dawned the fishermen, having caught nothing during the night, saw Jesus standing on the beach; he advises them to cast their nets on the right side of the boat. The disciple whom Jesus loved must for one last time identify the Lord for the unseeing Peter (21:7), who then is able haul the net with its 153 fish, the number meaning completeness, ashore. Thus far the text of chapter 21 has established that Peter's apostolic competence is dependent as in John 1:43 on another, his brother Andrew, the disciple whom Jesus loved.

Then as Jesus and Peter walk away from the lake, Jesus thrice asks Peter, "Do you love me?" and commands three times that Peter shepherd the flock Jesus has left behind. This command, with the Johannine recognition that it was Peter who first acknowledged Jesus to be the Son of God (6:68–69), and with the careful testimony that Peter was the first witness to the resurrection, secured Peter's place in the Church.

In the final action in the Johannine story, Peter turns to see the disciple whom Jesus loved following them and asked, "What about this man?" Jesus replied, "If it is my will that he remain until I come, what is that to you?" Misunderstood by hopeful believers as the promise that the Beloved Disciple would not die before the Lord's return, the author was required to remind the Church that the Lord had not made such a promise but had said, "If I will that he remain until I come, what is that to you" (21:22). Andrew the Beloved Disciple has a place and an authority of his own.[9]

The Gospel then ends with the reminder that that it is the Beloved Disciple who bears witness to these things, who, although now departed, has written them, that is, stands responsible for their being written (21:24). To appreciate the substitution in the Passion Narrative of "Beloved Disciple"

9 Chapter 21 has as its purpose establishing the place of Peter as the great fisherman, capable, if he believes steadfastly, of hauling in the great catch of 153 fish, while at the same time securing the place of Andrew the Beloved Disciple as independent in the sense that his relation to Jesus is direct, unmediated by Peter, and to do this in a way that corrects the misunderstanding of Jesus' words to Peter while at the same time not derogating Peter's place as the first witness to Jesus' resurrection and the one who first received the gift of faith that Jesus was the Son of the Living God (Matt. 16:16–17).

for the name of Peter's brother Andrew one must consider that the insertion of any personal name would have located John's Gospel at the center of a disqualifying argument. So successful was the device that the identity of the disciple who stood by the cross is still, after nearly two thousand years, popularly conceived to be John the Son of Zebedee despite a scholarly consensus that would be at best reserved or even skeptical. Yet Andrew's place as the authenticating witness to the composition of the Gospel by John and his fellow bishops was remembered by the author of the Muratorian Canon, in which the work of John and his fellow bishops receives the spiritual approval of the Apostle Andrew.[10] The near-miraculous existence of this outlier Gospel illustrates the mystery of the spread of the Gospel during the century after Pentecost, with a unanimity born of the one heart Irenaeus mentions, but relying upon many different historical memories.

This reading of the historical referents of the text saves the appearances while offering insight into the existence of a Johannine circle that was not familiar to the Synoptic authors. In the words of C. H. Dodd, "Behind the Fourth Gospel lies an ancient tradition independent of the other Gospels, and meriting serious consideration as a contribution to our knowledge of the historical facts concerning Jesus."[11] This reading contravenes the theory of Irenaeus that the author was the sons of Zebedee, a figure in whom the Gospel has little interest, merely mentioning the sons of Zebedee, "the ones of Zebedee," in the climactic appearance of Jesus to the seven apostles whom the text recognizes as representative of the twelve.[12] After Irenaeus' successful defense of the Gospel of John against gnostic claimants, until critical scholarship emerged in the nineteenth century, it was broadly

10 "The same night it was revealed to Andrew one of the apostles that with the consent of all John should write down everything in his name (eadem nocte reuelatum Andrae ex apostolis ut recogniscentibus cunctis Johannis suo nomine cuncta discriberet). Muratorian Canon, Metzger, *Canon of the New Testament,* 306; Lietzmann, lines 15–17.

11 C. H. Dodd, *Historical Tradition in the Fourth Gospel* (Cambridge: Cambridge University Press, 1965), 423.

12 The Johannine seven are Andrew, Peter, Philip, Nathanael, Thomas, "the ones of Zebedee." Like "the twelve," which the Gospel recognizes *en passant* as in 6:70 and 12:24, the sons of Zebedee have little interest for the author. The Gospel also mentions Judas (not Iscariot) in 14:22.

assumed that John the son of Zebedee was the Beloved Disciple of John's Gospel.

The history of the Fourth Gospel, whose author provided such tantalizing hints, will ever fascinate, but from the time when John's Gospel entered the cosmopolitan culture of the Church in the third quarter of the second century, the book was rightly valued not for the light it might cast on the history of the apostolic mission, engaging as the "Johannine question" always is, but for its achievement of its great purpose: that the reader, even those who will in the future believe without seeing, will know that "Jesus is the Christ, the Son of God, and that believing this will have eternal life" (Jn. 20:25).

The history through which the Gospel of John came into existence can be important to us because it was obviously important to its author. The worst that can be said of those critics who find it difficult to see the importance of Andrew/the Beloved Disciple for the Fourth Gospel is surely not that they lack erudition or critical insight, which they have aplenty, but that the trees of criticism make it difficult to see the forest, a book with an inner historical logic of its own, untouched, or touched only lightly, by Synoptic tradition.

# Seven
## *Apocalypse: In Heaven an Open Door*

Write what you see, what is and what is to take place hereafter.
Revelation 1:19

The word apocalypse means "unveiling" and what is revealed to the prophet John is the pattern of time and history, giving meaning to every Christian life as providence accomplishes God's promise. The Romans could at various times and in various ways encourage virtue and offer rewards to those who exemplified prudence in politics and courage in war, but in the end history was cyclical, life after death was murky, and in the background was always the belief that the universal sovereignty or Rome was the best that could be hoped for. Christianity on the other hand promised nothing less than the defeat of death and the gift of eternal life in the presence of the Creator in a renewed creation.[1] The cosmos, which had a beginning, would have an end and its end was its meaning. The great prophets, Isaiah, Jeremiah. Ezekiel, Joel, and Daniel, inspired by the Spirit of God, saw that the fruition of history, and of life, lay beyond this present world.[2]

Apart from words spoken against the idolatry and callous avarice of their contemporaries, the dominant theme in Old Testament prophecy was the coming of the Day of God. This is the day, culmination of the last days, whose coming Jesus prophesied, and which as fulfilling the creation God

1 The canonical image of Christian hope is the mosaic in Santa Pudenziana at the foot of the Esqueline, sometimes dated as early as 397, depicting Christ reigning in the New Jerusalem flanked by Peter and Paul, surrounded by the eleven, the four great winged creatures hovering overhead.

2 Isa. 61:2, 63:4, Jer. 12:3, Joel 3:18, Zeph. 1:15, Zec. 9:16, Mal. 3:17, Matt. 5 7:22, 1 Thess. 5:4.

saw as good, forms the historical framework within which the promise of God is realized. On that Day God will judge the world, rewarding righteousness and punishing disobedience, rendering pellucid the ambiguities of life and history. In the great prophets the themes of just punishment upon a fallen and rebellious people and the glorious fulfillment of God's promise beyond this world's history are contrapuntal, as in Isaiah. The serpent who deceived in the beginning will be punished by the Lord's "hard, great, and strong sword"; he will "slay the dragon that is in the sea" (Isa. 27:1, Job 40–41). On that day the Lord "will lay waste the earth and make it desolate and he will twist its surface and scatter its inhabitants. . . . The earth lies polluted . . . for they have transgressed the laws and violated the statutes and broken the everlasting covenant" (24:1, 5). But beyond God's just wrath lies blessing. "On this mountain the Lord of hosts will make for all peoples a feast of fat things" (25:6); "In that day this song will be sung in the land of Judah, 'We have a strong city; he sets up salvation as walls and bulwarks'" (26:1); "The Lord of hosts will be a crown of glory and a diadem of to the remnant of his people" (28:5).

It is a commonplace of the history of religions that such apocalyptic hopes are borne of political failure and oppression, as when, perhaps in the age of Tiberius, the author of *IV Ezra* predicts a reign of peace after the impending destruction of the nation. But a deeper root of the prophetic vision was the sense of incompleteness, indeed futility, bred by the apparent failure of justice in a fallen world.[3] The just might suffer and the unjust flourish like the green bay tree (Ps 35:37). Ecclesiastes depicts a people tempted to a near-cynicism fed by the disappointment that in the end death seemed to reign. Job's great reflection that if death is indeed the end for man he is less fortunate than a stump, which when spring comes may blossom (14:7–10), intimates a new hope, as does the taunt addressed to God: If you send me down to Sheol, who will praise you? From such considerations grew the thought that while justice would not be done perfectly in this world, Lazarus' day would come.

3 IV Ezra, chapters 3–14 of 2 Esdras, probably belongs to the first century AD. See the *Fourth Book of Ezra. A New Translation and Introduction*. Edited by James H. Charles, *The Old Testament Pseudepigraphia* (London: Longman, Darton, Todd), 1983.

In the background was always Genesis. God had willed life for mankind, planting in the garden the tree of life, which meant that while after the great disobedience death would be the common lot of humankind, death was nonetheless unnatural, being as it was the enterprise of the Serpent and the consequence of his lie. In a sense the entire Biblical story can be seen as God's determination to overcome death with life after the catastrophe, moral and natural, that sin had brought. Thus Saint Paul: "Creation waits with eager longing for the revealing of the sons of God, for creation was subjected to futility, not of its own will but by the will of him who subjected it in hope, because the creation itself will be set free from its bondage to decay into the glorious liberty of the children of God" (Rom. 8:20–21). "As in Adam all die, so in Christ shall all be made alive . . . . The last enemy to be destroyed is death" (1 Cor. 15:22, 26). This was the promise of Isaiah, that the day would come when nature itself would be pacified, "the wolf dwelling with the lamb and the leopard lying down with the kid" (11:6), when there would be no more hurt and destruction in all God's holy mountain. For the earth shall be full of knowledge of the Lord as the waters cover the sea (11:9–10, Rev. 21:3–4).

But this is the end of the story, a consummation depicted so beautifully in the concluding chapters of the prophet John's vision (21–22). Throughout the long history of the world, and throughout the story of the Hebrew Scriptures, two ideas had moved together: the prophetic vision of the day of God when nature would be restored, when God would judge the world, when the Messianic King would reign; and the conviction that for those who believed in God's promise there would be life in this new creation. This was explicit in canonical Daniel: "And many of those who sleep in the dust of the earth shall awake, some to everlasting life and some to shame and everlasting contempt" (12:2). Belief in the resurrection was so firmly established that prayers for the dead were offered, as when the noble Judas Maccabaeus, after the battle with Gorgias King of Idumea, believing that the Jews who had fallen had suffered because of their idolatry, sent 2000 drachmas to the Temple to provide for a sin offering. "In doing this he acted very well and honorably, taking account of the resurrection. For if he were not expecting that those who had fallen would rise again, it would have been superfluous and foolish to pray for the dead" (2 Macc. 12:43–45). When Jesus was sorrowful because Lazarus had died, Martha said to

Jesus: "I know that he will rise again in the resurrection at the last day," voicing the conviction common among the Pharisees (John 11:23–24).

These convictions, belief in life for the just in the new age and the glorious restoration of nature, rooted as they were in prophecy, and bearing the authority of Jesus, were to be given expression by the sole canonical prophet of the New Testament. John of Patmos was not the only prophet; as the letters of Paul tell us there were many, and prophets and prophecy were everywhere in the Church of the first three centuries (1 Cor. 14:1), but John was an extraordinary charismatic itinerant, not unlike the prophets known to the roughly contemporary author of the *Didache*: revered, honored, welcomed, and troublesome in the sense that their authority lay outside the terrain of the emerging episcopate with its goal of regular order. John, however, was given a distinctive mission; not only was he to prophesy, he was to write.[4]

The prophet John's situation is not unlike that of Clement of Rome, his near contemporary, who apologizes because recent events, often bloody persecution, have made correspondence difficult. For John is a victim of state repression of belief in Jesus, imprisoned on Patmos as a miscreant threat to the good order of the empire. Then when John was in spirit-filled prayer on the Lord's Day, he heard a voice from heaven commanding him to write to the seven churches. His prophecies were intended for his brothers, those who like him knew suffering "on account of the word of God and the testimony of Jesus" (1:9). For John Rome is not the underground Church of Peter and Paul but the woman seated on the seven hills, surfeited on the blood of the saints: "The woman that you saw is the great city that has dominion over the kings of the earth" (17:19). Whether the prophet survived Patmos we cannot know. Tradition assigns his vision to the reign of Domitian (81–96); Papias of Hierapolis wrote a commentary on John's apocalypse before 120, and in the 150s Justin Martyr described the author as "one who lived among us."[5]

What the prophet John saw when he was imprisoned on the island of

4 Many, most, of the images in John's apocalypse can be traced to the Hebrew Scriptures. This would not justify the conclusion that his book was a literary anamnesis, for what John saw was revealed to him.

5 *Dialogue* 81 (*ANF* 1:240).

Patmos revealed the providential pattern of history, showing "things that are and things that must come hereafter" (1:19). Like all true prophets John wrote under the inspiration of the Holy Spirit, called to prophesy by the touch of an angel and given the singular iconic vision of Jesus, who appears in the midst of the seven golden candlesticks representing the seven churches, a towering figure with hair white as snow and eyes as flames of fire, feet of fine brass, a voice as of many waters, and a face shining like the sun, holding in his hands the seven stars which are the angels of the seven churches. (Every nation, every part of creation, every person has an angel; stars are angels.) When John is terrified at the vision, Jesus offers reassurance as he had to the older prophets, laying his hand on the prophet, saying, "Fear not, I am the first and the last, alive and was dead, living for ever and ever and I have the keys of death and hell" (1:12–19).

John's vision of Jesus on Patmos recalls the appearance of God "high and lifted up" to Isaiah in the Temple, which evokes the prophet's words, "Woe, I am lost, for I am a man of unclean lips." Thus Jeremiah: "Ah, Lord God, I do not know how to speak, for I am only a youth" (1:6), and the prophet's complaint that the Lord has deceived him, making him a laughingstock as he prophesied punishment and judgment among a people who hate the word of the Lord (20:7). And again the protest of Amos: "I am no prophet nor a prophet's son, but I am a herdsman . . . and the Lord took me" (7:14–15). So the prophet John, when he saw one like a Son of Man, a sharp two-edged sword issuing from his mouth, his face like the sun shining in full strength, "the first and last," alive for ever more, holding the keys of death and Hades, at this sight "fell at his feet as though dead." But Jesus laid his right hand on the prophet John saying, "Fear not, I am the first and the last, the living one. Now write what you see" (1:17, 19).

John's vision is not history, but it presupposes a knowledge of his time and place beginning with the situation of the seven churches he addressed. These churches were clustered in western Asia. Two were connected by the road that led across Asia from the headwaters of the Euphrates to Ephesus. Sardis was an important city on the great road perhaps sixty miles inland from Ephesus on the Aegean. Philadelphia was thirty miles to the southeast. Smyrna was further along the Aegean coast, perhaps fifty miles north from Ephesus, and Pergamum, the old capital of the Lydia which had been left by will of its last king to the Romans in BC 133, yet further north along the aegean shore. Laodicea was inland from Ephesus, on the Lycus River not far from Colossae. Thyatira, remembered as the home of one of Paul's first converts (Acts 16:14), was eighty miles northeast of Smyrna. If these churches defined the territory John traveled in his role as prophet, it was extensive.

For each of the seven churches there was a prophetic message, based upon John's familiarity, which synoptically display the difficulties these churches faced. There is praise, correction, and a promise "to him who conquers," when conquering meant standing firm against heresy and bearing persecution. The Ephesians are to be praised for their endurance and faith under assault, and for their hatred of heresy as represented by the Nicolaitans, whose works John also views not with pity or regret but with hatred. Nothing is known of the Nicolaitans beyond their condemnation by John in 2:15,16. They are almost certainly a local representative of the "spiritual" religion that will be called Gnosticism. The Ephesians have endured, but they have lost their first fervor. Each of the seven letters ends not with a threat, although threats are always present, but with a promise, in Ephesians: "To him who conquers I will grant to eat of the tree of life which is in the paradise of God." The reference is to Genesis; this is the prophet's first reference to the principle that God wills the restoration of the natural order to an Edenic and more-than-Edenic state, one of the themes that unites Genesis with the revelation given John (21:1–5).

For the church at Smyrna, the church within which Polycarp had been born about 69, John has praise. The world will consider the church at Smyrna impoverished but John calls them rich in their poverty. John knows that some will be imprisoned. His advice, like that of Tertullian a century later, is "Be faithful unto death and I will give you the crown of life " (2:10). And this is the promise: he who conquers, he who is faithful unto death, "shall not be hurt by the second death," the second death being the consignment of the unjust to everlasting punishment at the return of Jesus.

Pergamum was a Greek city-state exceeded in importance among the great Hellenistic cities only by Rome, Antioch, and Alexandria. John has a tourist's image of Rome, which he had probably never visited, as an imperial power seated on its seven hills (17:19), but he knows Pergamum as Satan's throne, and it is this vision of a great trading center of luxury and impurity that provides background for John's vision of the falling, demon-infested, city in Revelation 18. The city is the seat of Satan, the place where Satan dwells. The church in Pergamum itself experiences internal divisions, suffering attacks on its faith by not one but two heresies. The Nicolaitans have visited Pergamum as they had Ephesus. Also present was the sin of Balaam. In Numbers 22 it is Balaam who viciously causes Balak to sin, an event mentioned again in Jude 11. The charge is that one commissioned by the Lord, a prophet indeed, caused the weaker brethren to sin, here specifically by eating meat offered to idols and by fornication. Here we are plunged into the nascent antinomian charge to which Paul was subjected and to the mysterious silence of John's revelation about Paul's teaching. Famously, Paul disapproved the practice on at least two grounds—it was bad witness and it indirectly involved the Christian in pagan sacrifices; "are not those who eat the sacrifices partners in the altar?"(1 Cor. 10:18). But Paul was not rigorous in the matter of sharing in (leftover) food offered to idols, perhaps because of this reluctantly tolerant view, more probably because of his rhetoric of grace superseding law. By the time Second Peter was written, Paul, his letters admittedly not always easy to understand, was charged with encouraging loose living (2 Pet. 3:15–17). As Second Timothy, chronologically one of the last of the canonical New Testament letters, roughly contemporary with Second Peter, records in Paul's voice: "All who are in Asia have turned away from me" (1:15). So, if this was more than disappointment at unjust criticism, by the sixties or seventies Paul believed he had lost his influence in the territory the prophet John knew best, the Roman province Asia. His doctrine may have been considered dangerous among Christians of Jewish background such as James of Jerusalem (James 2:14–26; Rom. 3:12, 4:7) and the prophet John, suspect of encouraging the body of heresy that fifty years later would begin to be consolidated around Maricon of Pontus, a bishop's son who made a deviant religion by rejecting the Old Testament with its God of law and wrath in favor of a religion of grace.

John's advice to Pergamum is "Repent, repent of both these heresies." His warning: "If not, I will come to you soon and make war against you with the sword of my mouth." This is a reference to 19:11–17, Christ the warrior "from whose mouth issues a strong sword with which to smite the nations" (19:15). Christ's weapon against error and rebellion is the truth.

The threat of a visit was high in the apostolic arsenal, as in John: "If I come, I will remember his deeds . . . prating against us with malicious words" (3 John 10). And then the promise to the faithful. "To him who conquers I will give some of the hidden manna." This may be an allusion to the manna that was kept "before the Lord" in the Holy of Holies of the tabernacle. This manna was placed in a "golden pot" within the Ark of the Covenant, hidden from the people but visible to God (Exod. 16:33; Heb. 9:4). The white stone, with a name written on it, promised by Jesus to the faithful at Pergamum (Rev. 2:17), which none but the one who receives it may know, is a reference to the Hebrew conviction that to name was to possess and indirectly, as in Genesis 2:19, to cause to exist. Thus at baptism Christians were, and still are, given a new name. Here there is also a reference to the Church as a building whose chief cornerstone is Christ (Eph. 2:20), made up of living stones built into a spiritual house (I Pet. 2:4), an image that at mid-second century will be central to the *Shepherd of Hermas.*

Thyatira, famous from this single reference, John praises for "your love, your faith and service, and your patent endurance." But here too there is disorder, the toleration of a prophetess whom John calls Jezebel after the treacherous wife of King Ahab, who is part of the movement, evident at Pergamum, to encourage Christians to be content with eating food offered to idols and with impure lives. Jezebel is not an abstraction; the prophet John knows her, he has warned her. She sounds like a forerunner to the hyper-Pentecostal movement that will beset the churches in Asia from the days of the prophet John to Tertullian, and indeed into the fifth century when its temper informed the Dontanist schism. This was probably in part a movement against the laxity that already beset the Church, the loss of first fervor, the Laodicean temper (3:14–19), but also a movement in defense of the exercise of prophecy at a time when the persistence of prophets and prophecy was requiring increasingly stringent control. Yet it is easy to forget the part played by Christian prophets. Already in the *Didache*, and even earlier in First Corinthians 12, the office was subject to abuse, while its importance was always brought forward. Prophets were one of the three original Christian ministries: apostles, prophets, teachers. Paul wished every Christian to possess the prophetic gift (1 Cor. 14:1). The *Didache* reminds: The prophets are your high priests (13.3). Ignatius says, "The prophets also do we love because they also have announced the Gospel" (*Phld.* 5:2).

Here the protest was not against gender; the prophetess Anna had foretold the birth of Christ, and the prophetic daughters of the Apostle Philp at Hierapolis were famous, but against the immorality that always seems to break out among the directly inspired hyper-moral. How the great and holy Tertullian, famous for his rigorism, could defend Maximilla, the iconic Montanist prophetess, while other orthodox writers considered her a moral scourge, is one of the puzzles of the second century. This is surely not unrelated to the fact that direct communication with God in the lives of ordinary mortals is only fruitful when there is a prior and unshakeable commitment to humility, self-criticism, and obedience to authority. But here, with the Jezebel of Thyatira, we are near the headwaters of a stream that will include in a relatively benign way the *Devotio Moderna* of the fourteenth century and in a decidedly harmful way the nuns of Port Royal in the seventeenth. The question of prophecy threatened the unity of the Church. Defended by Irenaeus on the apostolic authority of Paul in First Corinthians, Pope Victor denied the prophetic gifts of Maximilla, and shortly thereafter Tertullian left the communion of the Catholic Church for the Montanists. In Thyatira there are those who follow the prophetess, perhaps intrigued by her recounting of what "some call the deep things of Satan," a knowledge that on its face suggests a certain trafficking with evil. There are also those who do not. To them John's advice is, "Hold fast what you have, until I come" (2:19). And this promise: "He who conquers and who keeps my works until the end, I will give him power over the nations." The voice is that of Christ in Matthew 19:28 and 25:31, promising to share his throne with those who have witnessed faithfully. And again, "As I have received power from my Father, I will give him the morning star." The morning star is Jesus, not to be confused with the light-bearer, Lucifer, the rebellious son of the morning.

Sardis is the all-too-frequent image of a church that seems prosperous and popular but which is in fact spiritually dead. John does not charge Sardis with heresy but with faithlessness and that lethargy of the soul that predicts death. The church at Sardis has forgotten. "Remember what you received and heard; keep that and repent. If you will not awake, I will come like a thief. And you will not know at what hour I will come upon you" (3:3, I Thess. 5:2, 4, 2 Pet. 3:10). Happily, there were still a few faithful in Sardis, "people who have not soiled their garments; and they shall walk with me in white, for they are worthy." The promise: "He who conquers shall be clad in white garments and I will not blot his name out of the book of life; I will confess his name before my Father and before his angels." The book of life, which is different from the book of history with its twelve seals, is the catalog of the elect (13:8, 17:8, 20:12, 15, 21:27, 22:19). The white garment is the robe of baptismal purity (4:4, 7:9, 13, 14:16, 19:8, 14), white because it is washed in the blood of the Lamb.

Philadelphia deserves the prophet's praise. "The words of the holy one, the true one who has the key of David, who opens and no one shall shut, who shuts and no one opens. I know your works. Behold I have set before you an open door, which no one is able to shut." But this blessed congregation faces one difficulty. It has been an object of opprobrium on the part of those who say they are Jews but are not. This sounds like a battle between Johannine Christians and a congregation of believers who are reluctant to give up Jewish practices. If this is the case, they are to be identified with the Nazoreans of the third century, who used only the Aramaic or Hebrew Matthew. This battle in Philadelphia is a microcosm of the tensions caused by the broad Jewish rejection of the messiahship of Jesus. There would be Jews who were happy to see the heretics go but there would be others, newly converted Christians, who were reluctant to make the break. When Ignatius wrote to Philadelphia thirty years later there was still a concern: "If anyone interprets Judaism to you do not listen to him; for it is better to hear Christianity from the circumcised (Jews) than Judaism from the uncircumcised ('Jewish' Christians). But both of them (Christians who have broken with the synagogue and those who are reluctant to do so), unless they speak of Jesus Christ, are to me tombstones and sepulchers." John is bitter against these Judaizers, the "synagogue of Satan." "I will make them come and bow down before and learn that I have loved you." And this promise: "Because you have kept my word of patient endurance (2:19–21), I will keep you from the hour of trial that is coming on the whole world. . . . He who conquers, I will make him a pillar in the temple of my God; never shall he go out of it, and I will write on hm the name of my God, and the name of the city of my God, the new Jerusalem which comes down from my God out of heaven."

Laodicea has earned a special place in English imagination by giving us the adjective "Laodicean," descriptive of the lukewarm Christian temper which professes with the lips but not with the heart, neither cold nor hot, saying "I need nothing." On the contrary, says the prophet John, although you do not know it you are pitiable, poor, blind, and naked. Therefore, "I counsel you to buy from me gold refined by fire" and white garments to clothe your shame, and salve to anoint your eyes that you may see. Then the image that will be immortalized by William Holman Hunt in his "Christ the Light of the World" (1904); Christ stands at the door and knocks: "If any man hears my voice and opens the door, I will come in to him and eat with him and he with me. He who conquers, I will grant him to sit with me on my throne, as I myself conquered and sat down with my Father on his throne."

"He who has an ear, let him hear what the Spirit says to the churches" (2:29, 3:6). Not only is John acutely aware of the difficult situations the Asian churches face, beset as they are, as the Church ever is, by weakness and heresy; he knows the hostility of the imperial government, represented by the city seated on seven hills (17:9), surfeited with the blood of the saints (18:24), always jealous of its official religion, always willing to co-opt the hostility of the mob against the atheists.

John's mission to write to the churches fulfilled, there then follows the great image of the eternal, unfading glory of the kingdom, the unfolding of time and history, recounted in a book, but it is a book that no man can open and whose meaning is therefore hidden until the lion of the tribe of Judah, the root or origin of David and his kingship as well as the Son of David prevails, takes the book from the right hand of him that sits on the throne, and looses the seven seals (5:1–5). The one, the only one, who can know and form history is the Lamb standing as it were slain, from whom proceeds the seven-fold Spirit sent into the earth. This is the revealed image of God the Blessed Trinity: the Father the rainbow, the sevenfold spirit of God (Is 11:1–3), and the Lamb from whom the Spirit proceeds. "Thou art worthy, O Lord, to take the book and to open the seals thereof because thou wast slain and hast redeemed us to God by thy blood out of every tribe and tongue and people and nation. And hast made us to our God a kingdom and priests, and we shall reign on the earth." Then in a great cadenza, the living creatures, and the elders and the voice of many angels numbering myriads and myriads and thousands of thousands said with a loud voice, "Worthy is the Lamb who was slain, to receive power and riches and wisdom and might and honor and glory and blessing," and every creature in heaven and earth answer, "To him who sits upon the throne and to the Lamb be blessing and honor and glory and might for ever and ever," and the four living creatures said, "Amen!" and the elders fell down and worshipped.

The structure of the visions John is given in chapters 4 through 22 is almost, but not quite, a story with a beginning at 4:1, with a turning point or peripety at 11:15, and a grand comedic consummation in 21–22 with the marriage feast of the Lamb. The story moves from the vision of God in his majesty through the desolation of nature caused by the rebellions of angels and men, which evoke the wrath of the Lamb (6:17). The working out of that wrath is displayed through the pattern of the breaking of the seven seals by the Lamb, who alone came take up the scroll that is history and break its seven seals, beginning with the first seal, which discloses the famous four horsemen: conquest, war, famine, and death. Chapter seven depicts the protection of the elect that anticipates chapter 21: "Do not harm the earth or the sea or the trees till we have sealed the servants of God on their foreheads." There follows the great anticipatory vision of the elect, the multitude who have washed their robes in the blood of the Lamb (7:1-17).

Seven angels who stand before God then announce the punishment of the earth: "Woe, woe to those who dwell on the earth." The seven angels of the seventh seal possess the seven trumpets, the sounding of which mark out stages in the punishment of nature, for nature, like man, as in the great flood, lies under a curse. Broadly, chapters 5 through 11:15, with the exception of chapter 7, which is a kind of excursus cut out of the story to foresee the victory of the saints, tells the story of natural evil, the punishment of nature and of man through nature as a result of the rebellion of angels and men, a reiteration of the chaos of Genesis 1:2 and more extensively of Genesis 3:17–8:21–22. It is the story of fallen nature more than the story of fallen man.

Then the trumpet of the seventh angel signals the great peripety (11:15), the unexpected grace, the turning-point, proclaiming the victory of the lamb with great voices in heaven saying, "The Kingdom of the World is become the Kingdom of Our Lord and His Christ and he shall reign forever and ever." And the elders: "We give the thanks, Lord God Almighty, who art and who was, that thou hast taken thy great power and begun to reign." Then the temple of God was opened in heaven and the ark of his covenant was seen within the temple, "and the veil of the temple was torn in two from top to bottom" (Rev. 11:19, Matt. 27:51).

God will accomplish his victory with the birth of a child born of woman, a child whose birth represents the re-creating of the human race, a child caught up to God and to his throne, a child whose mother is clothed with the sun, the moon under her feet, and around her head a crown of twelve stars (12:1–2, 5). This birth signals the outbreak of open warfare between Satan and his angels and Michael and his angels. Satan, who has waited expectantly for the birth of the child that he might devour him, attacks the woman, who is Israel, the Church, and the Mother of God, pursuing her with a flood of water, the waters of chaos being Satan's native place. But God gives the woman the wings of an eagle and a secure place safe from the serpent in the wilderness, that is in the presence of God (12:6).

The woman, the mother of the child taken up to God's throne, is opposed by the dragon, who pursues the woman with a flood "like a river out of his mouth," who makes war on the offspring of those who keep God's commandments and bear testimony to Jesus and takes his stand by the sea, his domain. The glassy sea that stretches before the throne of the Lamb is now a sea beautiful and fixed, "of glass, like crystal" (4:6), no longer any place for the dragon whom the Old Testament knows as Rahab (Ps. 89:10, Isa. 51:9) or Satan, the snake or serpent, "the dragon that is in the sea" (Isa. 27:1); its only attribute now is beauty. When the New Jerusalem comes down out of heaven from God "the sea is no more" (21:1). The woman is protected by the earth, that is by nature, swallowing the flood when the dragon pours "water like a river out of his mouth" (12:15) to sweep her away. But she is given the wings of the great eagle that she might fly to the wilderness, that is to the presence of God.

The dragon, cast down upon the earth, creates a demonic trinity. The beast with ten horns and seven heads rises out of the sea. One of its heads had been wounded by Michael the archangel but the wound was superficially healed (13:3). Given power and great authority over every nation, the beast makes war on the saints. All who dwell on the earth will worship it except those whose names are written in the Book of Life. There is a second beast "which rose out of the earth," having two horns so that it imitates the Lamb, but it spoke like the dragon; it seduced all the earth and caused its inhabitants to worship the first beast, to bear its sign, and to make an image of the beast, so that the image, the third member of the demonic trinity, should speak. The mark given by the image of the great beast is the sign of the universal system that rationalizes and controls the world, without which no one can buy or sell (13:15–18).

The victory is now won in the heavens, which are now cleansed. The ambiguity of the angels, those angels who may appear in the heavenly court but who with God's permission tempt Job (Job 1:1–12), who may take to themselves the daughters of men (Gen. 6:1–5), or who may appear as messengers of the Incarnation (Luke 1:19, 26; 2:8–14) is now resolved.[6] Satan and those angels who follow him are cast out of God's presence. "Therefore rejoice you heavens but woe to you earth for Satan has come down upon you full of wrath for he knows that he has but a short time." The moral history of the world will be the history of the conflict of the saints with powers of secular omnipotence that present themselves as representatives of the Lamb, demanding allegiance to a secular idolatry whose erstwhile benefits are limited to those who bear the mark.

The sequence of visions then unfolds to display the warfare between the Lamb of God, the Child caught up to God's throne, and the dragons. The victory is won but the battle will rage until Christ returns, when the New Jerusalem comes down out of heaven from God. Now the Lamb stands on Mount Zion (14:1–5), surrounded by 144,000 of the chaste, who have lived in this world in anticipation of the new creation that is coming, who follow the Lamb wherever he goes. An angel then announces the eternal Gospel: "Fear God and give him glory, for the hour of judgment has come" (14:6–7). A second angel announces the fall of Babylon, the symbol of avarice and slavery (14:8). A third angel proclaims the fate of those who worship the beast and his image; these "drink the wine of God's wrath," and will be tormented with fire and brimstone "in the presence of holy angels and the presence of the Lamb" (14:10). But "blessed are the dead who die in the Lord" (14:13). So the hour has come to reap the harvest of the earth; the vintage

6 John Henry Newman came to believe that the angelic fall may have occurred over time, *Apologia Vita Sua and Six Sermons* (London: Yale University Press, 2008), 155–56. It may also be the case that sequence as the prophet John experiences it in his visions is not so much strictly sequential as full, time-full.

of the earth will be thrown into the one great winepress of the wrath of God. But those who have conquered the beast and not worshipped his image stand beside the sea, now like glass, beautiful but now no home for the dragon, and sing the song of the Lamb: "Great and wonderful are thy deeds, O Lord God Almighty." Rebellious nature now fails under the mighty wrath of God, as it failed with the coming of the flood in the days of Noah. "It is done" (16:17). Every mountain fled away and no islands were to be found. The heavens rained stones and men cursed God.

With chapter 17 the prophet's vision again touches history, for however one reads the enigmatic list of 17:10–11 the author clearly intends to indict the succession of persecuting emperors, each represented as one of the heads of the seven-headed beast first introduced in 13:1. But the deeper import is the defeat of the political order of the world that hates the saints, represented in chapter 17 as imperial Rome with its seven hills (17:9), "the great harlot, seated upon many waters, with whom the kings of the earth have committed fornication." The waters are "peoples and multitudes and nations and tongues," and the woman is "the great city that has dominion over the kings of the earth" (17:18).

Chapter 18 tells the story of the fall of Babylon, the city of man. Babylon, the world city, the place of the captivity of the elect, is busied with the arts of money, perfected in the purveying of every luxury, possessing gold and silver, jewels and pearls, cinnamon, spice, horses and chariots, and slaves, that is human souls, and surfeited with the blood of the saints. But now Babylon, the city who says, "I sit a queen, I am no widow, and sorrow I shall not see," will fall, bemoaned by the kings and ship captains and merchants who stand afar off weeping: "Alas, alas that great city Babylon, that mighty city: for in one hour thy judgment has come" (18:10). Chapter 18 is the great poetry of destruction; the voices of harpers and musicians shall fall silent, no craftsman shall be found, the sound of the mill shall no more be heard, the light of the lamp shall shine no more at all.

Then chapter 19 celebrates God's victory over the city that in scriptural terms is the world dominated by Satan: "Hallelujah! Salvation, and glory and power belong to our God, for his judgements are true and just. . . ." "Rejoice over her thou heavens and ye holy apostles and prophets, for God hath given judgement for you against her" (18:20). And at last the marriage feast of the Lamb comes, the consummation of the great comedy. "His bride, the Church, has prepared herself, and it is granted to her that she shall clothe herself in fine white linen. And the fine linen is the righteous deeds of the saints" (19:6–9). And then John sees the great image of Christ the Knight, mounted on a white horse, his robe dipped in the blood of his sacrifice (19:11–16). No man may name him, but he will reveal his name: he is called faithful and true; he is the Word of God, the King of Kings. The armies of heaven follow him.

Chapter 20:4–8 describes a kind of lacuna in the great war, the space of a thousand years during which Satan is chained in the bottomless pit while the martyrs, those whom John has known and among whom John may soon be, who had not received the mark of the beast, will live and reign with Christ.[7] These enjoy the first resurrection, the resurrection of the souls of those who had been beheaded "for their testimony to Jesus and the Word of God" (20:5). The second death, the death that for God's enemies will follow upon the judgment of God when Christ returns, has no power over these martyrs who "shall be priests of God and of Christ and shall reign with him for a thousand years." Whether this reign of the Saints takes place on this earth or in the presence of Christ, the text does not tell us. This vision has as its obvious purpose the rewarding of the martyrs, and perhaps this millennium of peace for the saints on earth is required by the fact that Jesus must have victory not only after time but in time, otherwise it could be argued that the "spirituals," the Gnostics, were right: the created order as God established it in Genesis would have proved irredeemable, having no end other than corruption and destruction.

The thousand-year reign of the martyrs is not the end but the prologue to the last battle. Satan is now freed, but he is freed only to be destroyed by the fire of God which comes down from heaven. The devil, the false prophet, and the beast are then cast into the lake of fire to be tormented forever (20:7–10). The dead stand before God's great white throne. The

7 This text became the *locus classicus* for millenarianism, for pre-millennialism, which holds that the millennium of the righteous will follow Christ's return, and post-millennialism, which holds that the reign of the righteous is an anticipation of the return and reign of Christ. Whatever else, it is a recognition of the glorious reward given the martyrs. See Jude 6 for the rebellious angels in chains.

created order marred by the dominion of sin has run its course: from God's presence "earth and sky fled away and no place was found for them" (20:11). Death and Hades, the underworld, Hades and Sheol, give up their dead to be judged by what they had done. Everyone is judged "by what was written in the books, according to his works" (20:11–13). With death and Hades those whose names are not written in the book of life, cowards, unbelievers, the abominable, murderers will be cast into the lake of fire.

With chapter 21 we come to the end of the story that is the great fruition of God's plan, for the prophet sees the new heavens and the new earth, which Isaiah (11:7–16, 65:17) and Blessed Peter had foretold (2 Pet. 3:11–13), coming down out of heaven from God. The sea is no more. The Jerusalem which is above comes down from God out of heaven, the new city, resting on the foundation of the twelve apostles of the Lamb, an image linking the very human labors of Peter and the eleven to the Kingdom of God in a way reminiscent of Christ's promise: What you bind on earth is bound in heaven.

Now the purpose for which man was created, that we might know God and be known by him, is fulfilled: "Behold the tabernacle of God is with men, and he will dwell with them"; not the tabernacle in which God might appear between the cherubim but the tabernacle that is God with us, incarnate in Christ, the eternal temple. And they shall be his people and God himself shall be their God with them. And God shall wipe away all tears from their eyes (Isa. 25:8) and death shall be no more, nor mourning nor crying, nor sorrow shall be any more, for the former things are passed away (21:1–4; Isa. 25:6–8). And he who sat on the throne said, "It is done. I am the alpha and the omega, the beginning and the end (1:8). To the thirsty I will give the fountain of the water of life freely. He who conquers shall have this heritage, and I will be his God and he will be my son" (21:6–7). But the cowardly and the faithless, murderers, fornicators, and liars, these will die not once but twice, condemned to rise only to face death in the lake that burns with fire and brimstone (8).

The prophet John then rejoices in the vision of the "the holy city, the new Jerusalem, coming down out of heaven from God" (21:10), walled about by the everlasting mission of the Twelve, who are the foundations of the new city. Israel is fulfilled; the names of the twelve tribes are inscribed on the gates (12). The coming aesthetic of the Middle Ages will reflect the influence of John's description; the city is adorned with the color and brilliance of precious stones, its streets made of "pure gold, transparent as glass." There is no temple, "for its temple is the Lord God and the Lamb" (22). There is no need of sun or moon, given in Genesis to light day and night, for "the glory of God is its light, and its light is the lamb" (23). The darkness that was upon the face of the deep when the story of creation opens (Gen. 1:2), the result of the rebellion of the angels, mitigated then by its separation into night and day by the informing Spirit of God, is now done away; there shall be no night (21:25). There remains only the vision of nature renewed. The four rivers are now "the river of the water of life, bright as crystal, flowing from the throne of God and of the Lamb," and on either side of the river growing abundantly the tree of life, the fruit of which Eve had rejected in favor of the forbidden tree of the knowledge of good and evil. There shall be no more anything accursed, but the throne of God and of the Lamb shall be in it, and his servants shall serve him. They shall belong to the company of the Lamb, whose name they shall bear on their foreheads. And they shall reign for ever and ever.

It is finished (16:17, John 19:30). And so John brings the reader to the end of the story, to the marriage feast of the Lamb that brings to perfection the divine comedy, his visions having traversed the blasted, parched territory of a world afflicted by the sin of angels and men, established an anchor in time when the woman clothed with the sun gave her fiat to the angel Gabriel, made a history for the elect, and created a people who look for the reign of the King. Then finally the promise of Jesus, "Surely I am coming soon," to which the Church responds: "Let it be; Come Lord Jesus!"

The Apocalypse of John was already well known when Papias of Hierapolis wrote his commentary at the turn of the century. Justin Martyr knew it as did Irenaeus. By mid-third century, given the increasing importance of Origen, Origenism, and the pre-Arian Alexandrian school, with their "spiritual" vision of the future, the prophet John's vision required defense. About 240 Dionysius of Alexandria wrote that the book could not be by the author of the Gospel and Epistles—style and vocabulary were too different—and, more tellingly, that it ought not be included in the canon because it was too Jewish and taught Christians to hope for un-spiritual, earthly things.[8]

8 *Church History* 7.25.22–25 (*NPNF*² 1:308–309).

Among the aspects of Christian life most foreign to modernity is the important place prophecy held in the church during the first three centuries. The most easily recognizable part of Jesus' work was his place as a prophet or teacher. Paul considered prophecy the most desirable of the spiritual gifts (1 Cor. 14:1). The earliest church manual, the *Teaching of the Twelve Apostles,* devotes disproportionate space to the managing of prophets and prophesy in the church. The place of prophecy was at the heart of the movement called Montanism which on balance seems to have been an exaggerated reliance upon prophecy, practices so sensational that the Roman authorities rejected the movement's phrophetesses, yet a movement in defense of which the great doctor Tertullian left the communion of the Catholic church to join what he considered a purer Christianity. In the first and second centuries the principal argument for the truth of the Gospel was the claim that Jesus had perfectly fulfilled to prophecies of the Old Testament.

Always at the heart of enthusiasm for and reservations about prophecy was one book that had made its way into the canon of scripture, the Apocalypse of the prophet John. It was not the only apocalypse written by those who called themselves Christians, but this book, called Revelation in English translations, was canonical for the whole Church, although there were always reservations. Dionysius of Alexandria represented the third-century opposition, and great doctors in the East maintained and perpetuated this reserve toward John's prophecy, so that while the book is often considered part of the canon in the East, it has no place in the liturgy in Eastern Orthodoxy.[9] The difficulty was and remains the temptation to see the images of the Apocalypse chapters 4–21 as claims to historical reality, when they are in fact revealed images seen through the door opened in heaven, constituting a divine typology that engages imagination even as it transcends created time, offering always a teleology of glory in which Christian imagination moves. Wherever the Apocalypse is understood as a simple history of the future, the objections of Dionysius of Alexandria will be raised. The

9 In the Stichometry of Nicephorus, Patriarch of Constantinople 806–815, which lists books received and those considered apocryphal, recording the number of lines or *stichoi* in each, Revelation is listed among New Testament Apocrypha.

history-like surface of the images always point toward realities the eye cannot presently see, toward times and places that are and are not like the things we now see as in a glass, darkly.

Paradoxically, John's book of prophecy won great favor in the West. In the 220s the Apocalypse was defended by Hippolytus of Rome in his lost works *On the Apocalypse and Gospel of John* and *Heads Against Gaius* and cited often in his work *On Christ and Anti-Christ.* About 290 Victorinus of Pettau published a work commenting on certain passages from Revelation.[10] As a catalog of revealed images, the Apocalypse soon became the basis of an iconography that predominated during the first millennium, displayed in apses; on triumphal arches, the great arches that marked the division between the nave or body of the church and the space usually terminating in a circular apse in which the altar stood, from Santa Pudenziana at the end of the fourth century to San Marco in the eleventh; on the facades of great Roman churches; and in sarcophagi.[11]

The inspiration for the reiteration across the centuries of Revelation 4–5, the order of heaven with Christ enthroned; 14:1–5, the lambs of Christ moving toward Mount Zion; and 21–22, Christ and the saints in the New Jerusalem, represent the inexpungable belief that Paul spoke truly, that Christ will return bringing the elect with him, that creation will be renewed, and so we will always be with the Lord. John's visions gave the Church the great image of the glory of God as the font of being, history, and salvation. They tell the story of the ravages of sin upon man and nature, of the birth of the child who is caught up to the throne of God and of God's protection of his mother from the enmity of the dragon, of the fall of the city of man and the coming of the new creation in which God's purpose is achieved.

John, writing as one who, already imprisoned on Patmos, may face

10 Quasten, 2:411.

11 Theodore Klauser, *Frühchristliche Sarkophage in Bild and Wort* (Olten, Schweis: Urs Graf-Verlag, 1966). Tafeln 23–24 [Arles], 25 [*Legem dat*], 30 [Ravenna], 40 [Verona]. The Arles sarcophagus shows Jesus standing on the mount with its four rivers, bracketed by Peter and Paul; the phoenix at the upper left. See also Joseph Wilpert, *La Fede della Chiesa Nascente secondo: I Monumenti dell'Arte Funeraria Antica* (Roma: Pontifico Instituto di Archeologia Christiana, 1938), figs 58, 59, and Walter Lowrie, *Monuments of the Early Church* (New York: Macmillan Co., 1923), 302–04, figs 161, 162.

death for the name, assures us that, just as our hearts had suspected, beyond and beneath this troublesome adventure, for those who have endured, there is the true city where Christ is king and the garden purified of sin and death and pain, where He who is the summary and meaning of creation will wipe away the tears of life so that we can see him as he is. Night, the darkness that was upon the face of the deep in Genesis, from which then the spirit of God separated the light to give form to night and day, is now done away because the Lord will be the light of the new city (Gen. 1:2,2:19, Rev. 22:4).

John's Apocalypse will always invite scholarly attempts to locate the text in the background of Old Testament prophecy and apocalyptic as well as contemporary non-canonical apocalyptic literature, as it should. But its meaning to the Church during the first millennium was found in the unshadowed conviction that Jesus would return, bringing with him the new creation. At Rome, until first, about 1100, the image of the Mother of God supervened as at Santa Maria in Trastevere, to be followed by sixteenth- and seventeenth-century Renaissance pictorialism, which might include anything from Domenichino's dramatic crucifixion of St. Andrew in San Andrea della Valle to Carlo Rainaldi's monumental apse painting of 1673 in Santa Maria Maggiore, to Bernini's Gloria and Chair of Peter in the Vatican basilica, the image that typically dominated liturgical space from the apse, commanding imagination Sunday by Sunday was Christ returning, welcomed by Peter and Paul, who had gone out to meet him in the air, an image conflating Revelation 21:3–4 and First Thessalonians 4:13–18 that answered to the cry of the faithful in the Apocalypse and the *Didache*: "Come, Lord Jesus."[12] John's Revelation is still read in the season of Advent in the Roman Church.

12 Rev. 22:20; *Didache* 10.6, 16.7.

# Part III
## *Writing the Christian Mind*

> Among many religious movements of antiquity, only Christianity and Judaism produced much literature at all. Roman religions appear to have been largely indifferent to the use of texts. . . . No Graeco-Roman religious group produced, used, and valued texts on a scale comparable to Judaism and Christianity.
>
> Harry Y. Gamble, *Books and Readers in the Early Church*

In the synagogue at Nazareth Jesus read from the Isaiah scroll, but Christian writings, both texts that would belong to the Sacred Scriptures and the non-canonical works of the first and second centuries, usually appeared in the more convenient book-form called the codex, sheets of papyrus stitched together and folded so that both the front and back of the gathered pages were accessible.[1] Christianity was always a literary religion, rooted in the Hebrew Scriptures, propagated by preaching and memory, by what Papias of Hierapolis, writing near the turn of the first Christian century, called the living voice, but also by written memoirs of the apostles, apostolic letters, and prophecy.

Beginning certainly by the time Paul wrote to the Thessalonians in the forties, there existed a Christian literature that would over time be considered canonical, regulative as proof of doctrine, but this small body of writing, the New Testament, would be surrounded by a much larger body of Christian literature, some of which while not canonical would be held in

1 See Glen H. Roberts and T. C. Skeat, *The Birth of the Codex* (London: British Academy, Oxford University Press, 1983). *Codex Sinaiticus* was originally a scroll, its text written in panels perpendicular to the edge so that the scroll could be folded into quire-like gatherings; a form transitional to the codex.

high esteem by the Church, while others that in the long run were not considered apostolic were sometimes read at the Eucharist, as were Clement's *Letter to the Corinthians* and the *Shepherd of Hermas*. These are called Apostolic Fathers and Apologists, although these titles are not given unqualified support by either content or chronology. The Apostolic Fathers, some recovered recently after centuries of oblivion, include now the seven letters of Ignatius and one of Polycarp; a manual of Church practice, the *Didache* or *Teaching of the Twelve Apostles*, a manual of faith and practice; and the *Shepherd of Hermas*, a kind of novella *cum* illustrative parables; and a homily, misnamed Clement's *Second Letter*. The Apologists include the two *Apologies* of Justin Martyr, the *Epistle of Diognetus,* Irenaeus' great work *The Refutation and Overthrow of the Knowledge Falsely So-Called*, Athenagoras of Athens' *Plea Regarding Christians*, Tertullian's *Apology*, and Tatian's *Discourse to the Greeks*. In the second and early third centuries writings by apologists such as Tertullian and Hippolytus against particular heresies and heretics—Valentinus and Marcion were favorite targets—constituted a special category of Christian texts. Before the Constantinian peace came in 313, Christians had created an extensive literature, of which surviving documents are only part, many of the writings known to Eusebius when he wrote his *Church History* in the 320s having subsequently been forgotten in the confusion following upon the collapse of Roman order in the West in the sixth century, under the pressure of the barbarian invasions of the fourth to the ninth centuries and the Islamic conquests of the seventh.

The autographs of the Apostolic Fathers, the texts as originally written in Paul's large letters, or dictated, written down by a secretary, and released to the copyist or to the messenger who will take them to their intended destinations are, like the autographs of the canonical books, lost, so we know these texts only as they were copied into later manuscripts. The best text of the letters of Ignatius, except Romans, is in an eleventh-century Greek manuscript, *Codex Mediceus Laurentianus*, in the Laurentian Library in Florence. The Muratorian Canon, which may belong to the late second or early third century, was preserved in a text of the eighth and lost until 1740. Survival is often fortuitous. Aristides' *Apology* was recovered only in 1889, when a Syriac translation was discovered in the Monastery of Saint Catherine on Mt. Sinai. Irenaeus' important *Demonstration of the Apostolic Preaching* was not recovered until it was found in an Armenian text in 1904.

The *Assumption of Moses*, probably a first-century Greek text, written perhaps originally in Hebrew or Aramaic, survived in a unique Latin text of the sixth century. The second-century *Epistle to Diognetus* survived only in one manuscript from antiquity, a 13th-century codex that included writings ascribed to Justin Martyr, which then was destroyed when the Louvain library was burned in 1914, by which time transcriptions had been made.

In addition to the writings considered part of the Christian patrimony there was surrounding these texts an extensive literature belonging to what Christians considered heresy, such as the Gnostic-Christian writings found among the texts discovered in Egypt, between 1890 and 1914 at Oxyrynchus, and at Nag Hammadi, where what looks like an entire Gnostic library, sixty-one works translated from Greek into Coptic, was discovered in 1945. Epiphanius wrote of the Gnostics, "They too have lots of books."[2] And not to be forgotten are texts belonging to Hebrew religious literature, books roughly contemporary with the early Apostolic Fathers that may have influenced Christian writers: *Enoch, IV Ezra,* the *Assumption of Moses* and the *Odes of Solomon.* The discovery at Qumran between 1947 and 1957 of the library of an Essene-like Jewish last-days movement, seven hundred and fifty documents including nearly all the canonical books of the Old Testament and several commentaries, offers evidence of the existence in Judaism in the Hasmodean and Herodian periods of a vibrant literary life.[3] Amid the contending influences represented by these texts, Christian writers, living always in the light of the faith engendered by the risen Christ, produced a literature that reflected the Christian mind, founding a tradition of thought, exposition, and defense that would persist into the Middle Ages, constituting in its earliest examples the intellectual manifesto of a quiet revolution that because it changed hearts changed the world.

The typical Christian's experience of the Gospel was aural. Christians were probably no more able to read a text than the general population, among whom it is estimated that only ten to twenty percent were literate. Over long decades, by a process still but partly understood, the written Gospels and letters became the canonical repository of Christian faith, but

2 *Panarion* 1.26.8.1 (Williams, trans., 1:96).

3 Frank Moore Cross, Jr., *The Ancient Library of Qumran and Modern Biblical Studies* (Garden City, N.Y.: Doubleday, 1962).

long before there were written Gospels, when such liturgical reading as existed relied heavily on the Hebrew prophets, Paul understood that "faith comes from what is heard, and what is heard comes from the proclaiming of Christ" (Rom. 10:17). The prophet John was commanded by the vision of Christ to write (Rev. 1:19) and blessed those who read (1:3). In the *Shepherd*, Hermas is commanded to write down what will be revealed to him, making two books which are to be given to Grapte, to be read to the widows, and to Clement to be forwarded to foreign cities, while Hermas is to read the book "to this city" along with the elders who preside over the Church. This reading constituted publication among first and second-century Christians. The one who read would not be a Christian reading casually—only in exceptional circumstances would he possess the codex or papyrus roll—but a reader, at first chosen informally for his literacy and later often the first step toward a clerical vocation. The public reading of a Gospel or one of Paul's letters in the assembly was no simple thing because the text was written *scripto continuo*, with no spaces between the words, so that the reader was required to grasp the syntax, rendering the text intelligible to the hearers as he read.

Christian writings of the first two centuries were addressed to widely varying audiences. The Gospels, known to Justin about 150 as memoirs of the apostles, were certainly read most commonly in the assembly to remind and to confirm conviction. There are hints that the Gospels found interest outside Christian congregations. The Gospel of John addresses those who believe and also those who would believe in the future (17:20, 20:31), and its text was studied carefully by Gnostics like Valentinus who strove to make it their own. The pagan apologist Celsus had obviously read the Christian scriptures, as had the subject of Justin's *Dialogue with Trypho*, a still-unbelieving Jew. Paul frequently commanded that his letters be read to the congregations to whom they were addressed and sometimes to those nearby. Apart from the Gospels, Acts, and the Apocalypse, the form of Christian texts was epistolary, including in addition to the Pauline corpus both Clement's letters, Ignatius' seven letters, and Barnabas. Paul's letters were addressed to churches and individuals across the empire, to be delivered by couriers or letter carriers (Rom. 16:1, 1 Cor. 16:10, Eph 6:21, Col. 4:7), as was the custom with other apostolic authors (1 Pet. 5:12; *Clement* 65.1; Ignatius, *Phil.* 11:2, *Smyrn.* 12:1).

At some time, probably during the third decade of the second century, Christianity would become a literary religion in the sense that its transmission and interpretation came to depend on writing as the living voice fell silent. By mid-second century there were not only letters and Gospels but apologies, Papias' exegetical books, and the beginning of history in the lost work of Hegessipus.[4] There was a rich literature of half-fictional acts and apocalypses.[5] The *Gospel According to Peter*, with its docetic undertone, and the *Gospel of Thomas*, with its Manichean tendencies and its romantic account of Jesus' childhood, illustrate the ways in which Jesus could be located in a Gnostic context. The popularity of the *Shepherd of Hermas* suggests that there was a readership for a popular Christian literature. This was the audience to whom the numerous apocryphal Gospels, Acts, and Epistles, some Gnostic, some miraculous, were addressed, all of which suggests that literacy among Christians was at the least not unusual. The Apologists sometimes made emperors their audience, a convention for gaining public notice. Aristides of Athens addressed Hadrian (117–138), Justin Martyr Antoninus Pius (138–161), and Melito of Sardis' lost *Apology* was addressed to Marcus Aurelius. There were controversial works, Irenaeus' *The Refutationn and Overthrow of the Knowledge Falsely So-Called* and anti-Montanist apologies by Miltiades and Apollinaris of Hierapolis.[6]

Before any of the Gospels existed in the form that we know them, and probably before the prophet John was given his visions on Patmos in the eighties, there existed a precious written witness illuminating an otherwise obscure period in the spread of the Good News, the *Teaching of the Twelve Apostles*, a church manual popular in its day, valued in the post-Constantinian Church and then lost for a thousand years. The *Didache*, to use the more common title, located somewhere between the letters of Paul and Clement of Rome to the Corinthians about 90, offers a picture of the teaching and life of Christians when the Jerusalem roots of Messianic Judaism were still near the surface, before the four Gospels were established as the public literature of the Church, and foreshadowing with impressive

4 Quasten, 1:284–86; *Church History* 4.22.8 (*NPNF*[2] 1:198–200).

5 Ibid, 1:106–57. And see James, *Apocryphal New Testament*, for the texts of apocryphal acts, gospels, and apocalypses.

6 Ibid, 1:228; *Church History* 5,18,1–13 (2 *NPNF*[2]1:236–37).

accuracy the faith and morals that would be characteristic of Christian life through coming centuries.

Also from the first century were Clement's *Letter to Corinth* establishing the order of obedient love in the Church. Then from the first quarter of the new century there were Ignatius of Antioch's letter to the churches in which the shape of the Catholic faith comes clear, and at mid-century Justin settled accounts constructively with philosophy and the pagan past.

# One
## *The* Didache: *Faith and Morals in the First Century*

> It has enriched and deepened, in an amazing way, our knowledge of the beginnings of the Church. Scholars, constantly drawn to its precious contents, have gained repeated enlightenment and inspiration from this little book.
>
> Johanness Quasten

The document that perhaps tells us more about Christian life in the first century than any other is *The Lord's Instruction to the Gentiles through the Twelve Apostles,* a fortunate find, known in the fourth century to Eusebius and Athanasius but subsequently lost, only to be rediscovered in 1883 in the library of the Greek Patriarchate at Jerusalem.[1] Its title represents an appeal to the plentitude of apostolic authority, for the twelve were the original witnesses, disciples called by Christ himself who in the words of Acts had accompanied him "during all the time that the Lord Jesus went in and out among us beginning with the baptism of John until the day he was taken up from us"(1:22).[2] In the prophet John's Apocalypse, which may be roughly contemporary with the *Didache,* the twelve are the foundation of the New Jerusalem, that is of the kingdom of God on earth and in heaven (21:14).

The name of the author or authors of the *Didache* who, claiming this high authority, compiled this short manual touching many aspects of

1 Quasten, 1:37.

2 The dating of the *Didache* is complicated by its reiteration of the first six chapters or the "two ways" portion of the *Epistle of Barnabas* (18–20). The "two ways" sections of *Barnabas* and the *Didache* may be versions of a document that with authorial changes—Barnabas uses the way of light and the way of darkness— circulated throughout the Church. Which is the original, which the copy, is hard to know.

Christian life, the morality of Christians, the order of Christian ministry, and sacramental and liturgical practice, is lost to us. It is nonetheless a work of power, rough beauty, and compelling gentleness that stands at the threshold of the culture its teaching foreshadowed. The *Didache* was written between two worlds. In the immediate background is Judaism; the author has not left the synagogue behind in imagination. The language of the Eucharistic thanksgiving recalls the language of temple thanksgivings. The Eucharist is an offering or sacrifice, recalling the action central to Judaism, and familiar as well to converted Gentiles. Christians are to come together on the Lord's Day to confess their sins, "that your sacrifice may be pure" (13.3, 14.1–2). God is the God of David (10.6). And there is the assertion that "The prophets are your high priests," which suggests that the author is not very far removed from the worship of the temple (13.3). Prophets and prophecy were part of the Church from the beginning, prophets being honored members of the order that linked them with apostles and teachers. There is a hint of the primitive sharing of goods as in Acts: "Share everything with your brother and call nothing your own" (4.8). Although he does not tell us who they are, the author is much concerned with "the hypocrites," whom he warns his readers not to imitate. These fast on Mondays and Thursdays, while Christians are to fast on Wednesdays and Fridays (8.1), a warning that even as it condemns insincerity suggests the complexity of a Christianity still not far from its Jewish roots in the 60s or 70s, the age of the Pauline Pastoral Epistles.[3]

The *Didache* mirrors a movement born in Palestine as it enters into the Greek world, carried there by Paul and Peter and others in the 40s and

3 The *Gospel of the Hebrews* exemplifies the interest in interpreting the apostolic mission as the authentic development of Jerusalem Judaism. See Quasten, 1, 111. The Ebionites and Nazarenes were sects whose members rejected the Pauline Epistles and taught the binding character of the Mosaic law. See *Dialogue* 47; *Against Heresies* 1.26, 5.1.3. And Revelation 3:9, the prophet John to Philadelphia, the Jews who say they are Jews but are not, against whom John displays the anger that often marks controversy between brothers. When Ignatius wrote to Philadelphia (6:1) thirty years later there was still this concern: "If anyone interprets Judaism to you do not listen to him; for it is better to hear Christianity from the circumcised (Jews) than Judaism from the uncircumcised ('Jewish' Christians)."

50s, so this manual of advice is addressed to readers, Greeks immersed in a pagan culture, who must be warned not to sacrifice to dead gods (6.3) and reminded that their Christian profession makes them members of a revolution that requires purity of heart and the rejection of pagan practices: adultery, the corrupting of boys, abortion, and infanticide (1.4, 2.1–2, 5.2). The readers and hearers of the *Didache* also require instruction regarding the right use of the sacraments (4.14, 9.5) and right order of Church government in an age when there are still apostles and prophets who must be honored. When the *Didache* was written, the order of apostles, prophets, and teachers was being succeeded by elected bishops and deacons, whose ministry is "identical with that of prophets and teachers" (15.1–2).[4] The author counsels respect for the recently established ministry of bishops and deacons, commanding that they not be despised because "they are deserving of your honor together with the prophets and teachers." "Day and night you should remember him who preaches God's word to you, and honor him as you would the Lord" (4:1). This chronological overlapping of apostles and bishops indicates a date earlier than the Ignatius epistles, in which the bishop is the essential sacramental center of the Church. When First Timothy and Titus were written these post-apostolic offices were assumed to be the centers of authority and good order (1 Tim. 3:1, Tit. 1:7).

The *Didache* knows and quotes written sources—the Septuagint, Deuteronomy, Wisdom, and Zechariah among others—but the great Pauline themes with their cosmic sweep and the concern for the relation between law and grace are absent, and while citations of the familiar Matthew or Matthew-like sources are frequent, the text displays no knowledge of the other Gospels. The introductory, and dominant, theme is the contrast between the way of life the readers have previously known and the Christian way: "There are two ways, one of life and one of death; and between the two ways there is a great difference."[5] This rhetorical pattern is

4 Clement 42 (Richardson, 62).

5 For the opinion that the "Two Ways" document of *Didache* 1.2–5.4 existed independently see Richardson, 161–62. And Ignatius, writing about 115, "There is an end to all, that the choice is between two things, life and death" (*Magn.*, 6:1).

rooted deep in the Hebrew Scriptures, in the way of life and the way of death described in Deuteronomy 30:15–20; in prophetic tradition, in Isaiah, Jeremiah, and Ezekiel; and is reflected in the Matthean text that prophesies the separation of the sheep from the goats, illustrating thereby the respective destinies of just and unjust (25:31–46). Isaiah prophesies two ways: "In that day the deaf shall hear the words of a book; the meek shall obtain fresh joy in the Lord, for the ruthless shall come to naught and the scoffer cease and all who work to do evil shall be cut off" (Isa. 29:19–20). The "two ways" is a staple of Old Testament apocalyptic, as in Enoch: "The spirits of you who have died in righteousness shall live and rejoice," but of sinners, "know ye that their souls will be made to descend into Sheol and they shall be wretched in their great tribulation" (5.103.7), and in Daniel: "Many of those who sleep in the dust of the earth shall awake, some to everlasting life and some to shame and everlasting contempt"(12:2). And in the Apocalypse: "He who conquers shall have this heritage, and I will be his God and he will be my son. But for the cowardly, the faithless, the polluted . . . their lot shall be in the lake that burns with fire and brimstone which is the second death" (Rev. 21:7–8). The Gospel of Jesus Christ is a gospel of division even in families (Matt. 10:34), and as in the Jewish-Christian Epistle of James the opposition between the Church and the world is finally absolute: "Friendship with the world is enmity with God" (James 3:9).

The moral instruction of the first six chapters of the *Didache* is an exposition of the dominical teaching of Matthew 5 and 6. The author is building a community distinguished by a new and distinctive kind of behavior, rooted in Exodus 20–24 and perfected by the Beatitudes of Matthew 5, a pattern characteristic of the new way of life that is an essential part of Christian witness, distinguished from the best of pagan moral teaching by a subjective note that presupposes not only the pursuit of virtue but conversion of heart.

Do not covet your neighbor's property, do not commit perjury, do not bear false witness, do not slander, do not bear grudges. Do not be double-minded or double-tongued, for a double tongue is a deadly snare. Your words shall not be dishonest or hollow, but substantiated by action. Do not be greedy or extortionate or hypocritical or malicious or arrogant. Do not plot against your neighbor. Do not hate anybody (2.2–7). Humility is the sign of Christian profession: "Be patient, merciful, harmless, quiet, and good" (3.8). The Father has lodged his sacred name "in our hearts" (10:2).

The author is addressing the Roman household, assuming that the father as head is the authority and political representative of the family. "Do not neglect your responsibility to your son or daughter, but from their youth you shall teach them to revere God."[6] Slaves belonging to the household have been baptized and would therefore be brothers. "Do not be harsh in giving orders to your slaves or slave girls. They hope in the same God as you . . ." Presiding over the order of life is the divine moral order which renders earthly station relative. "When he comes to us all, he will not respect your station, but will call those whom the Spirit has made ready" (5.10–11).

The *Didache* is addressed to readers, whether Jewish or Greek, who live in the ambiance of pagan culture and, Christians though they are, baptized and given the Pentecostal graces, have not reliably distanced themselves from Roman religious practice in which divination was an established, state-sponsored custom: "Do not be a diviner, for that leads to idolatry. Do not be an enchanter or an astrologer or a magician. Moreover, have no wish to observe or heed such practices, for it breeds idolatry" (2.4). It was a great claim of Christianity, as Ignatius would later write, that the star of Bethlehem, the birth of Christ, had broken the bonds of fatal necessity believed in classical culture to have dominated life through the influence of the circling planets.[7] Imitating the warning of Paul (1 Thess. 1:19, 1 Cor. 2.2) and John (1 John 5:21), readers are reminded "to keep strictly away from what is offered to idols, for that implies worshipping dead gods" (6.3). There is a new morality: "Do not commit adultery, do not corrupt boys, do not fornicate, do not steal, do not practice magic, do not go in for sorcery, do not murder a child by abortion or kill a new-born infant" (2.1–2), all practices common in the Hellenistic world.

The deliberate, reiterated, condemnation of the arrant sexuality of Roman life that ends in the destruction of children is the author's attempt

6 *Shepherd*, *Vis.*1.3: "Out of fondness for thy children thou didst not admonish thy family, but didst suffer it to become fearfully corrupt. For this the Lord is wroth with thee."

7 *Eph.* 19.

to separate decisively his readers from the culture in which they are immersed, in which passion born of casual carnality obscures the eye of the heart.[8] The condemnation of abortion is a moral necessity that flows from the fact that under the Christian dispensation, breaking with ancient Roman and Greek practice, each person belongs to God and is a brother or sister *in potentia*, so is not at the disposition even of parents and certainly not of the state. To be "murderers of children, corrupters of God's creatures" belongs, with neglect of the needy, oppression of the distressed, and advocacy of the rich, to the way of death (7:2). Christianity's tenderness toward childhood, rooted in the Lord's own regard for children and their exemplary trustfulness, developed quickly, in stark opposition to Roman callousness, because Christ was a child born of Mary and because Jesus had said that little children were especially beloved in the Kingdom, each having an angelic guard who beheld the Father's face and thus a destiny given by God which it was not the place of man to obviate (Matt. 18:10).

In stark contrast to the revolutionary teaching of the *Didache*, both Romans and Greeks, considering a child to be the property of the father, deemed it wrong, even unlawful, to bring an ill-formed child into the world and permissible for unwanted children to be exposed by the roadside, either to die or to be rescued into slavery or prostitution.[9] Such practices were tolerated and often considered unremarkable in the Hellenistic world. Ill-formed or unwanted children were an unnecessary burden. In Plato's perfect city envisioned in the *Republic* children were born for the good and service of the state, and the imperfect were to be hidden away, presumably left to die.[10] Aristotle, arguing on the basis of an imperfect biology that the child was not ensouled, becoming then a living being, until the ninth week, wrote in the *Politics* that when a couple had children in excess, abortion might be procured before life and sensation began.[11] The Twelve Tables of Roman

8 Tacitus noted with uncomprehending disapproval that among the Jews "it is a deadly sin to kill an unwanted child," attributing this prohibition, wrongly, solely to the Jews' desire for increasing numbers (*Histories* 5.5 [Wellesley, trans.], 272). Judaism's broad prohibition always admitted exceptions.

9 Justin 27 (Richardson, 259).

10 Plato, *Republic*, 5, 460b–c, 460e–461c (Jowett, 1, 722–23).

11 Aristotle, *Politics*, 1335b (McKeon, 1302).

law gave fathers the right of life and death over their young children and command that those born deformed be destroyed.

Although not explicit in the *Didache*, the Church had appropriated from Jewish tradition generally the belief that the world under God's providence bore the marks of sin and hence of imperfection, with the result that every kind of failure in nature could be seen in the light of Paul's great image in Romans of a world groaning and travailing, subjected always in hope (8:18–23). This was not fatalism; much could be amended by prayer, by just government, by human means, but until the return of Christ life would always be marked by an irreducible residuum of virulent evil that must be borne hopefully in remote imitation of the cross of Jesus.

Of all the aspects of the *Didache* that have engaged critics, it is the instructions it offers regarding baptism and the Eucharist that have commanded most attention. Prospective believers are to be instructed publicly, and then baptism is to be given in the name of the Father, Son, and Holy Spirit, this at a time when the word for God's consubstantial three-ness did not exist, baptizing preferably in running water, that is in a stream, but if this cannot be in cold water, and that failing then in warm, and finally if necessary requires in still water, by pouring water on the head three times in the name of the Father, the Son, and the Holy Spirit (7).

The instruction on baptism prefers one of the two metaphors typically used to explain baptism. One is that of washing, with the implication of the power of living water (John 3:5, 4:10–11, Rev. 21:6, 22:1, 17), which, along with historical precedent of Jesus' baptism in the Jordan and the remote references to the living waters of the perfected creation (Rev. 22:-5), is perhaps why the flowing stream is preferable.[12] The other is the Pauline metaphor; death to sin in the baptismal waters and resurrection to new life in Christ as one emerges reborn (Rom. 6:3–4). As it would happen, in an urban setting, it was usual that the one to be baptized stood in a shallow basin, with water poured over his or her body. Common baptismal practice would rely upon still water and the washing metaphor; at least this would be indicated by such surviving baptismal arrangements as may be seen in Roman churches, at San Clemente and the Lateran Baptistery. The common iconography of the baptism of Jesus by John the Baptist

12 Didache 7 (Richardson, 174).

depicts the Baptist standing in the stream pouring water upon Jesus from a vessel.

The protective discipline with which the Eucharist will be surrounded is already evident. As in Justin only the baptized who profess right belief and who walk in the way are to participate (9:5).[13] Confession, perhaps something like the commonly used *Confiteor* or perhaps public profession of specific sins, is required before communion.[14] Twice the author warns his readers that they are to make their confession not privately but in church, *ekklēsia*, and not to make their sacrifice without confessing their transgressions (4.14, 14.1). It is assumed by the text that the Eucharist is a sacrifice (14.1), but there is no mention of the body and blood of Christ, no reference to the institution narrative as described in the Synoptics and taught by Paul (1 Cor. 11:23–32). The Eucharist provides "spiritual food and drink" (11.3). The author is searching for a language that develops over time, as when Justin will say that Christians do not receive the Eucharistic elements as ordinary bread but "as the flesh and blood of that incarnate Jesus."[15] Oddly, the typical order in which the bread is offered before the cup is reversed, reflecting perhaps the influence of the pattern later assumed by Luke 22:17–20. The practice Saint Paul considered an abuse in Corinth, the celebrating of the sacrament in the context of a shared meal, was still the custom, for the text of 10:1 can be translated "after you are finished," or better "after you are satisfied." The prayers proposed are a pattern but not an inviolable pattern—any prophet might celebrate the Eucharist as he saw fit (10.7)—but are intended to regularize the practice of the churches.

That said, the *Didache* offers in the language of high liturgy the model that would have inspired the words said each Lord's Day over the cup and bread offered in the churches to whom the *Didache* was addressed:

> First concerning the cup, we give thanks to thee, our Father, for the holy vine of David your child, which thou didst

13 "No one is allowed to partake except those who believe the things we teach are true and has received the washing for forgiveness of sins and for rebirth and lives as Christ handed down to us" (Justin, 66 [Richardson, 286]).

14 1 John 5:16–17.

15 Justin 66 (Richardson, 286).

> make known to us Jesus thy Child; to thee be glory forever. And of the bread: We give thee thanks our father, for the life and knowledge thou didst make known to us through Jesus thy child; to thee be glory forever. As this broken bread was scattered upon the mountains, but was brought together and became one, so let thy Church be gathered together from the ends of the earth into thy kingdom. At the conclusion of the feast, when those present are satisfied: We give thanks to thee, our Father, for thy holy name which thou didst make to tabernacle in our hearts, and for the knowledge and faith and immortality which thou didst make known to us through Jesus thy child. To thee be glory forever. Thou didst create all things for thy name's sake, and didst give food and drink to man for their enjoyment, that they might give thanks to thee, but us thou hast blessed with spiritual food and drink and eternal life. Above all we give you thanks that you are mighty. To thee be glory forever. Remember, Lord, thy Church to deliver it from all evil and to make it perfect in thy love, and gather it together in its holiness from the four winds to thy kingdom which thou hast prepared for it. For thine is the power and the glory forever. Let grace come and let this world pass away. Hosanna to the God of David. If any man be holy let him come. If any man be not, let him repent (10.1–6).

The metaphor of the bread scattered and brought together lies deep in the Hebrew Scriptures, in the prophet Nahum's image of the people of Israel scattered on the mountains (3:18), in Isaiah's prophecy of the gathering together of all Israel on the Day (27:11), and in Jesus' prophecy that when the Son of Man returns the angels will gather the elect from the four winds and from one end of heaven to the other (Matt. 24:31). The thanksgiving celebrates the election of the holy faithful, gathered into the kingdom of Christ, which is foreshadowed in the Eucharist and perfected when Christ returns: "Our Lord, come!" (10.6, 1 Cor. 16:21). Why the Eucharistic prayers of the *Didache* neglect the recitation of Jesus' own words over the offered bread and wine, words well established, traditional when Paul wrote First Corinthians will remain a puzzle.[16] But then we cannot be certain that they were omitted for the fixed form of the liturgy was a work in progress. When Hippolytus wrote his *Apostolic Tradition* about 230 the bishop was invited to follow the model provided but was reminded that "it is not altogether necessary for him to recite the very same words which we gave before . . . but let each one pray according to his own ability."[17]

The writer's eschatology, Christ will soon return to call the Church to himself, is straightforward and fervent. There is nothing of the anxiety of the church in Thessalonica, whose members were concerned that those who had died before Jesus' return might be left out of that glorious event (4:13–18); or of the Johannine community, where the death of the beloved witness was perceived as a violation of the promise that he would live until Jesus' return, causing a crisis among the brethren (20:20–23). There is no apologetic recognition that envisioned missions to all nations as the patient work of time: "This gospel of the kingdom will be preached throughout the whole world as a testimony to all nations, and then the end will come" (Matt. 24:14), and no apology as in Second Peter: "The Lord is not slow as some men count slowness, but is forbearing toward you, not wishing that any should perish but that all should reach repentance" (3:9). One day with the Lord is like a thousand years and a thousand years like a day (cf. Psalm 90:4). The *Didache* shares the fervor of the Apocalypse, the dramatic ending of which, "Come Lord Jesus," is mirrored in the *Didache:* "Let grace come and let this world pass away" (10.6). The Church waits in expectation: "The Lord will come and all his saints with him. Then the world will see the Lord coming on the clouds of the sky" (16.7). The advice to watch for the Lord who would return unexpectedly, like a thief in the night, had not lost its force as the hope that, as in John's Apocalypse (22:20), conditions daily life.[18]

The coda to the Eucharistic prayer that allows the prophets "to hold Eucharist as they will," points toward the interest displayed in the last

16 "I received from the Lord what I delivered to you" (1 Cor. 11:23).

17 Hippolytus, *Apostolic Tradition* 10, as cited in Quasten, 2:189.

18 Jesus taught that no one knew the day or the hour, which undergirded his reiterated teaching that the disciples be always watchful, as in the parables of Matthew 25:1–30). The image of the thief in the night was a popular eschatological metaphor, as in 1Thessalonians 5:2, 1 Peter 4:15, 2 Peter 3:3, Revelation 3:3, 16:15.

chapters in regularizing a situation in which the ministry of itinerant apostles and prophets is being replaced by the settled ministry of bishops and deacons. These, apostles and prophets, are to be received as the Lord, but are to stay one day, or perhaps two, but if still present on the third day are false prophets. Prophets are one of the three original ministries providing a link with the prophets of Hebrew Scriptures (1 Cor. 12:28), with the ancient prophets such as Isaiah, and with John the Baptist, the prophetess Anna, and Philip's daughters, men and women directly inspired by God. As well as celebrating the Eucharist in whatever words they choose, the prophets' ecstatic utterances are not to be questioned or examined (11.7), for to do so is the sin against the Holy Spirit that cannot be forgiven (Matt. 12:31). No one can judge their behavior because they are judged by God (11.11). If a prophet foresees a great feast he is not to participate in it (11.9). If he asks for money, he is a false prophet (11.6). If he enacts an earthly mystery of the Church, if he does not teach others to do what he does himself, he shall not be judged by you, for his judgment is with God, for so it was the prophets of old (11.11–12). The reference is to the practice of the prophets of old, who, when commanded by God employed some dramatic action to symbolize their prophecy, as when Jeremiah wore the waistcloth (13:1–11) or carried the yoke about Jerusalem (28:10–11). Occasionally there might be a prophet who wished to give up itinerancy and settle in a community. Should a prophet do so, he was to be supported by the church; he would be the high priest of the community (13.2).

Among the early Fathers the argument from prophecy, the demonstration that what the prophets had prophesied Jesus had fulfilled, was ubiquitous and compelling. At Pentecost Peter argued that what the assembled pilgrims saw and heard represented the fulfillment of the prophecy of Joel (Acts 2:16–18, Joel 2:28–32). The same Spirit who had inspired the Church at Pentecost, enabling believers to discover Christ in the prophets' words, had inspired the prophets.

> The prophets who prophesied of the grace that was to be yours searched and inquired about this salvation; they inquired what person or time was indicated by the Spirit of Christ within them when predicting the sufferings of Christ and the subsequent glory. It was revealed to them that they were serving not

> themselves but you, in the things that have now been announced to you by those who preach the good news to you by the Holy Spirit (1 Pt 1:10-12).

Prophecy was widely practiced in the 180s when Irenaeus wrote his *Demonstration of the Apostolic Preaching*, and in his work *The Refutation and Overthrow of the Knowledge Falsely So Called* he defended prophecy against those who wanted it suppressed, a situation perhaps foreshadowed in the strictures of the *Didache* against questionable prophetic behavior (11:8–12). The prophetic gift had been an honorable and essential part of Christian life since Saint Paul, who considered it the most desirable of the spiritual gifts for the life of the congregation (1 Cor. 14:5). With the outbreak of the New Prophecy of the Montanists, perhaps as early as the 160s, the gift of prophecy had become controversial, with Victor of Rome (189–98) refusing to recognize the prophetic gifts of the leading Montanist prophets and Irenaeus defending prophesy as ancient practice in his work against the Gnostics in 185.[19] The difficulties caused by Spirit-inspired prophetic behavior, intimated in the *Didache*, would be realized in the future, when the ecstatic style of the New Prophecy of Montanus would trouble the church in Phrygia. The office of prophet as we find it portrayed in the *Didache* has obviously been subjected to the kind of abuse that would inevitably follow upon the conviction that prophets were inspired immediately by God and answerable only "to the spirits of the prophets." Spirit-filled and important as prophets were, unique as their status may have been, their ministry was typically itinerant. A stay of one day is ideal, three at the most.

The *Didache* gives us an invaluable picture of the Christian life, probably in the 70s or 80s, when the Eucharist might be celebrated *ad libitum*, when prophets were highly honored but their claims of privilege were viewed with reverent suspicion, and when the authority of bishops and

19 *Against Heresies* 3.11.9 (*ANF* 1:429). Tertullian says that the bishop of Rome, Eleutherius (175–89) or Victor (189–98), first accepted but then, inspired by Praxeas, rejected the Montanist prophets, (*Against Praxeas* 1 *ANF* 3:597). And see G. S. P. Freeman-Grenville, "The Date of the Outbreak of Montanism," *Journal of Ecclesiastical History* 5 (1954):7–15.

deacons required bolstering, presumably because these, although familiar in Roman cults, were novelties in Churches born of a Jewish context (15.1). The seeds of the Church Ignatius would know were already planted in the Church of the *Didache*. The way to life was known through references to canonical Matthew or its predecessor. The revolutionary, counter-cultural morality of Christianity was securely in place. The formative character of the sacraments was assumed. Prophecy would be valued and honored, but the life of the community was to be stabilized by overseers, *episkopoi*. Anticipation that Jesus would return very soon was high.

There is an appealing mildness of temper about the *Didache*. If you cannot use running water, use warm water, and if not warm then still water (7.2–3). "If you can bear the Lord's full yoke you will be perfect. But if you cannot, then do what you can" (6:2). "If anyone is holy let him come. If not let him repent" (10:6), yet one must be holy when Jesus returns; "a lifetime of faith will be of no advantage to you unless you prove perfect at the very last" (16:3). Its moral teaching became the teaching of the Church. Its liturgical formularies have a compelling beauty. The near-identity of the sacramental practice mandated in the *Didache* with the uses of the Church in the fourth century and later bears impressive witness to the consistency of the tradition.

How the *Didache*, known to Athanasius, could have been lost is a puzzle. Philotheos Bryrennios, Archbishop of Nicomedia, who found the *Didache* and Constantin von Tischendorf, the discoverer of *Codex Sinaiticus*, should be given prominent places among those who in an age of skepticism demonstrated the reliability of tradition and the trustworthiness of the Biblical text. Just as the Dead Sea Scrolls demonstrated the stability of the Hebrew text, the *Didache* offers evidence that the sacramental life and moral form of the Church were well in place in the age of Clement of Rome.

# Two
## *Clement: Counsel from Rome*

> Give us joy at this feast of St. Clement, the priest and martyr, who bore witness with his blood to the love he proclaimed and the gospel he preached.
>
> Collect for St. Clement's Day

Sometime in the 80s or 90s there was trouble in the church at Corinth, with one party in dispute appealing to Rome, where Clement, traditionally considered third successor to the Apostle Peter, presided over that church. There had been a schism pitting those who held office against rebels who wished, for whatever reason, to remove them. Clement's analysis is that the church in Corinth had misused the peace which had been granted. It had become prosperous, too prosperous, and thus too proud: "Hence came jealousy, and envy, strife and sedition, persecution and tumult, war and captivity. The dishonored rose up against those who were held in honor, those of no reputation against the notable, the stupid against the wise, the young against their elders. For this reason peace is far from you." The cause was "one or two individuals"(47:6), but those who had been thrust out may have included a bishop, for Clement references the expulsion of those who have "offered the gifts of the bishop's office blamelessly," indeed with "innocence and holiness" (44:5) as well as presbyters who were "living honorably." These had been appointed by the apostles or other men of repute who succeeded them and apparently confirmed in office by the consent of the whole church, which was the common practice.

Corinth was the important city at the isthmus joining Achaia to Megara and Attica on its north. Destroyed in the wars through which Rome annexed Greece in the 150s, it was refounded in BC 44, and when Paul visited Corinth it was the flourishing capital of Achaia. We know a good deal about the Corinthian church from Saint Paul's First Letter to the Corinthians. This letter is famous for the beauty of the treatise on love in chapter 13, and for the inspired exposition of the resurrection in chapter 12, but much of Paul's letter is taken up with difficulties that had been reported to him. There was tension between those who traced their faith to the teaching of Apollos and those who preferred Paul (3:5–6). Someone had presumed to marry his father's wife, his step-mother, thus committing incest and causing her to sin as well; a scandal which, Paul wrote, was not even to be found among the Gentiles (1 Cor. 5:1). The Corinthians had questions about the advisability of marriage in the light of the imminent return of Jesus, regarding which Paul permitted marriage but counseled celibacy as the higher way among Christians waiting for the day (1 Cor. 7:7–9). Paul's apostleship, hence his authority, was evidently questioned by some members of the congregation (9:1–2). The persistence of the love feast or common meal as the context of the Eucharistic sacrifice had led to various abuses, gluttony and drunkenness, which in turn led to Paul's exposition of the tradition he had received regarding the Eucharist and his warning about receiving the body and blood unworthily (1 Cor. 12:17–33). Finally, there were those who denied that the future resurrection would occur, probably because they believed like Alexander and Hymenaeus that it had already been realized (15:12–30, 1 Tim. 1:20, 2 Tim. 2:17). So when Clement in the address of his letter praised the spiritual excellence and steadfastness of the Corinthians, he may have been following the practice of saying the best that could be hoped for before entering the arena of argument.

The question as to why Corinthian Christians appealed to the Roman church at a time of crisis when Ephesus, even Alexandria, was nearer, is to be answered by the status of that church as the preeminent witness to the faith. Rome was the center of the empire and appeal to Rome was habitual, but the deeper reason was the character of the Roman church as the Church of Peter and Paul, within which recognition lay the still deeper awareness of the place of Peter as the center of the apostolic mission, and thus as the central witness to the apostolic preaching that emanated from the twelve. In this period there was not much appeal to Matthew 16:17, to Peter as the rock and possessor of the keys, but there is a profound awareness that it was Peter who, despite his weakness, had been given grace to name Jesus the Messiah (Matt. 16:16), had been the first witness to the Lord's resurrection (Luke 24:12, John 20:6), and had stood up as chief witness and spokesman for the twelve to proclaim the coming of the Holy Spirit at Pentecost (Acts 2:14). Even as Paul claimed an independent call sanctioned by his unique Pentecostal experience on the Damascus road, he was careful to assure himself that his Gospel was consonant with the Gospel taught by Peter at Jerusalem (Gal. 2:2).

The place of the Roman church at the stable heart of the apostolic mission was secured by two other circumstances. The living authority of Peter and Paul was established at Rome by the possession of their holy bodies, which Christians in Corinth surely knew. At least since 156, when Christians in Smyrna had tried in vain to secure the body of Polycarp, the bodies of the saints had been considered precious possessions.[1] This was rooted in the incarnational faith of the Church and specifically in the conviction that in possessing the body of one of the holy ones, one possessed the only human thing that could be known with certainty to participate in the life of heaven and the age to come.

Not much is known about the veneration of Paul's body before the great church on the Via Ostiensis was built in the 380s, but the spot by the red wall just outside the Circus of Nero where Peter had been buried after his death was a place of pilgrimage and prayer. Archaeology suggests that there was formal architectural recognition of its importance by 150. At the turn of the third century, about 200, a Roman presbyter Gaius, in an argument with Proclus, a defender of the Phrygian heresy later called Montanism, wrote, as Eusebius reports, "concerning the place where the sacred bodies of the aforesaid apostles are laid," adding, "But I can show the trophies [*tropaia,* victory monuments] of the apostles. For if you will go to the Vatican or the Ostian way you will find the trophies of those who laid the foundations of this Church."[2] Peter and Paul, who had taught and died

1 *Martyrdom*, 17–18. At Vienne in the principate of Verus (163–69) the ashes of martyrs were swept into the Rhone so that Christians could not revere their relics, guarding them in expectation of the resurrection (*Church History* 5.1.1–63 [*NPNF*² 1:212–16]).

2 *Church History* 2.25.7 (*NPNF*² 1:130). In an argument with Pope Victor (189–98) Polycrates of Ephesus cited the presence in Asia of the relics of great

in Rome, spoke in the Roman church. That church would remain unclouded by heresy, which was never charged against it until the pontificate of Callixtus (217–22), when in the controversy about the forgiveness of post-baptismal sin a culpable laxity was attributed to Callixtus. Characteristically the Roman bishop came to the defense of the orthodox under attack, which in a sense was what Clement was doing when he wrote to Corinth. Rome would be Athanasius' best friend in the fourth century.

Add to this awareness of the presence of the two great apostles as living voices the reputation of that church of right belief, rooted in the teaching of the founding apostles, a kind of acknowledgement of which one hears in the addresses of both Paul and Ignatius to that church. It was famous when Paul wrote in the 50s, "I thank my God through Jesus Christ for you all, that your faith is spoken of throughout the whole world." When, perhaps about 115, Ignatius of Antioch wrote to the Roman church urging them not to interpose themselves in his path to martyrdom, he described that church with admiration as "having the presidency of the country of the region of the Romans, being worthy of God, worthy of honor, worthy of felicitation, worth of praise, worthy of success, worthy in purity, and having the presidency of love, walking in the law of Christ and members in the father's name; which church I also salute in the name of Jesus Christ." Ignatius congratulated the Roman church because they were taught by Peter and Paul. "They were apostles, I am a convict. . . ."[3]

There must have been time in the late 50s or early 60s when both apostles were in the city. When Paul wrote to the Roman church he had a long history of proclaiming the Gospel in the great apostolic mission, from Jerusalem around to Illyricum on the eastern shore of the Adriatic (15:19). He was then on his way to Jerusalem, but he proposed, that duty done, to make for Spain and on the way to visit the Roman church (Rom. 15:24–25). We do not know when Paul arrived in Rome, but that he did so is related in the closing verses of Acts. Having been taken to Rome a prisoner, he was allowed to live in his own hired house, "and received all that came

saints, among them John the disciple whom Jesus loved, Polycarp and Melito of Sardis, as lending authority to his episcopal voice (*Church History* 5.24.2–5 [*NPNF*² 1:242]).

3 *Rom.* 4.3 (Richardson, 104).

to him, preaching the kingdom of God, and teaching those things that concern the Lord Jesus Christ, with all confidence, no man forbidding him" (28:31).

By then the Christian presence in Rome was enough to cause Nero (54–68) to blame the fire of 64 on the ever-unpopular Christians. The date of Paul's martyrdom is unknown, but tradition places it in the reign of Nero and considers the place where three springs flowed, now the site of the ancient monastery of S. Paolo alle Tre Fontane, the place where Paul was beheaded, execution by the sword being the prerogative of Roman citizens. Paul was buried outside the walls, where Constantine would build a church in the 330s. In 386 the Emperor Theodosius I began the much larger church that the present Saint Paul's, rebuilt after the disastrous fire of 1823, replicates, and when Paul's relics, long forgotten, were rediscovered in 2001, they were in a sarcophagus of the late fourth century.[4]

When Peter came to Rome is not known. He had been in Antioch before Paul, and the existence of a party of Cephas in Corinth attests his presence there (1 Cor. 1:12, 3:22). Peter was in Jerusalem about 45 when Paul met him there on the journey mentioned above, the occasion when Paul presented his Gospel to those who were "pillars" (Gal. 2:9). Whenever he arrived, the commonly accepted tradition, cited by Eusebius, is that Peter died under Nero, and most scholars associate his death with that persecution. The reference in John 21:18 to the death of Peter in old age with his armed stretched out, on the cross, may or may not be prophecy after the fact, but the evidence discovered attests to its truth. Every bone of what is thought to be Peter's body was found but his feet, suggesting that the tradition that he was crucified upside down may be accurate. The place of Peter's execution was the circus of Nero on the Vatican, and he was buried just outside the walls of a site later developed as a cemetery. The location of the obelisk, now relocated to the center of Bernini's colonnade, as it stood on the spina of the circus, is marked in the pavement of the Courtyard of the Roman Proto-Martyrs to the south of the basilica. The early popularity of his burial place as a place of pilgrimage can be dated from the coins

4 Maria Cristina Valsecci, "St. Paul's Tomb Unearthed in Rome," *National Geographic News*, 11 December 2006; Nick Squires, "Bone Fragments Determined to Be St. Paul's," London *Telegraph*, 28 January 2009.

found during excavations, and the evidence suggests that the *aedicula*,[5] the miniature building-like structure affixed to the red wall to mark the apostle's grave, was in place by about 150. One column of the pair that supported the altar-like table built into the aedicula can be seen *in situ* in the excavations beneath St. Peter's. The basilica that bears his name literally grew from the body of Peter, with altar after altar rising above that spot by the red wall.

Twenty years after the deaths of Peter and Paul, appeal to Rome meant appeal to its bishop Clement, who is associated with the church of San Clemente in Rome. The house at the lowest level of the three through which the present church was developed, opposite the narrow street from the Mithraeum, is traditionally considered Clement's house, the *titulus* from which the church grew.[6] Later there developed an elaborate hagiography that took Clement to the East, where he was martyred by being thrown into the Black Sea weighed down with a great anchor. But what we know best about Clement we know from his letter.

Clements's letter was written in response to a request from members of the Church in Corinth who objected to the putting aside of the duly appointed clergy, and it did not occur to the author that what happened in Corinth was none of his affair; the writer clearly expected his advice to carry great weight. The apology for the delay in turning to "the dispute that has arisen among you" had been caused by the "sudden and repeated calamities" that had befallen the Church, which must mean persecutions. Of how little worth the lives of Christians were held to be is indicated by Pliny's letter to Trajan, in which stubbornness, unwillingness to cooperate with the authorities, is punished with death and the torture of maidservants is a casual means to obtaining information.[7]

5 The "little building," the small open-air structure consisting of an altar-like table attached to the red wall, with an opening above that provided communication with the body below. It was the custom to lower objects to bring them near the body of Peter, thereby gaining the apostle's powerful blessing.

6 A *titulus* was a sign or plaque calling out the name of the owner of a house or property, in this sense the legal definition of property held for the Church in the name of a private person when Christians as a corporate body could not legally hold property.

7 Bettenson, 4.

The woman the prophet John saw seated on the seven hills in the Apocalypse 17–18 is not the then politically insignificant Roman church, meeting in a private house, seeking obscurity not publicity, but the imperial power, which upholds the city of merchants and ship owners and bankers John sees as the props of the city of this world and the enemy of the saints (Rev. 18). The prophet John saw that the city of God rested on the foundations of the twelve apostles of the Lamb (21:14); if he was aware of the condition of the church in the city of seven hills, there is no reason to believe, in an age in which Paul and Ignatius offered praise of the Roman church, that in the 80s the prophet John cannot have known of the witness borne by Peter and Paul in Rome.

Clement exercised episcopal authority in Rome. Historically, perhaps twenty or thirty years before Clement wrote, the first order of ministers in settled Christian congregations had been elders, in imitation of the synagogue. "Paul and Barnabas appointed elders for them in every church, with prayer and fasting, they committed them to the Lord in whom they believed" (Acts 14:28). Elders, *presbyteroi*, existed in the generation of the apostles and were the stable centers of their respective congregations. By the last quarter of the first century elders might be supported by the church: "Let the elders who rule well be considered worthy of double honor, especially those who labor in preaching and teaching. You shall not muzzle the ox while he is treading out the grain; the laborer deserves his wages" (I Tim. 5:17–18). These were the apostles' assistants and delegates, not their successors. Elders, like prophets and teachers, gave way to overseers, *episkopoi*, bishops as the Germanic word evolved, whose tasks it was to govern and teach. This is a Greek title; every cult had its *episkopos*. Their office belonged to the settled life of those Christian congregations whose existence represented the success of the itinerant apostles and prophets who were ever on the move. Presiding over the church in one city and its surrounding countryside, bishops did not speak under the dramatic inspiration offered by the prophets, which may have made Christians in the age of the *Didache* somewhat dismissive of the episcopal office, whose task it was to represent unfailingly the tradition they had received. Their assistants were deacons, or servers or servants, an office instituted in Acts to relieve the apostles of charitable works and later to assist at the altar. Whether the function of presbyters and bishops was ever identical is unclear; Titus 1:5–7, which seems to imply the identity of the two offices may be read in this way. But by the age of Clement and Ignatius, the period 80–120, the bishop was the superior office, bearing apostolic authority. The office of presbyter, unlike that of bishop, was integral to every synagogue, and would have been part of the life of every Jewish Christian congregation. The four and twenty elders of the Apocalypse, seated on thrones, clad in white garments, crowned with golden crowns, offering the prayers of the saints, would represent the living Church in the inspired imagination of a prophet (Rev. 4:4).

Clement's *Letter to Corinth*, concerned as it is with order in the Church, is the first straightforward mention of bishops as having been appointed by the apostles. "Preaching everywhere in country and town, they appointed their first-fruits, when they had proved them by the Spirit, to be bishops and deacons unto them that should believe" (42). This would have been done in the 60s or 70s, as the apostolic generation faded; one sees it happening in the *Didache* and it was accepted practice when Clement wrote, but twenty years later, when Ignatius wrote close after the turn of the century, the office was still required advocacy even within what Ignatius called the Catholic Church. There were still those who thought the celebration of the Eucharist did not require the authority of the bishop.[8] That would have included that vast spiritual Church, a kind of Gnostic sea of confusion in which the Catholic Church of Ignatius floated, among whose adherents there was no authority other than the authority of the great teachers such as Valentinus and the insight of the illuminated. So when Clement wrote to Corinth he was required to make an argument for what would be the normative order in a situation in which his assumptions were certainly not novel, but neither were they so firmly established that a faction in Corinth might not think it possible to remove the duly appointed bishop and presbyters, men who had after all probably not been appointed but elected or acclaimed. There had been jealousy over the office of bishop. Clement conducted at Rome the defense of what would become a bedrock of the government of the Church: persistent refusal to recognize the removal of duly appointed and consecrated ministers.[9]

8 *Smyrn.* 8.2 (Richardson, 115).

9 The Roman see, as in the case of Nicholas I (858–67), who risked tension with the East by his refusal to recognize the deposing of Ignatius (of Constan-

Having identified jealously and a too-comfortable prosperity as the causes of the schism, Clement makes his case, arguing not as the agent of law commanding obedience but as a teacher having authority and determined to convince, restoring the bond of charity that united the Church. Clements's letter set a standard for the tone letters from Rome would take: temperate, quick to praise, slow to pass judgment, given to persuading rather than condemning, and yet firm. Clement is deeply aware that the exercise of authority in the Church is marked not by arrogance, which he attributed to the Corinthian rebels, but to humility. "It is to the humble that Christ belongs, not to those who exalt themselves above his flock. The scepter of God's majesty, the Lord Jesus Christ, did not come with pomp or pride or arrogance, though he could have done so. But he came in humility" (16). To miss the fact that Clement considers this matter, which seems to concern Church order, as having profound moral implications is to misunderstand his letter. The Church, the body of Christ, is bound in unity by a common faith which is rooted in the bonds of living charity. The fruit of love is obedience. Rebellion and the schism that accompanies it is a spiritual disaster. Clement's argument in the first century would be Augustine's when he challenged the Donatists in the fifth.

The sources of Clement's argument are two-fold. There is "the rule (*kanōn*) of our tradition" (70). There is also Sacred Scripture, principally the Septuagint, with which Clement is so familiar that the text sometimes seems to be a texture of quotations from the Hebrew Scriptures and with references to several Pauline epistles as well. The rhetorical device Clement will employ is the appeal to examples or *epideigmata* that occupies much of the body of the letter, a technique found also in Hebrews chapter 11, which extolled examples of faith from Abel to David. There are examples of the destructive nature of jealousy (4–6), to which Clement attributed the deaths of Peter and Paul. There are examples of faith from Noah to Rehab (9:2–12), and even examples of noble pagans who out of humility offered themselves "to rescue their subjects by their own blood" with the

tinople) by Photius, would on principle resist the removal even of those it probably wished were out of the way: Ignatius was no favorite of the Roman bishop.

clear implication that the schismatics in Corinth should give up their rebellious wills and submit to duly constituted apostolic authority for the good of the Church (55).

There is an interest in and defense of that organic order that is eminently Christian but is also the political presupposition of every well-educated Roman (18:2–20). There is a beautiful order in the universe: "The sun and moon and choirs of stars roll on harmoniously in their appointed courses at his command. . . . He has decreed the earth become fruitful at the proper seasons. . . . The tiniest creatures come together in harmony and peace" (19:3–20:12). There was order in the worship in the temple; God "ordered sacrifices and services to be performed; and required this to be done, not in a careless and disorderly way, but at the times and seasons he fixed" (40.2). There is order in the empire. Not everybody is a general, colonel, captain, sergeant, and so on, but "each in his rank" carries out the orders of the emperor and of the generals (37.2). "The great cannot exist without the small, neither can the small exist without the great. All are linked together . . ." (37.4). Clement defends a hierarchical, organic order on the model of Paul's image of the body in I Corinthians 12:21–22, in which every man is called by God's providence into his or her state in life, strong or weak, rich or poor, exercising authority or subject to it. There are different bodies; the stars have different glories (1 Cor. 15:40–41). Reflecting the subjective principle, rooted in the second great commandment, that will complement the objective obedience that lies at the heart of Christian order, Clement writes, "Let each of us please his neighbor for his good, to edify him" (Rom. 15:2). Rebellion against this order as God has revealed it to the Church is rebellion against God. Obedience and humility are hallmarks of the Christian world; chapter 21 is Clements's image of Christians in this world: reverence for the Lord Jesus who shed his blood for us, respect for rulers, honor for the elders, children reared in the fear of God. The healing of schism will come when the rebels in Corinth accept the godly order of the Church in humility, when one or two arrogant persons and the faction they have generated no longer have any desire to persist in disobedience.

Clement's conclusion is crowned with his short treatise on love, perhaps the first extra-canonical treatment of what will be the reality and theme of Christian life, indeed the charter of the new creation.

> Who can describe the bond of God's love? Who is capable of expressing its great beauty? The heights to which love leads are beyond description. Love unites us to God. Love hides a multitude of sins. Love puts up with everything and is always patient. There is nothing vulgar about love, nothing arrogant. Love knows nothing of schism or revolt. Love does everything in harmony. By love God's elect were made perfect. Without love nothing can please God. By love the Master accepted us. Because of the love he had for us, in accordance with God's will, Jesus Christ our Lord gave his blood for us, his flesh for our flesh, and his life for ours (49:2–6).

Love is the ultimate gift, offered to the Corinthian rebels as the medium of their repentance.

The great concluding prayer is a reflection on God's omnipotence and majesty. Clement's attitude toward the imperial government deepens the mystery of Rome's intransigent, if intermittent, persecution. Clement wrote, "You, Master, gave them imperial power through your majestic and inscrutable might, so that we, recognizing that it was you who gave them glory and honor, might submit to them and in no way oppose your will" (61:1). Clement prayed, "Guide our steps and so that we walk with holy hearts and do what is good and pleasing to you, and to our rulers" (60:2). This civic duty as commanded by the apostolic mission can be traced to the teaching of Peter: "Be subject for the Lord's sake to every human institution . . . . Honor all men. Love the brotherhood. Fear God. Honor the Emperor" (1 Pet. 2:13–17) and Paul: "Let every person be subject to the governing authorities" (Rom. 13:1).

The petition of the Corinthians to Clement's Roman church and Clement's reply, with its mixture of firmness and gentleness, its appeal to common faith and common history, would exemplify the pattern of humble exhortation and claim to authority that would ever typify the charitable communication that bound believers to the church of Peter's successors. Clement's letter would be highly valued, so much so that it was read at the Eucharist in Corinth until the third century, and would find an audience far beyond dissident Corinthians, being included in the fifth century in

*Codex Alexandrinus*, one of the principal witnesses to the New Testament text, alongside the Gospels.

Clement would die at the hands of the imperial authority, perhaps not long after he wrote to Corinth, one of thirty-one bishops of the Roman church who would suffer for Christ before Constantine made Christianity legal in 313. The providential survival of Clement's letter gave evidence of the place of Rome and the manner of its witness and government fifty years after Pentecost, and anchored the judgement given by Irenaeus just a century later when he called it "that very great, oldest, and well-known church, founded and established at Rome by those two most glorious apostles Peter and Paul. . . . Every church must be in harmony with this church because of its outstanding pre-eminence."[10] Its authority derived in part from its fame, in part from the distinction of its founding apostles, but Rome's pre-eminence was always, as Ignatius wrote, "the presidency of love."

In the last decade of the first Christian century it was clear that those in authority in the churches had not volunteered, but had been sent, a situation much different that the reality among the Gnostics.

10 *Against Heresies* 3.2.2 (*ANF* 1:415).

# Three
## *Ignatius: Catholic Faith*

> Nobody must do anything that has to do with the Church without the bishop's approval. You should regard that Eucharist as valid which is celebrated either by the bishop or someone he authorizes. Where the bishop is, there let the congregation gather, just as where Jesus Christ is, there is the Catholic Church.
>
> Ignatius to the Smyrnaeans 8.1–2

The extant letters of Ignatius, Bishop of Antioch in Syria, were written to five Asian churches, three of which—Ephesus, Smyrna, and Philadelphia—had been addressed by the prophet John in his Apocalypse perhaps thirty years earlier, to Polycarp, bishop of Smyrna, and to Rome. As bishop of the capital of the old Seleucid Empire, Ignatius was a person of importance, obviously considered so by the imperial authorities, who arrested and arraigned him in Antioch as subversive to Roman authority. In chains, guarded by a cohort of ten soldiers, his "ten leopards" who "only grow worse when they are kindly treated," he, like Paul before him, as a Roman citizen was on the way to trial in Rome, his chains and guards a testimony to an effectiveness that made the authorities in Syria anxious for his death.[1] The church at Antioch over which Ignatius presided would have loomed large in Christian imagination at the turn of the century. It was the fruit of the first missionary endeavor of Peter (Acts 11:19–22), whose martyrdom at Rome was now famous, and it was there in Antioch that the brethren were first called Christians (Acts 11:26). As Ignatius traveled west, his movements determined by the plans of his captors, he was welcomed as the

1 *Rom.* 5.1 (Richardson, 104), *Eph.* 11.2 (Richardson, 91).

saintly representative of the famous church of Antioch. Ignatius received delegations and wrote letters of encouragement; at Smyrna he was visited by messengers from Ephesus and Magnesia.[2]

In the perhaps twenty years since Clement had written his letter to Corinth, the organization and faith of the Church had developed so that one could see in outline the Church of Irenaeus. There was now the evident influence of the ideas found in Paul's letters and more especially in the Gospel and letters of John, the influence of whose thought is not easily discerned in the first Christian century. Which Christian texts Ignatius had before him is debated—he certainly knew the Septuagint and Matthew—but even if he did not have the text of the Gospel of John before him, his appropriation of ideas formative of Johannine tradition is apparent. There is a new Johannine vocabulary. Some form of "love," the verb or cognate substantive occurs thirty-one times in John, twenty-one times in 1 John, only seven times in Matthew and five times in Mark, while "truth" is found twenty-one times in John, nineteenth times in the three epistles, once in Matthew, twice in Luke and three times in Mark. Love, *agape*, occurs at least thirty times in Ignatius' seven short letters.[3]

The mystery of the indwelling love of God illuminates Ignatius' letters; God's gifts of faith and especially love make union with Jesus the end and perfection of Christian life, "faith the beginning and love the end."[4] In John's Gospel Jesus had promised that the Counselor would dwell with those who believed; "he dwells with you and will be in you" (14:17). "You will know that I am in the Father, and you in me, and I in you" (14:20). Ignatius writes to the Ephesians that genuine life is "in Jesus Christ" (11:1). "Let us do all things in the conviction that he dwells in us. Thus we shall be his temples and he will be our God within us" (15.3). Sharing in the life of "the New Man Jesus Christ" makes every Christian the citizen of a new world in which death is being cast out (49).

2 *Magn.* 15.1 (Richardson, 97).

3 In addition to the striking similarities of vocabulary there are common grammatical uses, among them a preference for the perfect tense. See Morton Enselin, "The Perfect Tense in the Fourth Gospel," *Journal of Biblical Literature,* 55 (1936), 121–31.

4 *Eph.* 14.1 (Richardson, 91).

Union with Christ is effected through baptism and the Eucharist. Christ was baptized so that his death might hallow water, through which the new birth of John 3:5 is accomplished.[5] Ignatius will echo Jesus' words to the woman at the well: "There is living water within me, which speaks and says within me, 'Come to the Father'" (John 4:10).[6] As in John 6, "God's bread… is the flesh of Christ . . . I want his blood, an immortal love feast indeed" (Rom. 7:3). The Eucharist displays and causes the unity of the Church: "There is one flesh of our Lord Jesus Christ, and one cup of his blood that makes us one, and one altar, just as there is one bishop along with the presbytery and deacons, my fellow slaves. In that way what you do is in line with God's will" (*Phld.* 4.1). So complete is the union between Jesus and the Word that Ignatius will write of the "blood of God" (Eph.1.1). The spirituals "hold aloof from the Eucharist and from services of prayer because they refuse to admit that the Eucharist is the flesh of our Savior Jesus Christ" (Smyrn. 7.1).

From the beginning the Church had been defined not only by participation in its sacraments but by its beliefs or profession, constituted by its conviction that Jesus is Messiah and Son of God, the charge under which Christ died (Matt. 26:62–65). The Pentecostal profession was: "God has made him both Lord and Christ, this Jesus whom you crucified" (Acts 3:36). And Paul in Romans: "If you confess with your lips and believe in your heart that God raised him from the dead, you will be saved" (10:9). In the end every knee will bow and every tongue confess that Jesus Christ is Lord (*Phld.* 2:11). John required that his readers profess the Incarnation: that Jesus had not only come into the world, but that he had come "in the flesh," and the Gospel was written to convince the readers "that Jesus is the Christ," so that believing they might have life (20:31). This necessity for public profession made Christian witness no private matter; on a certain day it might be a matter of life or death, for it was the work of an inquisitor, when persecution was in season, to offer Christians their lives in exchange for denial of Christ. Pliny recalled, at a time not far distant from Ignatius' journey to Rome, that some in his provincial capital, accused of being Christians, had exonerated themselves by cursing Christ, which no true Christian would do.[7]

5 Eph. 18.2 (Richardson, 92).
6 Rom. 7.2 (Richardson, 103).
7 Bettenson, 3.

When Ignatius wrote, the Christian profession of faith was taking the familiar shape it would assume after the great councils of the fourth and fifth centuries. In the letters there are three summaries of Christian profession,[8] each asserting that Jesus is divine and human, the son of David and the Son of God; that he was a born of the Virgin Mary—her name occurs five times in Ignatius; that he was truly possessed of human nature, that he really suffered and died; that this took place at a specific time, under Pontius Pilate, and that he rose again from the dead. Failure to believe these truths put one outside the sanctuary. The Church was on the way to the great professions of faith by way of writers like Irenaeus, in whose *Refutation and Overthrow of the Knowledge Falsely So-Called* their outline is clear,[9] through the creeds of Nicaea and its clarifications, and finally to what is the longest, and perhaps the loveliest of all, the fifth-century creed given Athanasius' name, beginning *Quicunque vult*: "Whoever would be saved, it is necessary that he profess the catholic faith" and going on to name the relations and missions of the three divine persons.

By the turn of the century the Church had taken the hierarchical structure that would be characteristic. Bishops, no longer as in the *Didache* slighted as mere functionaries lacking the charismatic gifts of apostles and prophets, appear in Ignatius as the stable centers of the churches, the chief teachers and liturgical officers of their respective communities, bulwarks of right faith in an ocean of heresy that threatened to destroy the Catholic faith. Communion with them, which meant love issuing in obedience, Ignatius considered an essential mark of the Church. "I cried out when I was among you; I spoke with a loud voice, 'Give heed to the bishop and the presbytery and the deacons.'"[10] "Without the bishop's supervision, no baptisms or love feasts are permitted" (*Smyrn.* 8:2). This carefully defined liturgical and theological office, held as in Clement's *Letter to Corinth* to be of apostolic origin and authority,[11] developed

8 *Eph.* 20.1–2 (Richardson, 93), *Trall.* 8:2–3 (Richardson, 100), *Smyrn.* 1.1–2 (Richardson, 112–13).

9 *Against Heresies* 1.10 (*ANF* 1:330).

10 *Phld.* 7:1–2 (Richardson, 109–10); *Didache* 15.1–2.

11 Clement 42 (Richardson, 62). The use of the commonplace title "overseer" or "supervisor" found also in pagan cults was unremarkable and almost inevitable. The Germanic "bishop" mildly mystifies the Greek sense.

originally to perpetuate the apostolic mission, would prove in the post-apostolic age to be the bulwark against the threat of a shadow church that used Christian-like vocabulary but with very different meanings. The New Testament Epistles, and probably one of the four Gospels, John, is marked by an awareness of the existence of contending missions and of a great movement set against the incarnational theology of glory that would be represented by Ignatius, Justin, and Irenaeus. The episcopal office, with its canons of regular nomination and election, the mutual recognition of other bishops and of the authority of the great sees, its insistence that those who governed must have been sent, was calculated to confirm the faith and to establish sacramental unity in love. The episcopal office, to which the Roman bishop belonged, was to emerge as the honored and weighty example.

The episcopacy was given apostolic authority, as maintained by Clement and assumed in the pastoral epistles of First Timothy and Titus, and even recognized in the *Didache*.[12] This proves to be the balance-wheel of teaching, yet the exercise of the office was not immune from desolating difficulties, as in the war between Hippolytus and Callixtus in the early third century, the conflict between bishop and bishop in the Donatist controversy of the early fifth century, and the dispiriting opposition of the Anti-pope Laurentius to Pope Symmachus in the early sixth. Later centuries would bring their own difficulties, such as the existence of two, on one occasion three, Roman bishops during the Avignon schism of 1317 to 1478 rooted in the investiture controversy.[13] There have always been grounds supporting an unromantic view of many of the occupants of the Chair of Peter, but the episcopal office itself was despised by the Gnostics on the systematic grounds that there could be no visible Church; "Others, outside our number, call themselves bishops and deacons as though they received their authority from God. . . .

12 Clement 42.4 (Richardson, 62); 1 Tim. 3:1; Tit. 1:7; *Didache*, 15:1–2 (Richardson, 178).

13 Avignon is a commune in southern France purchased by Pope Clement VI from Johanna I of Naples in 1348, over which the papacy maintained control until the revolution in 1791. The removal of the papacy from Rome to Avignon, although it had complicated political causes, at least enabled the French king to influence papal elections and to appoint French cardinals, thus to confute the doctrine of Boniface VIII in *Unam Sanctam* (1302).

These people are waterless canals."[14] When Tertullian finally left the Catholic Church, disgusted with the laxity of its members, he repaired to, and became an early advocate for, the "spiritual church," defining the Church as a number of persons joined together in the Spirit, "not the Church which consists of a number of bishops."[15] The treasure was in earthen vessels.

Often the chaotic nature of the world from which the Church emerged is obscured by the sixteenth-century historiography that posits a period of primitive purity, a period which, if it is intended to describe pervasive sanctity and doctrinal unanimity, is largely an illusion, for the first two Christian centuries were marked by dissent, theological confusion resulting from insufficient development of revealed truth, moral failure, and rebellion. There were alternative hierarchies, or at least mutually hostile missions, and there must have been some close relation between the existence of different hierarchies or schools and the existence of Gospels as different as John and Valentinus' *Gospel of Truth*. Saint Paul was harassed by "false apostles, deceitful workers, who had transformed themselves into apostles of Christ" (2 Cor. 11:13). Second Timothy 3:1–11 is an energetic condemnation of those traitors to the Gospel of corrupt mind who are ever learning and never coming to the truth, and Second Peter is strong against those who bring in damnable heresies (2:1), while Revelation 2:2 describes those who say they are apostles but are not. The author of the Johannine Epistles is challenged by those who will not even receive his emissaries (3 John 9). The text of the Epistle of Jude is mostly a diatribe against those who have secretly gained admission, "ungodly persons who pervert the grace of our God into licentiousness and deny our only master and Lord Jesus Christ" (4).

While notice of these difficulties is ubiquitous, few New Testament texts recount the content of these errors, and to the regret of historians Ignatius refuses to record their names.[16] The prophet John is bitter against the Nicolaitans (Rev. 2:6, 15), whose doctrine he hates but never describes. There is always the jealous ambition that seeks Church office. Then there is Diotrephes of 3 John 9, who desires preeminence, presaging, or perhaps endeavors to

14 Quoted from the *Apocalypse of Peter* as cited by Elaine Pagels in *The Gnostic Gospels* (New York: Vintage Books, 1979), 40.

15 Tertullian, *On Modesty* 21 (*NPNF*[2] 4:100).

16 *Smyrn.* 5.3 (Richardson, 114).

imitate the rebellion in Corinth addressed by Clement. The argument of the Johannine Epistles infers a complex of interrelated issues: denial that Jesus came in the flesh (1 John 4:2), salvation by insight or knowledge rather than by repentance and regeneration (1 John 2:4), and uncertainty regarding the moral requirements for communion (1 John 5:16–18). The gainsayers of Second Peter (3:4) question the Second Advent: "Where is the promise of his coming?" When Paul wrote to the Corinthians there was an apparently pervasive opinion that denied the resurrection of the body (1 Cor. 15:12).

The existence within the Church of confusions such as these, reinforced by the generic dualism of vernacular Platonism and the anti-incarnational assumptions of Hellenistic culture, would find context by the time of Ignatius of Antioch in a pervasive "spiritual" religion called in modern scholarship Gnosticism. This taught, among other opinions, that Jesus Christ had come as a heavenly savior who had no part in a fallen created order, and who therefore did not suffer, did not die and was not resurrected, as well as the doctrine that the promises of Jesus were fulfilled in a kind of illumination or recognition properly called knowledge. Without exception these systems take as a unifying presupposition not the testimony of the prophets, with which the account of Paul and Ignatius, Justin and Irenaeus, always begin, but some form of theosophical dualism. At best subject among Gnostic teachers to allegorical interpretation, at worst rejected outright by Marcion as the work of an evil deity, the prophetic writings were the very foundation of the Church Ignatius knew: "And for the prophets, let us love them too as they anticipated the gospel in their preaching and hoped for and awaited him, and were saved by believing in him. Thus they were in Jesus Christ's unity. Saints they were, and we should love and admire them, seeing that Jesus Christ vouched for them and they form a real part of the gospel of our common hope" (*Phld.* 5:2).

Hundreds of books have been written to attempt to describe the "spiritual" heresy that challenged the apostolic mission from the beginning and to discover its origin. Gnosticism is a title used by scholars that does not appear in the contemporary literature. John hints at its appositeness when he contrasts those who say "I know him," with the way of confession and repentance, and indeed 1 John can be read as a subtle defense of one kind of knowledge, the knowledge that, inspired by the Spirit, accompanies love and obedience, while gainsaying the presumptuous *gnosis* of those who have gone out from his fellowship because they were not really of one mind and heart with it (1 John 2:19). Irenaeus does call the opponents of his theology Gnostics, a title that might be more accurately if awkwardly translated "knowers" or perhaps "intellectuals," for the faculty with which they grasped revealed truth was mind or reason, not understanding made receptive by the humbled heart. When we meet Gnosticism in Irenaeus' great book *The Refutation and Overthrow of the Knowledge Falsely So-Called,* written about 185, it is a complex of systems with several variants of such currency and power as to be able to threaten the Catholic Church which Ignatius and Irenaeus represent. Perhaps it was finally the Constantinian sponsorship of the Catholic Church that rendered Gnosticism jejune, but its principles would survive to form a succession of heresies form the Paulicians of the second century to the Albigensian of the thirteenth and to influence the anti-sacramental side of reformed and Anabaptist theologies in the sixteenth century.

When the descriptive term "catholic" appears in Ignatius, it is a Greek compound of a preposition *kata*, which here may mean "according to" or "throughout" and the adjective *holos,* here functioning as a substantive, which means "entire, complete." It does not imply that this Catholic faith represents a majority or a geography, although later "catholic"' would have both those connotations, inasmuch as it suggests that the faith is the common property of right believers throughout the world, coherent and whole in itself, a possession of the elect, the Church, which is the Greek *ekklēsia*, meaning those called out of the general population to the assembly in Athens, or in Christian theology out of the world to enjoy the privileged status of saints-in-the-making, sharing in the life of Jesus Christ. The Catholic faith was not the property of any place or bishop but lived in the hearts of the faithful and was witnessed and in that sense defined especially by the great sees, among which, as early as Irenaeus about 185, Rome stood first.[17]

17 The Roman Catholic Church as the unique magisterial authority was a work of time requiring the loss of Alexandria, Jerusalem, and Antioch to Islam beginning in the seventh century and the alienation from the Roman see for theological cause of most Greek-speaking Christians in 1054. Insistence on the word Roman was a nineteenth-century English rebuttal fielded when the Church of England claimed a Catholic heritage under the influence of the Oxford Movement. When Theodosius defined the Christianity of the empire he referenced the faith of the churches of Rome and Alexandria.

Certainly "catholic" did not describe a creed universally held by all those who considered themselves in some way followers of Christ, but by the orthodox, right believers, who were in communion and communication with one another. Surrounding this Catholic Church there was a vast religious underworld, its existence attested by the perennial complaints of the apostolic authors and the existence, as at Nag Hammadi and Oxyrynchus, of the theosophical detritus of Hellenistic religious culture. When we meet this virulent anti-incarnationalism in its developed form in the late second century, Gnosticism so-called had effloresced into several distinguishable but conceptually related varieties. There was a kind of hyperbolic Paulinism represented by Marcion of Pontus that was based on an ecstasy of grace so compelling, so freeing, that the just God of the Old Testament was rejected as the creator of an order marked by cruel and constraining necessity.[18] When Peter warned that the writings of Paul were deliberately being twisted into heretical shape, he surely had in mind a Marcionite-like distortion of Paul's preaching into an antinomian dualism (2 Pet. 3:15–17). And Marcionism is dualistic; there is a god of grace and a god who made the present world, and also illuminist salvation is secured through a one-time ecstatic or quasi-ecstatic enlightenment. The degree to which Marcionism depends on a cosmic, intellectual or spiritual monism, the idea that the only, single reality is "spiritual," all else is illusion, remains unclear. More probably the Marcionite faith was a practical conclusion from the experience of a joyous release from a world bound under necessity and death.

Not so with Valentinus, Irenaeus' main opponent, who had developed an underlying philosophic dualism, rooted in Platonism and commonly represented by the idea that the body is a tomb, in Greek the cleverly alliterative *sēma soma* (tomb, body), into the culturally pervasive religious idea that the natural order is the illusory production of a secondary creator called the demiurge. What Valentinian and Marcionite dualisms share is a conviction that the historical order and man as part of that order are by nature irredeemable, either because they are the productions of an evil deity or because these things of mere matter lack reality to such a degree that in comparison with the world of spirit that *gnosis* teaches, they are nothing or because of the common cultural conviction that the flesh is destined for

18 Blackman, *Marcion*, 72.

corruption and decay. These variant Gnosticisms also shared a kind of illuminism, or the belief in an ecstatic enlightenment that ends the tension of personal history, an experience before which one is a lost and anxious wanderer but after which the Gnostic soul is perfectly united with the Savior in the great *pleroma* or fullness.

In addition to the adherents of great teachers like Valentinus and Ptolemaeus, who claimed to represent the true teaching of the apostles, there were outliers in this Gnostic world—systems so bizarre, Ophites, Cainites, Sethians, so infected with pagan mythology, that it is difficult to understand their currency.[19] But none of these could have been effective without the omnipresent underlying philosophical dualism rooted in a kind of vernacular Platonism, the skepticism of the new academy that saw everything created as unreal and illusory, knowledge of this world of shadows as at best merely probable and every argument capable of more than one conclusion. Into this illusory world the gnosis of Valentinus and the other Gnostic teachers brought psychological certainty while imputing to the knowers a status far above that enjoyed by ordinary believers; it was the difference between being enlightened spirits or *pneumatikoi* and being mere animal souls or *pseuchikoi.*[20]

On the facts it is difficult to think of a system more obviously antithetical to the religion built upon the Old Testament and the apostles. Yet there *is* a certain dualism in Christianity, technically called finite dualism to distinguish it from the absolute, all-pervading dualism of the Gnostics and Manicheans. Christians are assured that although he who is in them is greater than the one who rules this world (I John 4:4), God's work is ever beset by the devil, that fallen angel who rebelled at the instant of creation, and who, with his accomplices, still goes through the world like a roaring lion, seeking whom he may destroy, tempting and accusing (1 Pet. 5:8). Satan, incarnate in the serpent in the garden, challenges Christ in the wilderness (Matt. 4:1–11), plays an indispensable role in the great vision

19 Part of the challenge of understanding Gnosticism is reconciling the appearance of the movement in the second century in Irenaeus as deceptively near-orthodox with Epiphanius' late fourth-century description in the *Panarion*, where Gnostic practices are described as bestial.

20 *Against Heresies* 1.7.5, 1.8.3–4 (*ANF* 1:326–27).

of John, opposes the woman and her child who is caught up to God's throne, then is cast down upon the earth to seek and destroy until Christ returns (Rev. 12:7–17; 1 Pet. 5:8). Baptism begins with an exorcism, prayers that by the power of the Spirit the one to be baptized will be released from the influence that Satan seeks to exercise over every child of Adam, and the Eastertide renewal baptismal promises include the renunciation of Satan and all his works.

This language of very real but finite dualism may have given Gnostic doctrine a hold. "All that is in the world is not of the Father" or the assertion of Paul that the fashion of this world is passing away (1 Cor. 7:31, 1 John 2:17), that "flesh and blood cannot inherit the kingdom" (1 Cor. 15:39), or the assumption of Hebrews that this world is the shadow of good things to come (Heb. 8:5, 10:1; Col. 2:17). This language is countered by the contrapuntal assertion of the Johannine prologue: "All things were made through Him, and without him was not anything made that was made," and by the whole tenor of the Pauline-Johannine theology of glory. But because this present order is flawed and not final, it could be understood in the "spiritual" way by those who were seeking evidence of its essentially evil or illusory nature. These Gnosticisms were not obvious religious failures any more than the spiritualisms of contemporary popular religion are failures. Gnosticism of the Valentinian variety persisted into the fourth century, and some form of Marcionism or of the "spiritual" faith persisted by way of the Paulicians, the Bogomils, the Cathari or the pure ones, the Albigensians, making its way up the Danube and finally into the Rhineland and France, and it may be said with caution that this system infected to some degree the reformed religions of the sixteenth century in a material if not in a formal way, especially the Anabaptists but also the Reformed tradition, among some of whom it is a principle that the Eucharistic gifts do not become the body and blood of Christ.

Along the way these spiritual movements appeared again and again to solve the perennial question of personal and cosmic evil by offering the plausible, and often welcomed, explanation that we are beset by sin not because of the primordial and existential involvement of our own wills in chosen rebellion against God our Father, but because we are implicated in an evil cosmic system that, rooted in the createdness and bodiliness of the world, has enslaved us unknowingly and from which bondage we are released by initiation into the true spiritual world. Paradoxically, it was a system that over time expressed itself on one hand in a creation-denying asceticism of varying degrees, as with the twelfth-century Albigensians in France, and on the other in an antinomian acceptance of human sin and folly as unavoidable and therefore indeed unremarkable. But with Ignatius we are near the beginning of the story. Three centuries later this dualism, always capable of relieving the conscience of the imputation of sinfulness by locating its cause outside the self, intrigued Augustine in the form of Manichaeism.

That these dualistic systems existed throughout the Hellenistic world of the first and second centuries is not in contest. The Hermetic literature of Egypt which knows nothing of Christ or Judaism and the Gnostic texts in the Nag Hammadi library are among the evidences that a kind of pervasive spiritual religion existed apart from its parasitic attachment to Christ the savior figure. The gateway through which this system made its bid to be the defining theology of those who considered themselves Christians will always be contested. Tertullian wrote that it was all caused by philosophy, referring implicitly to Platonic dualism,[21] and dualism of a kind was to be found in the faith of the Church.

The occasion on which this anti-incarnational theology began to challenge the defenses of the early Church is perhaps to be found along the road that led from the experience of Pentecost to the eschatological crisis that occurred as the first Christian generation died without witnessing the return of Jesus. The Gospels attest a tradition that denies any knowledge of the day and hour, but that did not obviate the belief of the brethren in the Johannine community that their beloved witness would live to see the Parousia (John 21:23) or the anxiety of the Thessalonians that those who slept had already missed the great event (1 Thess. 4:13–18). First Corinthians 15:12–56 attests the existence—and surely they were not alone—of Christians in good standing who in the light of Pentecostal gifts considered the hope of a future resurrection of the body unimportant if not misguided. Gnostics as much as Montanists considered themselves spirit-filled.

Pentecost, the coming of the indwelling Holy Spirit promised by Jesus, is an event that changed and changes lives, but it does so in a way that

21 Tertullian, *Prescription of Heretics* 7 (*NPNF*[2] 3:246).

complements but in no wise abolishes belief in the historical or supra-historical future foretold by the great prophets of the Old Testament, developed by the highly colored apocalyptic of the Maccabean period, Daniel, and texts like *Baruch*, the *Book of Enoch*, and the *Book of Ezra*, and woven into Christian belief by canonical apocalyptic, as in Matthew 24–25 and Revelation 21–22. One can suspect that when Ignatius wrote "Let us either fear the wrath that is to come or love the present grace, one or the other, provided only that we be found in Jesus Christ" (Eph. 11.1), he may have been speaking to the contemporary argument between those who found fulfillment in the indwelling presence of the Paraclete and those who looked forward expectantly to the return of Jesus to judge, bless, and vindicate. For Ignatius, union with Jesus in love was the meaning of the present, his sure return the anchor of hope. "It is the last days" (Eph.11:1). Like the author of the *Didache,* writing perhaps thirty years earlier, Ignatius knew that every life took one of two paths; "Everything is coming to an end, and we stand before this choice, death or life, and everyone will go to his own place. One might say in a manner of speaking that there are two coinages, one God's, the other the world" (*Magn.* 3:5).

When the Fourth Gospel was written, its author presupposes a Church in which attention was focused on life with Christ in the Holy Spirit, but never to the exclusion of belief in Jesus' imminent return, an event anticipated by the Johannine community with such fervor that the death of their Beloved Disciple before Christ's return, seemingly in contravention of Jesus' promise, caused consternation (John 21:21–33). It was inevitable that, as it would happen again in the late nineteenth century, some or many would come to the belief that the future resurrection was fulfilled by the believer's present participation in the life of the Spirit, Christ's promise having been fulfilled at Pentecost.[22] Thus Paul condemned Hymenaeus and Philotas in the passionate rhetoric of 1 Corinthians 15:12–

22 The thesis of Johannes Weiss in his 1892 study *Jesus' Proclamation of the Kingdom of God* that the essence of Jesus' teaching was his imminent return, a failed hope, provided background in different ways for the "realized" eschatology of the Gnostics, realized insight rather than regeneration and future hope, and encouraged the historicist-realized eschatology of Walter Rauschenbusch's *Social Gospel* (1917) and its early twentieth-century adherents.

28 not for denying the power of the resurrection but for believing that the resurrection was already past (1 Tim. 1:20, 2 Tim. 2:17), that the spiritual, soul-transforming fact fulfilled Jesus' promise; the kingdom is within you (Luke 17:21). The Corinthians who denied the resurrection of the body would not have considered themselves un-Christian. In Second Timothy Paul also condemned the "empty and worldly chatter" of the resurrection-deniers; the Gnostics were full of theories and consequently were prolix writers, producing works that competed with Christian books into the fourth century. The belief that the resurrection had already taken place was represented in the Nag Hammadi library by the *Treatise on the Resurrection* (*Epistle to Rheginos*), the *Exegesis on the Soul*, and the *Gospel of Philip*.[23] Paul warned the Thessalonians not to be deceived by a forged letter "purporting to be from us, to the effect that the day of the Lord has come" (1 Thess. 2:2).

This way of thinking tends to the conclusion that the created order, itself the work of the demiurge who opposes the One, has no future while the spiritual, "psychological" order is reality, and if it was not full-blown Gnosticism, the doctrine of Hymenaeus and Philetus was on the way. It followed that Jesus was not a participant in the created order that was illusion or hopelessly infected with evil, encouraging the attendant conviction that Jesus was a spiritual messenger from the real or "spiritual" world who did not suffer and did not die and was not resurrected in the bodily way attested by Thomas in the Gospel of John (20:25–29).

At this point, about the turn of the second century, the contradiction between the spiritual theology and the theology of glory became public and unavoidable, and the refutation of the pervasive spiritual heresy became a major interest of the second and third century Fathers and Apologists, becoming the theme not only of Irenaeus' great book but of works by Justin and by Tertullian, notably in his *Against Marcion,* and occupying significant parts of later comprehensive refutations of *gnosis* such as the *Dialogue on the Orthodox Faith* (279) by Pamphilius of Caesarea and Epiphanius' *Panarion,* published in 377. There is evidence that in his letters Ignatius was anxious not only to defeat the "spiritual" heresy, but also to refute the Judaizing error so roundly denounced by Paul in Galatians and elsewhere,

23 Robinson, ed., *Nag Hammadi Library*, 4–5.

but it was Gnosticism that would challenge most successfully the faith Ignatius taught throughout the second century.[24]

In the five letters Ignatius addressed to churches as he moved up the coast of Asia his principal concern was the defense of the faith he called catholic from this spiritual heresy. His tools are the assertion of a creed in which we see the outlines of the great creed of Nicaea and an insistence on the principles of the Pauline-Johannine theology of glory or *doxa,* as well as the requirement of communion with and obedience to the bishop. Christianity is an incarnational, not in the common sense a "spiritual" religion, and its end is not "spirit" in the Gnostic sense but *doxa* or glory. The Church, writes Ignatius, is "predestined from eternity to enjoy forever continual and unfading glory" (*Eph.* pref.).

To grasp the terms of the controversy that would go on from the late first century to at least the early third century, it is important to understand that glory or *doxa* represented that dimension of reality existing always in God and fulfilled historically, or supra-historically, in Christ, the Saints, and in the New Creation. This world of glory *is* the world of Spirit, but Spirit in the Pauline-Ignatian sense is more real than flesh, not less real. When Paul says that Christians belong to spirit and not to flesh he is saying nothing remotely like the Gnostic claim that salvation is immaterial; Irenaeus derides Valentinianism as "invisible" salvation.[25] The Holy Spirit is made known ultimately in glory, which is the antithesis of the modern spiritual, as in Genesis 1, perfectly full of form, light, and being. Glory belongs to the character of God and whatever exists in his presence. Giving or attributing glory to God means recognizing him as the font of all being, expressed as goodness, beauty, and truth in their ultimate terms. By his promise, says the apostle Peter, Christians are called into the realm of God's eternal glory (1 Pet. 5:10). Because of God's salvific will, the fallen world, through the travail of history, is making its way from corruption or failure of form toward the glory that will be revealed in us (Rom. 8:18). We presently suffer what Paul called "light affliction" (2 Cor. 4:17) and "the sufferings of this present time" (Rom.

24 *Magn.* 8 (Richardson, 96).

25 "Their tradition respecting redemption is invisible and incomprehensible" (*Against Heresies* 1.21.1 [*ANF* 1:345]).

8:18) but these are not to be compared with the weight, the reality, of that glory in which we will share.

No image of the realm of glory is adequate, but the modern writer well-known to the English-speaking who has come closest to imaging this is C. S. Lewis, one of whose great contributions was the standing upon its head of the Puritan, and ultimately Gnostic, illusion that goodness of the real world which God inhabits is pale and empty, where goodness is by disengagement from the created order, when in fact the created order was made to reflect, and finally to bear, the consummate glory of God. From this poverty Lewis released the northern European religious imagination.

That said, the theology of glory and the life of the Spirit were, and indeed throughout history always will be, required to fight for their lives in the unending contest with "spiritual" religion. Ignatius says to the Ephesians: "I have learned that some from elsewhere have stayed with you, who have evil doctrine; but you did not allow them to sow it among you."[26] These Ignatius elsewhere describes as those who "make a practice of carrying about the name with wicked guile, and do certain other things unworthy of God . . . . These men you ought to shun as wild beasts; for they are mad dogs, biting by stealth, against whom you ought to be on your guard, for they are hard to heal."[27]

An age in which knowledge, unless it is scientific, tends to be at best opinion, it will always be difficult to understand the energy with which the apostles and early Fathers denounce the act of knowingly preferring one's own enlightened beliefs to the teaching of the bishop and the Church, this being heresy, which means in its Greek origin, the act of choosing from the catholic faith whole and entire what one will or will not believe. When Ignatius asks, "If those who act carnally suffer death, how much more shall those who by wicked teaching corrupt God's faith for which Jesus Christ was crucified. Such a vile creature will go to unquenchable fire along with anyone who listens to him."[28] When he makes this judgment he is imitating St. Paul, who twice declared those who taught a variant gospel "accursed" (Gal. 1:8, 9) and John the Evangelist who warned that those who abandoned the doctrine he had taught were without God, and that no emissary

26 *Eph.* 9 (Richardson, 90).
27 Ibid., 7.1 (Richardson, 89–90); *Smyrn.* 4.1 (Richardson, 113).
28 Ibid.,. 16.2 (Richardson, 92).

of wrong doctrine should be welcomed or wished Godspeed, warning that anyone who wished such a one well "was a partaker in his evil deeds" (3 John 8, 9). The Apostle Peter described "false teachers" who bring in "damnable heresies, even denying the Lord who bought them," as "natural brute beasts, made to be taken and destroyed," who speak evil of things they do not understand (2 Pet. 2:1, 12).

These apostolic witnesses spoke in this decisive and forceful way not out of hatred for heretics but out of hatred for heresy, and, more importantly, out of a sense of their duty to protect the once-revealed, life-giving truth of Christ whom they loved. Following the witness of Paul that there is no other name whereby men may be saved, Ignatius wrote, "Let no one be misled. Heavenly beings, the splendor of angels, and principalities, visible and invisible, if they fail to believe in Christ's blood, they too are doomed."[29] "There is one physician only, of flesh and of spirit, born and yet not born, who is God in man, true life in death, Son of Mary and Son of God, first capable of suffering, then beyond suffering, Jesus Christ Our Lord" (Eph. 5:7). Ignatius' creed-like statements always include the assertion in Ephesians that Jesus Christ "our God" was conceived by the Holy Spirit and born of Mary (Eph. 7:2 ). To the Trallians (9) he writes of "Jesus Christ, who was of the family of David, of Mary, who was truly born, both ate and drank, was truly persecuted under Pontius Pilate, was truly crucified and died in the sight of those in heaven and earth and under the earth, who also was truly raised from the dead, when his Father raised him up, as in the same manner his Father shall raise up in Christ Jesus those who believe in him, without whom we have no true life,"[30] and in similar words in the opening lines of the letter to Smyrna. In these Ignatian affirmations one sees the creed on its way from the simple profession that Jesus is Lord to the creeds known to Irenaeus which ring with the words and phrases of Nicaea and of the Roman baptismal creed we know as the Apostles Creed.

One may maintain that the traditional doctrine of the Eucharist is mistaken, that somewhere between the upper room, John 6, and Ignatius, the tradition went wrong, but it is difficult to deny either that Ignatius' doctrine is an exposition of the doctrine of John 6, the text in which Jesus teaches

29 *Smyrn.* 6.1 (Richardson, 114).
30 *Trall.* 9 (Richardson, 100).

that the elect must eat the flesh and drink the blood of the Son of Man, or that this teaching is ancient, rooted in the earliest accounts. To Smyrna he wrote, "They [the troublers of the Asian churches] abstain from the Eucharist and prayer, because they do not confess that the Eucharist is the flesh of our Savior Jesus Christ who suffered for our sins, which the Father raised up by his goodness. They then who deny the gift of God are perishing in their disputes; but it were better for them to have love, that they also might attain to the Resurrection" (7:1). Quite consistently, the Gnostic denial that the Eucharist is the flesh of Christ was rooted in the insistence that Jesus only appeared to die on the cross. "If it is merely in semblance that these things were done by our lord I am also a prisoner in semblance" (*Smryn.* 4). There was and is ultimately no mediating moment between the "spiritual" philosophy of the Gnostics and Ignatius' theology of glory.

It is in Ignatius that the Church emerges, by at least 115, as a communion centered around the bishop, to whom the Church is united by the bonds of charity. Ignatius says simply that the Roman bishop holds the primacy of love. It is the bishop's acknowledgement that makes the Eucharist lawful, and his permission is required even for an *agape*, that troublesome Church supper originally associated with the Eucharist itself, regarding the abuse of which St. Paul complains in First Corinthians (11:20–22). Ignatius' conviction that unity with the bishop would preserve right faith was to prove only partly effective, for over time the occasional bishop would make a schism, and it would take the advice of Irenaeus, and the centuries of practice based upon it, to establish the claim that it was upon the apostolic sees, and especially the witness of Peter in the city of Peter and Paul, that ultimate responsibility for teaching and witness had devolved.[31] The Roman church, Ignatius wrote, cleaved to Christ's every command, observing not only the letter but the spirit, "being permanently filled with God's grace purged of every stain alien to it."[32]

With the beautiful text of Ignatius' *Ephesians* 19 building on John 19: 26–27 and Revelation 12, Mary the Mother of Jesus finds her place in the economy of salvation as the early second-century Church knew it. In Ephesians Ignatius names three mysteries that shout aloud although they were

31 *Against Heresies* 3.3.2 (Richardson, 372).
32 *Rom.*, pref. (Richardson, 103).

wrought in the stillness of God: the virginity of Mary, the birth of Jesus, and the death of the Lord; the Virgin birth, the Incarnation, and the Passion. Although it will always be a source of argument, it may be plausibly pointed out that in the Virgin birth is strictly implied the later doctrines about Mary. If Jesus is born of a Virgin who conceived by the Holy Spirit, that Virgin must be without the stain of sin both for the sake of fitness and so that she can give Our Lord his sinless humanity. And if, through the merits of the cross of Christ foreseen, that Virgin does not owe the penalty of death imposed by our participation in original sin, she will not die as we do but will fall asleep, her soul taken to the arms of Jesus to join her body (the East) or was taken up body and soul into heaven (the dogma of the Assumption of the Blessed Virgin). Such formal conclusions from the fact of Mary's virginity belong to a later age, but the seeds from which the teaching grew, that Mary, ever-virgin, Mother of God, preserved from the stain of original sin, taken body and soul to the presence of Christ, are here, in Ignatius' letter to the Christians of Ephesus.

Ignatius lived and wrote just as the oral tradition was being replaced by written Gospels. He is insistent that the prophets because they predicted Christ belong to him, but, he says, "The Gospel is the crowning achievement forever" (*Phld.* 9:2). Ignatius uses the word gospel or good news or good announcement as the summary of the saving teaching of the Church, but not to describe a book or books. When Ignatius quotes from the Gospels it is Matthew that he cites; he is also familiar with much of St. Paul. But in the letter to the Philadelphians Ignatius writes that he prefers the living voice to the documents, original documents, because when one appeals beyond the common tradition to a text, the argument then turns on the accuracy and appositeness of the text.[33]

Ignatius stakes out the incarnational theology that Justin Martyr and Irenaeus will defend, making his famous refutation of the "spiritual" gloss on the teaching of the apostles, the position that the Asian Church would affirm in the second and third centuries, and which the Roman Church would take up as soon as it enjoyed public peace. Defending the theology of glory was no easy task, because its mythic and revealed presupposition ran counter to an alternative theology that considered the hope of the New

33 *Phld.* 8:2 (Richardson, 110).

Creation "unspiritual" and Jewish, the Apocalypse that supported these beliefs incredible. The controversy would center, as the reader of Ignatius might have foreseen, on the doctrine of resurrection of the body, or, more dramatically, the resurrection of the flesh, the affirmation of which passed into the great creeds, gainsaying the truly insidious doctrine of "spiritual" resurrection and "spiritual" restoration that was intrinsic to a greater or lesser degree in the theology of the Alexandrians, Clement, Origen, and Dionysius. The theologians for the defense would be the great Asians: Ignatius, Justin and Irenaeus, with Melito of Sardis, Methodius, and the little-known Nepos. The story of this long-running controversy belongs to the story of Alexandria before Arius.

One's understanding of the issues involved is perhaps assisted by a consideration of the place of the Apocalypse in the mind of the church, for it was admired and derogated or ignored as the theology of glory was admired or ignored. The Apocalypse, however obscure its pattern and teaching may seem with texts like 2 Peter 3:12–13 and Romans 8:22, made the theology of glory normative for the Roman church and hence for the West. The theology of glory represented, among other things, the Christian commitment to the Old Testament that Hellenism and Platonism never decisively weakened.

In addition to his six letters to the churches, Ignatius also wrote to Polycarp, bishop of Smyrna, shortly after his visit to that city had inspired his letter to that church there. The letter to Polycarp is not much concerned with the dangers of heresy but offers the bishop of Smyrna the weighty advice of the older bishop of a famous city who is on his way to martyrdom. Scholarly opinion almost unanimously locates Ignatius' journey in the reign of Trajan, 98 to 117. The tone of Ignatius' advice to Polycarp suggests that he was writing to a young man, perhaps not long in the episcopate, so perhaps a date near the turn of the century is best. Since Polycarp was born in 69, one of the few dates certain in the fragile chronology of the late first century, Ignatius may have been addressing a Polycarp still in his thirties, who would live until 155, when he would die a martyr in his see city of Smyrna. Ignatius' summary advice to Polycarp was: "Do not let anything be done without your consent, and do not do anything without God's." (*Pol.* 4.1).

Ignatius' own desire to fight for Christ with the beasts of the arena was fulfilled, for his death has ever been celebrated in the calendar of the Roman church. The special burden of Ignatius' letter to the Romans is the personal request that no one attempt to secure his freedom, the assumption being that someone in an official or personal capacity might be able to have the charges brought against him quashed; "If you are silent and leave me alone, I am a word of God, but if you desire my flesh I shall be a mere noise." He requests that no one interfere; he does not order it as Peter and Paul, who were apostles, might have done (4:3). Ignatius' zeal in this matter, his evident desire for martyrdom, his description of the well-known possibilities, "fire, cross, battling with wild beasts, wrenching of bones, mangling of limbs," to which he looks forward, has always encouraged the thought that his readiness to die in the arena seems to modern ears almost pathological. One might argue that Ignatius on merely human considerations, to say nothing the zeal born of his supernatural love for Jesus, has little choice (Rom. 6.3). Were he to be set free, it would forever be said that Ignatius had bought his way out or been released through influence, and his witness would have been discredited by those detractors who always look on from the shadows. And besides, Ignatius is in love. "That is whom I want—the one who rose for us."

> Grant me no more than to be a sacrifice for God while an altar is at hand. Then you can form yourselves into a choir and sing praises to the Father in Jesus Christ that God gave the bishop of Syria the privilege of reaching the sun's setting, when he summoned him from its rising. It is a grand thing for my life to set on the world, and for me to be on my way to God, so that I may rise in his presence.[34]

34 Rom. 2.2 (Richardson, 103–104).

# Four
## *Justin: Whatever Is True*

> Philosophy is indeed the greatest possession, and most honorable before God, to whom it leads us and alone commends us, and these are indeed holy men who have bestowed attention on philosophy. What philosophy is however, and the reason it has been sent down to men, have escaped the attention of most.
>
> Justin Martyr, *Dialogue with Trypho* 2

From the beginning, Christians considered themselves in possession of a universal religion with a mission to all mankind. Its apostles and teachers, which understanding that it is God who calls the elect, sought to convince the world that the ideas it proposed to the intellect was true and therefore deserving of, first, consideration and, finally, acceptance. The first apologist was Paul, who appealed not only to principles found in the Hebrew Scriptures, but to tradition, conscience, nature, and poetic insight, arguing in Romans that Gentiles should learn from nature the power and existence of God and from human nature that the existence of conscience is enough to establish the claims of righteousness. Paul sought by quoting the pagan poets and noticing the unknown god to make an apology for Christianity on the Areopagus.[1] Christian literature before Ignatius tends to be didactic as in the *Didache,* or disciplinary as in First Clement, but there survives a fragment of the lost *Apology* of Quadratus, probably written as early as 124.[2]

Justin wrote his *First Apology,* addressed to Antoninus Pius, about 150. In his *Against the Greeks* Apollinaris of Hierapolis addressed the Emperor Marcus Aurelius, and Miltiades' lost, nearly contemporary *Apology*

1 Rom. 1:18–22, 2:14–16; Acts 17:22–31.

2 Quasten, 1:191; *Church History* 4.3.1–2 (*NPNF*²1:175).

*for Christian Philosophy* and Athenagoras of Athens's *Plea Regarding Christians,* written after the Emperor Commodus was associated with his father Marcus Aurelius in 176, followed. The anonymous *Epistle to Diognetus* and Tertullian's *To the Heathen* and *Apology*, belong to the early third century.[3] Underlying their intellectual, theological, and moral arguments was always the conviction that Christianity, far from damaging the Empire by teaching a degrading superstition, was the agent through which religion was rendered reasonable and morals lifted above the turpitude that characterized popular culture in the age of the Antonines, 138–92 AD.[4] Augustine, in the wake of the Ostrogothic incursions of 410, would deny that God willed permanent triumph to any empire, but Melito touched a theme not far from the heart of almost all the Apologists when he wrote during the good days of mid-second-century: "The most convincing proof that the flourishing of our religion has been a boon to Empire . . . is the fact that the Empire has suffered no mishap since the reign of Augustus, but on the contrary has increased in splendor according to the universal prayer."[5] Clement, a century before, provided an example of that universal prayer:

> Grant that we may be obedient to your almighty and glorious name, and to our rulers of earth. You, Master, gave them imperial power. . . Grant them, Lord, health, peace, harmony, and stability, so that they may give no offence in administering the government you have given them. For it is you, Master, the heavenly king of eternity, who give the sons of men glory and honor and authority over the earth's people.[6]

Justin, always named Justin Martyr because he died a victim of imperial persecution about 165, was born near the turn of the first century in Flavia Neapolis, now Nabulus, in Samaria, so Judaism would not be foreign to him. Justin knows its books and its contemporary history, mentioning in

3 Quasten, 1:187–252.
4 Justin 27 (Richardson, 259).
5 *Church History* 4.26.7–8 (*NPNF*[2] 1:205).
6 Clement 61.1 (Richardson,72).

his *Dialogue with Trypho* the second Jewish revolt of 132–35 as recent.[7] Just when Justin was converted to Christianity he does not tell us, but his vocation to philosophy preceded that conversion, and it was philosophy, its search for truth, that began his journey to Christ. He argues from Scripture and tradition as well as from reason. Like his Christian contemporaries he knows Matthew best, Luke next best, and Mark slightly. He does not name the Gospel of John but may quote John 3:5: "You must be born again." He knows the Apocalypse of John with its prophecy of Christ's thousand-year reign on earth.[8] Justin is steeped in knowledge of the Old Testament; the Psalms and Isaiah are favorites. Always the philosopher, he engaged the world of pagan thought just as Stoicism gained its finest expression in the *Meditations* of the Emperor Marcus Aurelius. Plato is very much part of Justin's intellectual arsenal.[9] Albinus, who wrote a prologue to Plato, the *Didaskalikos*, was Justin's contemporary. Justin did not live to see the renewal of Aristotelian thought by Alexander of Aphrodesias at the turn of the second century; he does in the *Second Apology* mention Epicurus, the flourishing of whose school he attributes to the wicked demons.[10] Justin does tell the reader that Crescens, against whom the *Second Apology* was in part written, was a Cynic, one who "makes indifference his end," and who therefore can know no good but indifference.[11]

Standing as he does midway in time between Ignatius about 115 and Irenaeus who wrote in the 180s, Justin is our best witness to the shape of Christianity at mid-second-century, and his descriptions of the sacramental life of the churches he knew in Ephesus and Rome, as well as his references to Scripture, are indispensable testimonies. For Justin baptism is the act whereby those who would believe are reborn, "washed in the water in the

7 *Dialogue* 1 (*NPNF*[2] 1:194).

8 Ibid., 81 (*NPNF*[2] 1:240).

9 Ibid., 2 (*NPNF*[2] 1:195). Justin "mentions Socrates positively nine times in all in the first and second *Apology*; he quotes Plato's *Dialogues* fourteen times, five of them [from] the *Republic*" (Hengel, *Four Gospels*, note 13).

10 Justin, *Second Apology* 7 (*NPNF*[2] 1:190).

11 Ibid., 3 (*ANF* 1:189). The indifference Justin rebukes was indifference to convention, tradition, property, and social status, these being irrelevant to the physical and mental discipline necessary for self-fulfillment. See A. A. Long, *Hellenistic Philosophy*, 110.

name of God the Father and master of all, and of our Savior Jesus Christ, and of the Holy Spirit." Its effect is that, "being illuminated within, we should not remain children of necessity and ignorance but become children of choice and knowledge, attaining remission of the sins we have already committed."[12] Justin says of the Eucharist that "no one is permitted to partake unless he has received the washing for the forgiveness of sins and for rebirth and lives as Christ commanded us to live," seconding the discipline surrounding the Eucharist, evident in the *Didache*, that would remain into the present. The Eucharist, "consecrated by the word of prayer which comes from him," is not common bread or common drink, but is "the flesh and blood of that incarnate Jesus."[13] Justin does not name the four Gospels, but he knows the memoirs, remembrances or recollections of the apostles, which with the prophets were read at length at the Sunday Eucharist. Among the prophets was John, author of the great Christian vision of things to come, who, Justin wrote, lived among us in time of Domitian (81–96).[14]

A philosopher by profession, proudly wearing the philosopher's dress,[15] Justin's writings are efforts to establish the intellectual credibility, as well as the political utility and moral superiority, of Christianity. In his three apologies, two addressed to Greeks, one addressed to the Jews, Justin undertook the task of giving the Christian religion a place in the intellectual firmament of mid-second-century paganism, while at the same time arguing in his *Dialogue with Trypho the Jew* that Christianity was the divinely appointed fulfillment of Old Testament prophecy, so that failure to accept Christianity derogated the very prophets in whom Trypho professed belief. "We do not think that there is one God for us, another for you, but that he alone is God who led your fathers out of Egypt."[16]

Something of Justin's own intellectual formation can be understood from the *Dialogue with Trypho,* which, although subsequent to *First Apology*, is a two-part work recounting first Justin's own conversion, beginning with an account of his study of philosophy and providing in the second

12 Justin 61 (Richardson, 282).
13 Justin 65–66 (Richardson, 285–86).
14 Ibid., 67 (Richardson, 287); *Dialogue* 81 (*ANF* 1:241).
15 *Dialogue* 1 (*ANF* 1:194).
16 Ibid., 11 (*ANF* 1:199).

arguments as to why Trypho should listen to his own prophets who predicted the coming of Christ, the two parts together offering an effective example of the engagement of the Church with both the philosophic past and with the witness of the Hebrew Scriptures.

The *Dialogue* begins with Justin's explanation to Trypho of his attempt to find the truth through the study of philosophy. The setting is perfectly Socratic. Justin, wearing his philosopher's gown, is walking along a public way when he is greeted, "Hail, O philosopher," by one who has himself studied philosophy under Corinthus the Socratic in Argos. Justin replies with the conversation-opener, "What is important?" Trypho answers that philosophers are always to be respected and that mutual benefit may come from philosophic conversation. Trypho, describing himself as a Hebrew of the circumcision who has fled from the war of Bar Kochba, invites Justin, "Tell us your opinions of these matters and what your philosophy is."[17]

Justin then gives an account of his search for truth. He had canvassed the philosophical schools. The Stoics were unable to give Justin any knowledge of God. The Peripatetics wanted the fee settled before instruction began. The Pythagoreans required that Justin first master the quadrivium, the study of the mathematical arts, mentioning "music, astronomy, and geometry." But then Justin came upon "a sagacious man, holding a high position among the Platonists. The perception of immaterial things quite overpowered me, and the contemplation of ideas furnished my mind with wings… and such was my stupidity that I expected forthwith to look upon God, for that is the end of Plato's philosophy."[18]

Justin had become the perfect Platonist, but he needed more than ideas. Explaining his philosophic conversion to Trypho, Justin writes, "Just at this moment, when, seeking quietness, walking by the sea" he came upon "a certain old man, meek and venerable who was concerned about some of his household who had wandered away from him." The old man is the heaven-sent guide toward conversion, the prototype of the angelic guide in the *Shepherd,* and is prophetic of Boethius' Lady Philosophy. He asks Justin "Are you a philologian but no lover of deeds and of truth," a lover of words but not of reality and virtue? Justin replies with something of the knowingness that

17 *Dialogue* 2 (*NPNF*[2] 1:194).
18 Ibid., 2 *(NPNF*[2] 1:195).

besets philosophy unchastened, "What greater work could one accomplish than this, to show the reason that governs all, and having laid hold of it, and being mounted upon it, too look down upon the errors of others and their pursuits." But Justin also understands that without thought virtue is impossible: "Without philosophy and right reason prudence would not be present to any man." There follows an exchanged in which the old man echoes Aristotle. Some knowledge comes to us by learning, the intellectual virtues, and some by practice, the moral virtues, but there is also knowledge that comes by sight, and the philosophers cannot speak correctly about God because they have not seen him. But, says Justin, God cannot be seen by human eyes but is discernible to the mind alone. Knowledge of God is knowledge of a different kind, a knowledge borne of insight.[19]

Plato, Justin believed, had taught "that the mind is of such nature, and has been given for that end, that we might see that very being when the mind is pure itself. Thus it might occur that this knowledge of a God who is unutterable and ineffable might come into souls well-dispositioned on account of their unity with him and their desire to see him." But it is not merely the man of intellect but the virtuous man who is able to see God: "It is not on account of his affinity that a man sees God, nor because he has a mind, but because he is temperate and righteous."

Justin is arguing an unexceptionable Platonism, the possibility of access to God through the ideas the mind of every man shares with the divine mind, the position taken by Plotinus in the next century, accompanied by a settled pessimism regarding the corruptible body, the offer of philosophic certainty while simultaneously obviating the very possibility of the incarnation. These ideas the old man dismisses: "It makes no difference to me whether Plato or Pythagoras held such opinions, for these do not know what a soul is. The soul lives but it does not possess life as its own but it has life caused by something other than itself. The soul partakes of life because God wills it to live"; "to live is not its attribute, as it is God's."

The old man has cleared Justin's mind of the propositions that lie at the heart of Platonism: its beliefs, first, that the mind is a common term between God and man, and the closely related idea that the soul is by its

19 *Dialogue* 3 echoes Aristotle's *Nichomachean Ethics* 1103a (McKeon, 952); Robert M. Grant, "Aristotle and the Conversion of Justin," *JTS* 7(1956):246–48.

own nature, not by the will of God, eternal.[20] "Thus it will not even partake of life when God does not will it to live, for to live is not its attribute." These two ideas, rejected by Justin at the beginning of his career as a Christian philosopher, are at the heart of every system of emanations, behind Gnosticism, behind Plotinus, Origen, and Arius, providing an alternative to creation *ex nihilo*, creation by God of the world that bears the impress of his hand and whose human crown bears his image.

Abandoning Plato as the sufficient way to knowledge of God, Justin asks how, if there is no truth in philosophy, anyone can be helped? The old man replies: "Long before this time, certain men who are more ancient than all those who are esteemed philosophers, both righteous and beloved by God, who spoke by the divine Spirit and foretold events which would take place, and which are now taking place. . . . Their writings are still extant. . . . They did not use demonstration in their treatises, seeing that they were witnesses to truth above all demonstration." The Christian Justin's principal argument for the truth of the Gospel would be that Christ had been foretold in the prophetic writings, the truth of which would be confirmed by the presence of the same Spirit who had inspired Isaiah and Jeremiah in the believer's heart.

After the old man had left him, "A flame was kindled in my soul and a love of the prophets and of those men who are friends of Christ possessed me." The words of the Savior "possess a terrible power in themselves and are sufficient to inspire those who turn aside from the path of rectitude with awe; while the sweetest rest is afforded those who practice them."

Managing the true and beneficial aspects of systematic or dogmatic Platonism,[21] its epistemological optimism, the belief that the mind can know truth, and its certainty that the world known by the senses comprehends exhaustively neither experience nor reality, while suppressing the tendency to collapse thought about God into an anti-incarnational emanation

20 This difficulty haunted theology. Augustine wrote in his *City of God*: "Surely in matters which the mind of man cannot penetrate it is better to believe what God tells us, namely that the soul is not co-eternal with God but is created out of nothing" (10.31).

21 As distinct from the skepticism of the dialogues. The Neoplatonist Numenius, writing perhaps fifty years after Justin, faulted the late Academy's "notorious reserve of judgement" (Guthrie, trans., 62).

theology, would challenge theologians throughout the third century, when brilliant thinkers such as Clement of Alexandria and Origen would be drawn to Platonism's beautiful and explicatory but intrinsically anti-incarnational principles. Justin at the beginning of his life as a Christian philosopher had rejected its errors while accepting its anti-skeptical claims. The ancient man, his work done, departs, and the love of Christ is kindled in Justin's soul. Philosophy has led Justin step by step to Plato and then, the difficulties of Platonism acknowledged, to the threshold at which the Prophetic Spirit could make Justin a Christian.

Justin Martyr's conversion as described in his *Dialogue with Trypho the Jew* is the earliest account of reason in search of faith. The philosopher would become a theologian, and Justin's attempt to clarify the Christian doctrine of the Trinity, a word not yet in use,[22] is an important stage in the development of theology, for it is here, in Justin's *First Apology*, that the teaching that the Eternal Son is also the Logos, or Word, is developed into an, admittedly nascent, Trinitarian doctrine.[23]

Justin's *First Apology*, addressed to the Emperor Antoninus Pius, is directed toward a Greek-reading audience and entertains a larger purpose than mere toleration. Justin first argued that it was unjust to punish for the name when the accused had broken no law, a question that had vexed Pliny fifty years earlier, and then went on to coopt ideas native to pagan philosophy to show that Christians did not derogate the philosophic wisdom of the past.[24] Though Christian belief towered above paganism, there were similarities; since paganism taught doctrines similar to the doctrines of Christ, the doctrines could hardly be repugnant to religion or reason, although that pagan wisdom was derivative, borrowed from the prophets, who had taught long before Plato. "Moses was earlier than Plato and all the Greek writers" and with regard to the reason (*logos*) of whom the whole human race partakes those who live according to reason are Christians, even

22 Theophilus of Antioch's use about 180 of *triados* with reference to "God, his Logos, and his Sophia" in *Ad Autolycum* 2.15 is often cited as the first reference to the Trinity. See Robert M. Grant, *Theophilus of Antioch, Ad Autolycum*, 53.

23 Justin 13, 22 (Richardson, 249, 256).

24 Ibid., 58–59 (Richardson, 280).

though they are accounted atheists, since in everything they said about immortality and punishments after death "they took hints from the prophets."[25] This incipient unity between Christianity and certain themes native to the best of pagan philosophy was possible because whatever the poets, philosophers, and historians had written rightly derives truth from the logos sown throughout the world, which these grasped darkly, and conversely, since these authors shared in the Word they were worthy of attention.

When the *Dialogue* was written Justin had already penned the words that would become the classic representation of the relation between Christ and the philosophers:

> We are taught that Christ is the first-born of God, and we have shown above that He is the reason (*logos*) of whom the whole human race partakes, and those who live according to reason are Christians, even though they were accounted atheists, as were Socrates and Heraclitus among the Greeks, and those like them.[26]

The Church would never claim that Socrates and Plato and Aristotle were Christians unaware, but Justin established in imagination their indispensable role in the life of the Christian mind and inaugurated an indefeasible sympathy, so that in the thirteenth century Aquinas would begin his great *Summa* by asking, not disingenuously, whether any discipline other than philosophy was necessary, and in the fourteenth century Dante would make an honored place for the philosophers, safe from the frozen inferno. Given that God's *logos* is spread throughout creation, whatever has been said truly by any men in any place belongs to us Christians.[27] This claim, proposed by Justin perhaps about 150, established the principle that would make Christianity the religion of humanity, preventing its becoming a fideistic cult, with its revelation alienated from all that had been considered philosophy and natural wisdom. The light that is Christ,

25 Ibid., 44 (Richardson, 270).
26 Ibid., 46 (Richardson, 272).
27 Justin, *Second Apology*, 13.4 (*ANF* 1:192–193).

although it does not furnish union with him apart from the sacraments, lightens every man coming into the world. The claim to this God-sent, universal rationality forestalled thinkers such as Tertullian, who believed that the divine revelation given Jerusalem should stand apart from the corrupting philosophy of Athens. What, asked Tertullian, has Jerusalem to do with Athens?[28] Justin and his successors answered that apart from the fruits of natural reason, the house of revelation would be built on sand. The remainder of the *Dialogue* is an unsuccessful attempt on Justin's part to convince Trypho and his friends that the Hebrew Scriptures lead to Christ, that his own prophets, lifting the wisdom of the philosophers above the frustration they inevitably enjoyed, opened the gate to truth and happiness. Justin and Trypho become partners in a lengthy dialogue in which Justin argues the truth of Christianity from the prophets while Trypho defends the Jewish rejection of the messiahship of Jesus. The argument, as the arguments between unbelieving Jews and Messianic Jews would always be, is an argument over the rightful interpretation of the Hebrew Scriptures.

After Justin the glory of divine revelation would ever be rooted in and would ever elevate toward glory the broad experience of the best of philosophers: the Stoics, Aristotelians, and Platonists. Christ who had no part in the world dominated by Satan and organized against God, the world to which Christians stood opposed, was the Word in whom every man participated, "enlightening every man coming into the word" and the bright form of every creature. "In him all things were created. . . . He is before all things, and in him all exist." Justin in his *Apology* and in the *Dialogue* is saving philosophy from itself, giving natural wisdom a propaedeutic place in the adventure of the soul even as it provides for revealed wisdom a root in nature and in the broad experience of mankind.

Justin knew that despite reason's essential place in the household of faith, reason was not enough. He had become a Christian, in his words, because after reading the prophets "a flame was kindled in my soul," the flame of Pentecost. Fifty years later another philosopher, recognizing that

28 Tertullian, *Prescription of Heretics* 7 (*ANF* 3:246). And see Theophilus of Antioch, who shared Tertullian's conviction that the poets and philosophers taught "useless and godless notions" (*Ad Autolycum* 3.2 (Grant, trans., 103).

the best among the Greeks and Romans had taught righteousness and acknowledged God, would write that Christian doctrine:

> Although in itself true and most worthy of belief, is not sufficient to reach the human heart, unless a certain power is imparted to the speaker from God and a grace appear upon his words. . . . If then it should be granted that the same doctrines are found among the Greeks as in our own Scriptures, yet they do not possess the same power of attracting and disposing the souls of men to follow them.[29]

29 *Origen against Celsus* 6.2 (*NPNF*[2] 4:573).

# Five
## *Irenaeus: The Theology of Glory*

> In this new order man will always remain new, in converse with God.
>
> *Against Heresies* 3.36.1

About 185, before any council had published a creed, at the beginning of his great work *The Refutation and Overthrow of the Knowledge Falsely So-Called*, Irenaeus professed the faith he had received.

> The Church, though dispersed throughout the whole world, even to the ends of the earth, has received from the apostles and their disciples this faith: She believes in one God, the Father and almighty maker of heaven, and earth, and the sea, and all things that are in them and in Christ Jesus, the son of God, who became incarnate for our salvation; and in the Holy Spirit, who proclaimed through the prophets the dispensations of God, and the advents, and the birth from a virgin, and the passion, and the resurrection from the dead, and the ascension into heaven in the flesh of the beloved Christ Jesus, our Lord, and his future manifestation from heaven in the glory of the Father to raise up anew all flesh of the whole human race, in order that to Christ Jesus our Lord and God and Savior and King, according to the invisible will of the Father, "every knee should bow, of things in heaven and things in earth and things under the earth," and that he would execute judgment toward all.

With respect to what will be the faith of the Church at Nicaea in 325, only "conceived by the Holy Ghost" is missing, but this was never controversial.

Much of the last two paragraphs as these stood in its final conciliar form of 381—the Holy Catholic Church, the communion of saints, one baptism (only) and the forgiveness of sins—answer concerns belonging to a time slightly later than Irenaeus, the pontificates of Zephyrinus (198–217) and Callixtus (217–22), during which these questions, the matter of re-baptizing the fallen and the forgiveness of post-baptismal sins, became pressing problems. The words that put down Arianism: God of God, Light of Light, and the famous *homoousion*, of one substance with the Father, belong to the fourth century, and the later controversial *filioque* (and the Son) belongs to the fifth century, first cited at the Council of Toledo in 447. But the faith of the Church expressed in the form of a creed, already evident in outline in Ignatius, was substantially in place when Irenaeus wrote his long book.

Irenaeus did not claim that this faith had been derived from the Church's books, although he found proofs of its truth in them, but rather wrote that "the Church although scattered in the whole world, carefully preserves [the faith] as if living in one house, she believes these things as if she had but one heart." The Catholic faith shines everywhere like the sun, illuminating "all men who wish to come to knowledge of the truth."[1] Those who preside in the churches—he is thinking of the bishops who by now are its guardians—do not prescind from this faith for "no one is above his teacher," and adherence to it is not a work of intellect but of a faithful will: "He who can say much about it does not add to it, nor does he who can say little diminish it." These complex references are to the tradition, the rule of faith, that lives in the heart of the Church.

Irenaeus learned the faith as a boy in Asia. We know Irenaeus spent his first years there because he reminisces with Florinus, a friend who would finally turn to the *gnosis* that Irenaeus so deeply opposed, about the days when together they heard Polycarp's witness to Christian tradition in his own house in Smyrna. Polycarp was martyred in 156. Irenaeus must have been born before about 140, so he was perhaps fifteen, a *pais* as the Greek runs, when he heard Polycarp of Smyrna speak of his encounters with apostolic witnesses, among whom, as Irenaeus remembered it, John was preeminent.[2] Much ink has been spilled on the thesis that the John whom

1 *Against Heresies* 1.10.2 (*ANF* 1:331).

2 *Church History* 5.20.4–8 (*NPNF*², *2*:238–39).

Polycarp knew was the Apostle John and the Beloved Disciple. But scholarship has largely, if not quite universally, given up that belief in favor of the idea that Polycarp's John was another, perhaps John the Presbyter, author of the Johannine Epistles, who, because of striking similarities of language and ideas, should be associated in some way with the writing of the Gospel. However that may be, Irenaeus was proud of his memories of Polycarp, memories not written down but cherished in his heart, and because of his knowledge of the bishop of Smyrna Irenaeus considered himself a member of an Asian tradition of great antiquity and unchallenged authority. This was the tradition represented by Polycrates of Ephesus in his controversy with Victor bishop of Rome over the date of Easter. Polycrates reinforced his argument by claiming the relics of John, "who reclined upon the bosom of the Lord," without giving the reader any local evidence of John's identity beyond the assertions that John slept in Ephesus and had been "a priest wearing the breastplate."[3]

This connection with Asia Minor goes far in explaining Irenaeus' staunch defense of prophecy; the opponents, Montanists he wrote, themselves pseudo-prophets, would not accept either the outspoken advocate of prophecy Paul, or that aspect "presented by John's Gospel in which the Lord promised that he would send the Paraclete, but set aside at once both the Gospel and the Prophetic Spirit."[4] Irenaeus' criticism came at a time when prophets and prophecy had been identified with the New Prophecy, a reform movement named for the famous prophet Montanus, much given to ecstatic prophecy, marked by a rigorist bias, and convinced that the millennial kingdom would be realized in the villages of Pepuzza and Thymion in back-country Asia Minor. When Irenaeus left Asia for Gaul is not known, but in 177, when he was about thirty-seven, he was commissioned by the martyrs of the Church in Lugdunum (Lyons) to carry to Eleutherius of Rome their plea on behalf of the Montanist prophets, whose miracles "caused their prophesyings to be credited by many."[5] The New Prophecy of the Montanist prophets and the prophesying Irenaeus approved occupied much common ground and, it could be argued, had a common root in

3 *Church History* 5.23-24 (*NPNF*[2], 1:242–43).

4 *Against Heresies* 3.11.9 (*ANF* 1:429).

5 *Church History* 5.3.4 (*NPNF*[2] 1:219).

apostolic practice, in the experience of the Church, in the *Didache* and in Paul. The anonymous historian of the movement quoted by Eusebius includes a list of "those who had prophesied under the new covenant," among them Ammia of Philadelphia, Quadratus, and the daughters of Philip.[6] In 177 Irenaeus was a willing advocate for toleration, holding that prophecy belonged in the Church and that the authorities ought not be quick to expel those practicing a gift commended by Paul and long encouraged among Christians.[7] Later Irenaeus would again justify his name, which means "peace," by mediating the end-of-century dispute between Victor of Rome and Polycrates of Ephesus about the date of Easter.[8]

Presumably Irenaeus was successful in his mission of 177. He returned to a church rejoicing in the martyrdom of their bishop Photinus and was soon elected to his place. As a Greek-speaker of good education, Irenaeus considered himself a kind of exile among the Gauls, whom he served faithfully until his death by martyrdom, as tradition holds. Just eight years after his Roman mission Irenaeus had finished his great anti-heretical work, the *Refutation and Overthrow of the Knowledge Falsely So-Called,* in which the catholic faith, as he, following Ignatius, named it, was defended against what must have been the credible and imminent threat posed by the "spirituals" or "knowledgeable" or "insightful" in Gaul.[9]

Irenaeus' principal targets in the *Refutation and Overthrow of the Knowledge Falsely So-Called* were Valentinus, a religious genius and gifted writer, and his disciple Ptolemaeus, although Marcion of Pontus and others are also in his sights.[10] Along the way he gives the reader much insight into the history of the Church and necessarily brings forward in some detail and with rhetorical force the great theological principles with which he opposed the systems of Valentinus and the other great Gnostics: Basilides,

6 *Church History*, 5.17, 2–3 (*NPNF*[2] 1:234).

7 Eusebius does not detail the content of the letter from Lyon to Eleutherius, but it is usually assumed to have urged toleration of prophecy. Irenaeus himself was prophecy-friendly (*Against Heresies* 1.13.1, 2.32.4), and critical of those who rejected a gift promised in John's Gospel and approved by Paul (*Against Heresies* 3.11.9).

8 *Church History* 5.24.11 (*NPNF*[2] 1:243).

9 *Smyrn.* 8.2 (Richardson, 115).

10 *Against Heresies* 1.27 (*ANF* 1:252).

Saturninus, Cerithus, Carpocrates, and Marcion.[11] Valentinus' system Irenaeus considered especially dangerous because it could so easily be made to look like a slightly different but cleverly constructive adaptation of the faith of the Church. It was, he wrote, like a fake jewel which cast doubt on the real thing.[12]

The ordinary exponents of the Gnostic system when Irenaeus wrote against it did not always have separate congregations, but, like the Corinthians who denied the future resurrection, were often especially insightful thinkers standing among the "unenlightened" believers at the Eucharist. In fact, despite the rhetorical ambiguity, Gnosticism, even in Valentinus' sophisticated version, denied or implied the denial of every tenet of the faith. Creation was the flawed work of a secondary god called the demiurge. Salvation was to be gained by insight or knowledge not by repentance and regeneration. The future belonged not to the New Creation envisioned by the prophet John in his Apocalypse but to the soul's ascent to the pleroma or the fullness. The Gnostics had their own books but they also claimed many of the Church's books; for Valentinus these were John and the writings of Paul especially, and for Marcion, Paul and Marcion's own version of Luke.

The power of Gnosticism lay in its claim to release those properly instructed from the world of necessity and moral conflict by offering an all-encompassing insight rooted in the belief that the soul was a divine spark already united with the pleroma, hence placing the enlightened beyond the claims of this world. Valentinus' great book begins: "The gospel of truth is joy." Although the basis of Marcion's system seems to have been belief rather than insight, his *Antitheses* began "O wonder upon wonder, rapture, power, amazement!"[13] The ecstatic joy of union with the divine and abrogation of the judgment of the Old Testament God by the loving heavenly Savior, would inevitably be compared with the slow and sometimes painful transformation of the baptized person by the grace of the Holy Spirit which the Catholic Church offered. The tendency of Gnosticism to resolve all moral questions in a process of insight might well seem

11 *Church History*,1.24–28. (*ANF* 1:348–52)

12 Ibid., 1.pref.2 (*ANF* 1:315).

13 Blackman, *Marcion*, 109.

at least superficially attractive when compared with the Gospel of the Great Church which for all its gifts of blessedness rested upon the foundation of love-inspired self-denial. The necessity of submission to revealed truth might seem credulous and simple-minded when Valentinus made the knowingness that encourages pride into a virtue, so that Gnostics called Catholics mere animal souls in contrast with the *pneumatikoi*, the "spirituals" of their own congregations.[14] Marcion's followers "make fun of us," Justin wrote.[15]

Irenaeus' other important extant work was the *Demonstration of the Apostolic Preaching*, in which he first sets forward the catholic faith and then offers a strong defense of the argument that the fulfillment of prophecy shows the authenticity of Christianity. Apart from these two great works there were several letters, some works noticed in Eusebius' *Church History*, and a work *Concerning Knowledge*, now unfortunately lost. That one of Irenaeus' surviving letters was addressed to a contemporary, Florinus, who had sat with him at the feet of Polycarp but who had later gone over to the gospel of *gnosis*, illustrates the fluid nature of the several movements called Christianity at mid-second century.[16] With reason one may wonder if among those who claimed belief in Jesus Christ around 180, a near majority may not have shared the faith of Valentinus or Marcion to one degree or another.[17]

We know something of the sources that fed Irenaeus' theology. He was an indefatigable advocate for the Gospel of John, regarding which Christian authors had for the most part previously been silent, an interest rendered more intense by his youthful memories of Polycarp's discourses.[18] He rarely cites synoptic texts that lie outside the agreements of Matthew and Luke. In *Against Heresies* he cites John, who had moved into the mainstream of Christian thought, more than one hundred times, Matthew at least twice that often, and Mark perhaps twenty times. Yet Irenaeus is a great defender

14 *Against Heresies* 2.30.1–2 (*ANF* 1:403-404)

15 Justin 36 (Richardson, 280).

16 *Church History* 5.20.4–7 (*NPNF*² 1:238–39).

17 Epiphanius, writing in 377, drawing partly on literary sources and partly on his own knowledge, enumerated 156 heretical Christian sects in his *Panarion* or *Medicine Chest*.

18 *Church History* 5.20.4–5 (*NPNF*² 1:238).

of the fourfold Gospel canon, arguing its completeness from the, to us unconvincing, facts that there are four winds, that the earth has four zones, and John's Apocalypse four living animals.[19] Irenaeus considers the Gospel canon closed and holds Gnostic works like Valentinus' *Gospel of Truth* to be false gospels.[20] Irenaeus cites Plato's *Laws*, which he uses as evidence that the philosopher, who believed God was both good and just, was more religious than the gnostics.[21]

The most important literary influence on Irenaeus' thought is the Hebrew Scriptures, from which he derived a set of interrelated principles: that the world was created by the one God *ex nihilo* or out of nothing, that it was created good, and that God's promise rests ineluctably upon it, so that it must be brought finally to the fulfillment for which it was destined in the beginning. At the end of the third book Irenaeus explains the great principle that shapes his thought:

> Since men are real, they must have a real existence, not passing away into things which are not, but advancing among things that are. Neither the substance nor the essence of the created order vanishes away, for he is faithful and true who established it, but the pattern of this world passes away, that is, the things in which the transgression took place, since in them man has grown old. Therefore God, foreknowing all things, made this pattern of things temporary, as I showed in the book before this, pointing out, as far as I could, the reason for the creation of the temporal universe. But when this pattern has passed away, and

19 *Against Heresies* 3.11.8 (*ANF* 1:428). Irenaeus identified the eagle with Mark, the man with Matthew, the lion with John, and the ox with Luke. Of these only the identification of Luke with the ox would persist, with Victorinus of Pettau, Jerome, and Augustine offering different schemes. The identification of Mark with the lion by Victorinus and Jerome came to be important in the civic mythology of Venice.

20 Quasten, 1:128. Valentinus' *Gospel of Truth* was recovered in the Nag Hammadi find and published by Robert M. Grant, *Gnosticism: A Source Book of Heretical Writings from the Early Christian Period* (New York: Harper and Brothers, 1961).

21 *Against Heresies* 3.25.5 (*ANF* 1:459).

> man is made new, and flourishes in incorruption, so that he can no longer grow old, then there will be a new heavens and a new earth. In this new order man will always remain new, in converse with God. That this state of things will remain without end, Isaiah says, as follows: "As the new heavens and the new earth which I will make, remain before me, so shall your seed and your name."

This commandingly beautiful passage develops ideas central to the Old Testament (Isa. 11:1–10, 25:8). The Word of God going forth into the world will fulfill God's purpose, not returning to him empty but accomplishing God's promise. This theme is developed fully by Irenaeus, relying on the Pauline image of man and nature passing from the reign of disobedience that issues in corruption and death into the realm of Spirit-inspired obedience that leads to life and glory (Rom. 8:18, 23). For Paul the realm of the supernatural, a word he does not use, is the realm of glory, where Christ who is the Lord of Glory reigns (1 Cor. 2:8). For Irenaeus history is the scene in which God accomplishes his purposes, not with some grand Hegelian march through time to which individuals are irrelevant but in the restoration of human nature and nature.

This decisive moment of restoration begins when a woman chosen by God says to his messenger: "Be it unto me according to your word." Thirty years before Irenaeus' *Against Heresies* Justin had written:

> Christ became man by the virgin in order that the disobedience which proceeded from the serpent might receive its destruction in the same manner in which it derived its origin. For Eve, who was a virgin and undefiled, having conceived the word of the serpent, brought forth disobedience and death. But the Virgin Mary received faith and joy when the Angel Gabriel announced to her the good tidings that the Spirit of the Lord would come upon her and the power of highest overshadow her. . . . And by her he has been born . . . by whom God destroys both the serpent and those angels and men who are like him.[22]

22 *Dialogue* 100 (*ANF* 1:249). See also Justin 33 (Richardson, 263).

Recapitulation, *anakephalaiosis*, (ana=re, kephalē=head) as Irenaeus' doctrine would be named, meant that the Blessed Virgin Mary sums up, heads up anew, or perfects the destiny of the Virgin Eve. "The former was seduced to disobey God, but the latter was persuaded to obey God, so that the Virgin Mary might become the advocate of the virgin Eve. As the human race was subjected to death through a virgin, so it was saved by a virgin." And analogously Christ, the second Adam, recapitulates in obedience the rebellion of the first. Then indeed "the sin of the first formed man was amended by the chastisement of the First-begotten."[23]

The golden thread running through Irenaeus' thought is his faith that the promise of God, his salvific will, is always kept and fulfilled. The conviction that mankind was created for companionship with God issues in Irenaeus' belief that God became man in order that we might enter into that companionship promised in the Eden, before sin caused our flight into the desert of alienation over which the Serpent wanders. "The Word of God, Our Lord Jesus Christ . . . through his transcendent love, became what we are, that he might bring us to be what he is himself."[24]

As compellingly beautiful as it is true, *theosis* or divinization means not that Christians become divine, for it is not God's revealed purpose to subsume our human life into himself, but to fulfill that singular unrepeatable creature for whom he died, whose name he knew in the beginning. By participation in Christ, our humanity is fulfilled in his, and our knowledge of the Father in the mirror of his knowledge causes us to become the creatures he had foreseen when the morning stars sang together. The means is baptism: "He came to save all through means of himself—all I say who are born again to God—infants, and children, and boys and youths, and old men."[25] Irenaeus reiterates Justin's doctrine that bread and wine in the sacrament of the great thanksgiving become the body and blood of Christ.[26] And if these things, taken from nature and having a natural uses, can thus be transformed into the body and blood of Son of God, and given to

23 *Against Heresies* 5.19:1 (*ANF* 1:547).
24 Ibid., 5.Pref.(*ANF* 1: 527),
25 Ibid., 2.22.4 (*ANF* 1:391).
26 Justin 66 (Richardson, 286).

believers as real food, how can the gnostics say that "the flesh cannot receive the free gift of God, which is eternal life?"[27]

These ideas of the goodness of creation, of God's indefeasible will not to abolish what he had made but to perfect it, ran counter to the sensibilities of the Hellenized world, in which milieu the corruptibility and transient nature of the body was stubbornly presupposed. The obvious point of contention was the doctrine of the resurrection of the flesh, a dramatic defeat of death in which the body was proved to be the bearer of the weight of glory. It was a first principle of Gnosticism that the body could not inherit salvation, and the Catholic insistence that the body would inherit a glorious eternality and incorruptibility established the division that separated the religion of Irenaeus from the religion of Valentinus. "Vain, likewise, are those who say that God came to those things that did not belong to him," wrote Irenaeus, reflecting the assertion of John: "Without Him was not anything made that was made" (1:3); "He came unto his own" (1:11). The great Gnostic insight was the nothingness, the illusory or evil nature, of the created order. But, Irenaeus wrote, "Vain in every respect are they who despise the entire dispensation of God, and disallow the salvation of the flesh, and treat with contempt its regeneration, maintaining that it is not capable of incorruption." Then, following the syllogism of 1 Corinthians 15:12–20, "If there is no resurrection then Christ is not raised from the dead," Irenaeus wrote: "But if this [the body] indeed does not attain salvation, then neither did the Lord redeem us with his blood, nor is the cup of the Eucharist the communion with his blood, nor the bread which we break the communion with his body. For blood can only come from veins and flesh."[28]

Defense of the resurrection of the flesh was the lynchpin of the theology of glory. Eighty years earlier Ignatius of Antioch had denounced those who argued that Jesus was resurrected as a bodiless spirit; "I believe that he was in the flesh even after the resurrection."[29] Thus in the Gospel of John Jesus invites Thomas to put his hand into the Lord's wounded side (20:24–29). There are many interpretations of John 1:14: "We beheld his glory, the glory as of the only begotten son of the Father." Perhaps this is the generic

27 *Against Heresies* 5.3.3 (Richardson, 388).
28 Ibid., 5.2.2 (*ANF* 1:528).
29 *Smyrn.* 3.1.

reflection of the Church on the glory of the Lord. Perhaps it is recollection of an event like the Transfiguration. Perhaps the risen Christ had appeared to the author. But however one reads this text in Jesus' resurrection the glory of the world that is being born was revealed, and this was the glory Saint Paul knew would be revealed in the New Creation (Rom. 8:18, 2 Cor. 5:17) and the glory which the prophet John knew belongs to the Jerusalem that will be (Rev. 21:11). That glory will be revealed in us. In the second century, belief that the soul somehow survived required no defense. That the body would be raised from death necessarily engaged the attention of Christian apologists. Eusebius knew the treatise *On the Resurrection* by Sextus.[30] Tertullian wrote *On the Resurrection of the Flesh,* Methodius of Olympus *On the Resurrection,* Athenagoras *On the Resurrection of the Dead,* and Hippolytus *On God and the Resurrection of the Flesh.* The first creed of the Roman Church asked, "Do you believe in the resurrection of the flesh?" which asks for the affirmation "I believe in the resurrection of the body."

The theology of glory brought into the world an optimism that would be realized in the great moral adventure that compasses the presence of God in this life and ends before his throne. Men are now set free by grace, through baptism, able to face God, to honor and love him, truly his sons and daughters, not his slaves, but his sons. This is the note of newness struck by the earliest Gospel in the figure of the new wine that required new wine-skins (Matt. 9:17), by Paul in Second Corinthians when he writes that to be in Christ is to be a new creation; "the old things are passed away, the new has come" (5:17), by Ignatius in Ephesians 19, when he wrote of the new star, the star of Bethlehem, brighter than the other stars, around which the sun and moon and other stars arranged themselves, amazed that this new thing had arisen.

> As a result all magic lost its power and all witchcraft ceased. Ignorance was done away with, and the ancient kingdom of evil was utterly destroyed, for God was revealing himself as a man, to bring newness of eternal life. What God had prepared was now beginning. Hence everything was in confusion as the destruction of death was being taken in hand.

30 An ecclesiastical writer otherwise unknown (*Church History* 5.27).

And the one who sat upon the throne said: "Behold I make all things new" (Rev 21:5).

Irenaeus was a true Asian in his belief in the thousand-year reign of Christ in the renewed creation, in prophecy, in the importance and authenticity of the Gospel of John and the Apocalypse. This influence was perpetuated into the early third century in the writings of the great Hippolytus, who wrote *On the Gospel of John and the Apocalypse, The Antichrist, On the Passover,* and *A Commentary on Daniel,* all expressing interests Irenaeus would have shared.

Among others Irenaeus' great book answers this great question: Why, unless the soul is sick beyond measure, do we love beauty and order and the fullness of being that expresses itself always in a kind of superabundance? Because these are the things for which we are made, and these finite glories are the reflections in creation of the beauty and form and fullness that reflect the glory of God. There are finally three and only three conclusions that can be drawn regarding man as we are, being as we are the crown of nature and of the created order. Irenaeus would not have known the modern counsel of despair which teaches that the vast labor of nature comes to more vast labor leaving nothing but death in its wake. He was of course familiar with the "spiritual" position that the created order and man as much as he is part of it is futureless although something survives, a conclusion that persists in the all-too-common modern idea of heaven.

Finally there is Irenaeus' own brilliant exposition that the created order is not only about our resurrection but about God's drawing his creation toward the perfection for which he intended it, a perfection that is not in the first instance about humankind as we are, but about Christ in whom we live and in whom all things consist, and thus has as its final cause the glory of God. Because of our participation in him we and the world will be changed from glory to glory until we see his face in the fruition of a love affair that began with our baptism. Irenaeus looked forward to that future when the pattern of this world formed in sin is done away, when "man is made new and flourished in incorruption, so that he can no longer grow old. Then there will be a new heavens and a new earth. In this new order man will always remain new, in converse with God."[31] And so God's will that when he calls our name we should answer is after the long catastrophe

31 *Against Heresies* 5.30.1 (*ANF* 1:566–67).

of sin achieved, and our desire that we know the voice and the face that calls us is fulfilled.

With Irenaeus the outlines of the Christian theology were set firmly in place, with the conclusions drawn from revelation and from Scripture developed into a coherent system including the fallen nature but essential goodness of creation, the life-giving power of the sacraments, the person of Jesus Christ and the efficacy of his sacrifice, the reality of the resurrection, and the supernatural purity given the Mother of God. The long future of the constant renewal and development of the Christian mind would bring no addition that was not presaged by Irenaeus. Overarching all these is the great fact that the end of things is life and glory, when the first-fruits of newness given at Pentecost burst into fulfillment, when all things are made new at the return of Christ. Come, Lord Jesus.

# *Bibliographical Notes*

In the footnotes references are frequently made to Cyril C. Richardson, *Early Christian Fathers* (New York: Touchstone, 1996), and to Henry Bettenson, *Documents of the Christian Church*, 3rd ed. edited by Chris Maunder (Oxford: At the University Press, 1999) as being the most easily and inexpensively accessible sources for many texts of the first two centuries. The translation of Scripture usually quoted is *Revised Standard Version, Catholic Edition* (San Francisco: Ignatius Press, 1966), with occasional appeals to the Greek text.

## Christian and Jewish Writers and Texts


Anti-Marcionite Prologues. Dom Donatien De Bruyne, "*Les plus anciens prologues latins des Êvangiles,*" *Revue Bénédictine* 1(1928), 192–214. Engelbert Gutwenger, "The Anti-Marcionite Prologues," *Theological Studies* 7 (1946): 343–409.

*Ascension of Isaiah.* Translated by R. H. Charles. London: Adam and Charles Black, 1900. Reprinted London: SPCK, 1917.

Arnobius of Sicca. *Against the Gentiles, ANF* 6:401–572; *The Case Against the Pagans.* Translated by George Engelbert McCraken. Westminster, Md.: Newman Press, 1949.

*Assumption of Moses. The Assumption of Moses: A Critical Edition with Commentary.* Edited by Johannes Tromp. New York: Brill, 1963.

Athenagoras. *A Plea Regarding Christians,* Richardson, 290–340.

Clement of Rome. *Letter to the Corinthians. ANF* 1:6–21; LCL 1: 1–121; Richardson, 43–73.

*Didache.* Richardson, 171–82; LCL 1: 305–33. *Epistle to Diognetus. ANF* 1:23-30; Richardson, 205–224; LCL 1: *The Book of Enoch.* Translated by R. H. Charles. Oxford: At the Clarendon Press, 1912.

Epiphanius. *The Panarion of Epiphanius of Salamis*, translated by Frank Williams. *Book I* Sections 1–46). Atlanta: SBL Press, 2009; *Books II and III: De Fide*. Boston, Mass.: Brill, 1998.

Eusebius. *Church History*, *NPNF*[2] 1:73–287; *The Church History*. Edited by Paul L. Maier. Grand Rapids, Mich.: Kregel Publications, 1999.

IV Ezra. *The Fourth Book of Ezra. A New Translation and Introduction*. Edited by James H. Charles. London: Longman, Darton, Todd, 1983.

Hippolytus. *The Treatise on Apostolic Tradition.* Edited by Gregory Dix and Henry Chadwick,1968. Reprint, New York: Routledge, 2006. *The Apostolic Tradition of Hippolytus.* Translated by Burton Scott Easton. New York: Macmillan Company, 1934. *Refutation of All Heresies*, *NPNF*[2] 5:9–153; Pinkerington, O.: Beloved Publishing, 2016. *On Anti-Christ*, *NPNF*[2] 5:204–209.

Ignatius of Antioch. The seven letters of Ignatius are in Richardson, 87–126, and the Greek-English text is in LCL 1:156–276.

Irenaeus. *Refutation and Overthrow of the Knowledge Falsely So-Called*, *NPNF*[2] 1:315–578; Reprint edition. Pickerington, O.: Beloved Publishing, 2015; Richardson, 358–97. *Demonstration of the Apostolic Preaching.* Translated from the Armenian by J. A. Robinson. London: SPCK, 1920.

Josephus. *The Works of Flavius Josephus*. Translated by William Whiston. Halifax, Nova Scotia: Milner and Sowerby, 1852. Reprint. New York: Thomas Nelson, 1998.

Justin Martyr. *Dialogue with Trypho the Jew*, *ANF* 1:194–270. *First Apology*, Richardson, 225–89; *ANF* 1: 159–87. *Second Apology*, *ANF* 1:188–93. *Second Apology, Dialogue with Trypho.* Washington, D. C.: Catholic University of America Press, 2008.

Lactantius. *The Death of the Persecutors*, *NPNF*[2] 7:301–22.

Melito of Sardis. *On the Pascha and Fragments*. (Oxford: Oxford University Press, 1979).

Muratorian Canon. Bruce Metzger, *The Canon of the New Testament.* Oxford: Clarendon Press, 1987, Pp. 305–307, abbreviated in Bettenson, 31–32; Henry Gwatkin, ed. *Selections from Early Writers Illustrative of Church History to the Time of Constantine.* London: Macmillan and Co, 1937. Pp. 82–88.

Novatian. *The Trinity, the Spectacles, Jewish Foods, In Praise of Purity, Letters.* Translated by J. R. Russell. Washington, D.C.: Catholic University of America Press, 1972. Reprint 2008.

*Odes of Solomon.* Translated by J. H. Bernard (Cambridge: At the University Press, 1912).

Origen. *On First Principles.* Translated by G.W. Butterworth. New York: Harper and Row, 1966; *NPNF*[2] 4:395–699.

Polycarp. *The Martyrdom of Saint Polycarp, Bishop of Smyrna*, Richardson, 149–58.

Socrates. *Church History, NPNF*[2] 2:236–427.

Tertullian. *Against Praxeas, NPNF*[2] 3:597–627. *Apology, NPNF*[2] 3:17–55. *Concerning Flight in Persecution, NPNF*[2] 4:116–25. *On Modesty, NPNF*[2] 4:74–101. *The Prescription of Heretics, NPNF*[2] 3:243–65. *The Resurrection of the Flesh, NPNF*[2] 3:545–94.

Theophilus of Antioch. *Ad Autolycum.* Translated by R. M. Grant. Oxford: At the Clarendon Press, 1970.

## Philosophers

Greek and Roman philosophers are generously represented in the Loeb Classical Library and there are critical editions of most authors. The texts cited below are readily available English translations referenced in the text.

Aristotle. Since its publication in 1941, Richard McKeon's one-volume *Basic Writings of Aristotle* (New York: Random House) has been a common text for English readers. *Metaphysics,* McKeon, 681–926. *Nichomachean Ethics,* McKeon, 927–1112. *Politics,* McKeon, 1113–1315.

Celsus. *On the True Doctrine: A Discourse Against Christians.* Translated by Joseph R. Hoffmann. New York: Oxford University Press, 1987.

Cicero. *The Nature of the Gods and on Divination.* Translated by C. D. Yonge. Amherst, N.Y.: Prometheus Press, 1997. *The Republic and the Laws.* Translated by Niall Rudd. Oxford: Oxford University Press, 1998.

Dio Chrysostom. *Discourses* II, XII-XXX. LCL. Translated by J. W. Cohoon. London: Heineman, 1939.

Epictetus. *Discourses, Fragments, Handbook.* Translated by Robin Hard. Oxford: University Press, 2014. *The Moral Discourses of Epictetus.* Translated by Elizabeth Carter. New York: E. P. Dutton, 1926. Reprinted often.

Epicurus. *The Essential Epicurus: Letters, Principal Doctrines, Vatican Sayings and Fragments.* Translated by Eugene O'Connor. Amherst, N. Y.: Prometheus Books, 1993.

Lucretius. *On the Nature of Things.* Translated by H. A. J Munro. New York: Washington Square Press, 1965.

Numenius of Apamea. *Works, Biography, Message.* Translated by Kenneth Sylvan Guthrie. London: George Bell and Sons, 1917.

Plato. Benjamin Jowett's two-volume *Dialogues of Plato*, first published in 1892 and reissued by Random House in 1947, is a standard English text. *Timaeus,* Jowett, 2:3–70. *Phaedo.* Jowett, 1:441–501. *Laws,* Jowett, 2:407–729.

Plotinus. *Enneads.* Translated by Stephen McKenna and B. S, Page. (Encyclopedia Britannica) Chicago: William Benton, 1952.

Polybius. *Histories.* Translated by Robin Waterfield. Oxford: University Press, 2010.

Salustius. *Salustius Concerning the Gods and the Universe.* Translated by Arthur Darby Nock. Cambridge: At the University Press, 1926. Paperback edition 2013.

Tacitus. *The Histories.* Translated by Kenneth Wellesley. Baltimore, Md.: Penguin, 1964

## Gnostic Sources

*The Nag Hammadi Library in English.* Edited by James M. Robinson. Revised edition. HarperCollins, San Francisco, 1990. This translation publishes the texts found there in 1945, including the *Epistle to Rheginos* and Valentinus' *Gospel of Truth.*

*Epistle to Rheginos: A Valentinian Letter on the Resurrection*. Translated with commentary by Malcolm Lee Peel. Philadelphia: Westminster Press, 1969.

*Gnosticism: A Source Book of Heretical Writings from the Early Christian Period*. Robert M. New York: Harper and Brothers, 1961. *Heracleon's Exegesis of John*, 195–208. *Ptolemaeus' Exegesis of John*, 182–83. Valentinus, *Gospel of Truth*, 146–61.

## Secondary Sources

*Part One: A Waiting World*

The world of thought that provided context for the making of the Christian mind compassed Hellenistic philosophy, Roman and Greek Religion, and the history and religion of the Jews. For the philosophical background, in addition to the primary sources cited above, see John Burnet's frequently reprinted *Early Greek Philosophy* (London: Adam and Charles Black, 1892, 4th ed., 1930, repr. 1971), a sure guide to Greek philosophic thought from the sixth-century BC Milesians, physicists who attempted to find a foundation for thought through an analysis of nature, to the Pythagoreans, who through their interest in mathematics directed philosophy toward the study of the mind and how we know. Among helpful sources for the period from Cicero to Sallustius are A. A. Long, *Hellenistic Philosophy* (New York: Charles Scribner's Sons, 1974). See also Harry A. Wolfson, *The Philosophy of the Church Fathers* (Cambridge: At the University Press, 1956). Among the many interpretations of Plato see G. M. A. Grube, *Plato's Thought*, and A. E. Taylor, *Plato: The Man and His Work*, and also Taylor's *Aristotle* (1919, repr. New York: Dover Publications, 1955).

Insofar as its sources were literary, first-century Christianity was founded on the Hebrew Scriptures most commonly known to Christian writers through the third-century BC Greek translation called the Septuagint, and through second-century AD translations by Theodotion of Ephesus and Aquila of Sinope. Jewish apocalyptic, which contained the seeds of the Messianic expectation that informs the apostolic writings, began in the age of the great prophets Isaiah, Jeremiah, and Zephaniah. See R. H.

Charles, *A Critical History of the Doctrine of the Future Life in Israel, Judaism, and Christianity* (London: A. and C. Black, 1913). The apocalyptic theme was intensified in the period of the second temple (BC 515–70 AD) and especially during the Maccabean ascendency (after BC 167), for which see canonical Daniel, *IV Ezra*, the *Book of Enoch*, trans. R. H. Charles, and M. R. James, *The Apocryphal New Testament* (Oxford: Clarendon Press, 1960).

On Judaism the two-volume *History of Israel* by Theodore Oesterly and William Robinson (Oxford: At the Clarendon Press 1932; repr. 1957) has never been supplanted. See also Michael Grant's *History of Ancient Israel* (London: Weidenfeld and Nicholson, 1984; repr. 2002), and D. S. Russell, *The Jews from Alexander to Herod* (Oxford: Oxford University Press, 1967), and his *Method and Message of Jewish Apocalyptic 200 BC–AD100* (Philadelphia, Pa.: Westminster Books, 1964). See also Frederick C. Grant's *Ancient Judaism and the New Testament* (New York: Macmillan, 1959) and A. H. M. Jones, *The Herods of Judea* (Oxford: At the Clarendon Press, 1938; repr. 1967), and Martin Hengel, *The Zealots: Investigations into the Jewish Freedom Movement in the Period from Herod I until 70 A.D.* (Edinburgh: T. & T. Clark, 1989).

The essay on Roman religion relies on Cicero, Dio Chrysostom, and Sallustius cited above, and on R. M. Ogilvie, *The Romans and Their Gods* (New York: W.W. Norton, 1969), as well as J. H. W. G. Liebescheutz's *Continuity and Change in Romans Religion* (Oxford: At the Clarendon Press, 1979) and Frederick C. Grant, *Hellenistic Religions* (New York: Bobbs-Merrill, 1953).

*Part Two: Revelation*

Recent decades have seen a renewed interest in the history of the first-century Church and in the process whereby memory became texts. Helpful are Martin Hengel, *Acts and the History of the Early Church* (SCM-Canterbury Press, 1979), *Between Jesus and Paul: Studies in the Earliest History of Christianity* (Fortress Press, 1983), and *Conflicts and Challenges in Early Christianity* (New York: T & T Clark, 1999); and the first two volumes of James D. G. Dunn's *Christianity in the Making: Jesus Remembered* (2000) and *In the Beginning* (2009), both published at Grand Rapids, Michigan by William B. Eerdmans. For an eccentric but insightful view of the relation between the written and remembered traditions and the formation of the

Gospel canon see J. A. T. Robinson's *Redating the New Testament* (London: SCM, 1976) and *The Priority of John* (London: SCM, 1963). The modern quest for Gospel origins begins with Burnett Hillman Streeter's *The Four Gospels* (London: Macmillan and Co., 1924), which brought to life the theoretical source Quelle or Q, which if a ghost, is a ghost hard to exorcise. See also Frederick C. Grant's *Growth of the Gospels* (New York: Abingdon Press, 1933) and *The Earliest Gospel: Studies in the Evangelic Tradition at the Point of its Crystalization in Writing* (New York: Abingdon, 1943). See also Martin Hengel, *The Four Gospels and the One Gospel of Jesus Christ: An Investigation of the Collection and Origin of the Canonical Gospels* (London: DSCM Press, 2000). For the argument that Matthew and Mark were standalone traditions see John M. Rist, *On the Independence of Matthew and Mark* (Cambridge: Cambridge University Press, 1978).

The bibliography generated by the letters of Saint Paul is immense, partly because Paul has been at the center of an argument since he wrote Galatians and since Peter came to Paul's defense in Second Peter 3:15–17. Paul is best understood through the text of the letters themselves, then through a consideration of their chronology, and finally through contexts and influences. Classic studies include Edgar J. Goodspeed, *Paul* (Nashville: Abingdon Press, 1950) and *Chapters in the Life of Paul* by John Knox (Macon, Georgia: Mercer University Press, 1987), and more recently James D. G. Dunn's comprehensive *The Theology of Paul the Apostle* (Grand Rapids, Mich.: William B. Eerdmans, 2006). For Gnostic influence on Paul see W. Schmithals, *Paul and the Gnostics* (Nashville, Tenn.: Abingdon Press, 1972), and especially Elaine Pagels, *The Gnostic Paul* (Harrisburg, Pa.: Trinity International Press, 1975).

The chapter on the Gospels relies upon *The New Testament in the Apostolic Fathers* by the Oxford Society of Historical Theology (Oxford: At the Clarendon Press, 1905) as a source for determining the use of the New Testament books by first- and second-century writers. This project was updated and expanded by Andrew Gregory and Christopher Tuckett in the two-volume *Reception of the New Testament in the Apostolic Fathers* (Oxford: Oxford University Press, 2005). For the technical and sociological background of Gospel-writing see Harry Y. Gamble, *Books and Readers in the Early Church: A History of Early Christian Texts* (New Haven, Conn.: Yale University Press, 1995), Colin H. Roberts and T. C. Skeat, *The Birth of the*

*Codex* (London: British Academy, Oxford University Press, 1983). See also Brian J. Wright, *Communal Reading in the Time of Jesus* (Minneapolis, Minn.; Fortress Press, 2017), which makes the case that public reading of Biblical texts was a common means of publication in the early Church.

The Gospel of Matthew is embroiled in the Synoptic Problem as it has been understood since the publication of Burnett Hillman Streeter's *The Four Gospels: A Study in Origins* (London: Macmillan and Co. 1930) with its advocacy of a hypothetical proto-Gospel Q. The view taken above that Matthew, if not chronologically the first of the Gospels, which cannot be known, was certainly the most referenced before 150, finds a natural sympathy for, but is not logically necessary to, the arguments put forward for Matthean priority by William R. Farmer and Dom Bernard Orchard, for which see Farmer's *Synoptic Problem* (Macon, Ga.: Mercer University Press, 1981). See also Austin M. Farrer "On Dispensing With Q," in D. E. Nineham (ed.), *Studies in the Gospels: Essays in Memory of R. H. Lightfoot* (Oxford: Blackwell, 1955), 55–88. For the argument that Matthew and Mark were stand-alone traditions see John M. Rist, *On the Independence of Matthew and Mark* (Cambridge: Cambridge University Press, 1978). The important place held by the Sermon on the Mount in the making of the Christian mind, historical and sociological studies being not particularly helpful, is best understood from the text itself, perhaps with the assistance of an intelligent commentator sympathetic to the purpose of the Beatitudes, such as Fulton J. Sheen's *The Cross and the Beatitudes* (New York, P.J. Kennedy & Sons, 1937), still in print, or John Stott, *The Beatitudes: Developing Spiritual Character* (Intervarsity Press, 2008), or better yet the commentaries of the Fathers, Leo the Great's Ninety-Fifth Sermon, or Augustine's *Commentary on the Sermon on the Mount.*

On John see C. H. Dodd's two magisterial works: *The Interpretation of the Fourth Gospel* (Cambridge: At the University Press, 1958), and *Historical Tradition in the Fourth Gospel* (Cambridge: At the University Press, 1965), and more recently Raymond E. Brown, *An Introduction to the Gospel of John* (New York: Doubleday, 2003). On the existence of an independent Johannine tradition see Robinson's *Priority of John* (Eugene Oregon: Wipf and Stock, 2011) and Dodd's *Historical Tradition.* The view of Johannine origins refines my *Andrew of Bethsaida and the Johannine Circle* (New York: Peter Lang, 2013). Charles E. Hill's *Johannine Corpus in the Early Church*

(Oxford: Oxford University Press, 2004) does much to establish the influence of John in the first half of the second century. The reading of the Anti-Marcionite Prologues as in part historically reliable depends on Dom Donatien De Bruyne's "*Les plus anciens prologues latins des Évangiles*" in *Revue Bénédictine* 40 (1928), 192–214. The notes and documents on which De Bruyne's research was based were published in 2015 as *Latin Prefaces to the Gospels* (Turnhout, Belgium: Brepols, 2015). The early date assigned by De Bruyne, 160–80, was contested by Engelbert Gutwenger in "The Anti-Marcionite Prologues," *Theological Studies* 7:343–409, and remains controversial. On the anti-Marcionite prologues see B. W. Bacon, "The Latin Prologue of John," *Journal of Biblical Literature* 32 (1913):194–217. E. S. Buchannan, "The Codex Muratorianus," *JTS* 8 (1906–1907): 537–45, and especially Eckhard J. Schnabel, "The Muratorian Fragment: The State of Research," *JTS* 57 (2014):231-64. And see Hill, *Johannine Corpus*, 128–38.

John's Apocalypse may, with reason, be seen a prophetic history, as an allegory, or as a mythic pattern with some contemporary historical underpinnings, which last informs the essay in Part Two above. See Austin Farrer, *The Apocalypse of St. John the Divine* (Oxford: Clarendon Press, 1964) and *The Rebirth of Images: the Making of St. John's Apocalypse* (Westminster: Dacre Press, 1949; repr. Eugene, Ore.: Wipf and Stock, 2006). On the history of interpretation see William C. Weinrich, *Revelation* (Downer's Grove, Ill.: InterVarsity Press, 2005). See also Stephen L. Cook, *The Apocalyptic Literature* (Nashville, Tenn.: Abingdon Press, 2005).

*Part Three: Writing the Christian Mind*

The *Teaching of the Twelve Apostles* or *Didache,* well known in the early Church but then lost until 1883, is the earliest non-canonical text current in the first century. A good authority is Anton Milavack: *The Didache: Text, Translation, Analysis, and Commentary* (Collegeville, Minn.: Liturgical Press, 2003) and *The Didache: Faith, Hope, and Life in the Earliest Christian Communities* (New York: Newman Press, 2003).

For the history of the literature see F. L. Cross, *The Early Christian Fathers* (London: G. Duckworth, 1960; repr. Bundora, Vic.: Burchardt Library, 1985); Edgar J. Goodspeed, *History of Early Christian Literature* (1942; rev. ed., Chicago: University of Chicago Press, 1966); Helen Rhee,

*Early Christian Literature: Christianity and Culture in the Second and Third Centuries* (New York: Routledge, 2005), and Morton Scott Enslin, *The Literature of the Christian Movement* (New York: Harper and Brothers, 1938).

The anchor for modern critical study of the Apostolic Fathers in English is the scholarship of Joseph Barber Lightfoot. For reference see his *Apostolic Fathers, Part I* (1860) and *Part II* (1885–90), a more recently published recension of which is *The Apostolic Fathers: A Revised Text, with Notes, Introductions, and Translations* (Hildesheim, N. Y.: G. Olms, 1973). See also Robert M. Grant, *Greek Apologists of the Second Century* (Philadelphia: Westminster Press, 1988), and Nicholas L. Thomas, *Defending Christ: the Latin Apologists before Augustine* (Turnhout, Belgium: Brepols, 2011). On Ignatius see Grant's *Ignatius of Antioch* (Camden, N.J.: Nelson, 1966) and Cyril Richardson, *The Christianity of Ignatius of Antioch* (New York: Columbia University Press, 1935); on Irenaeus, Grant, *Irenaeus of Lyons* (New York: Routledge, 1997, repr. 2011; Denis Minns, *Irenaeus* (Oxford: Oxford University Press, 2009); and Eric Osborn, *Irenaeus of Lyons* (New York: Cambridge University Press, 2001).